BROADCAST NEWS WRITING

GRID SERIES IN ADVERTISING AND JOURNALISM

Consulting Editors
ARNOLD M. BARBAN, University of Illinois
DONALD W. JUGENHEIMER, University of Kansas

Barban, Jugenheimer & Young, *Advertising Media Sourcebook and Workbook,* Second Edition
Burton, *Advertising Copywriting,* Fifth Edition
Burton and Ryan, *Advertising Fundamentals,* Third Edition
Burton and Sandhusen, *Cases In Advertising*
Fletcher & Bowers, *Fundamentals of Advertising Research,* Second Edition
Fletcher & Jugenheimer, *Problems and Practices in Advertising Research: Readings and Workbook*
Howard and Kievman, *Radio and TV Programming*
Jugenheimer & Turk, *Advertising Media*
Leckenby and Wedding, *Advertising Management: Criteria, Analysis and Decision Making*
Pickett, *Voices of the Past: Key Documents in the History of American Journalism*
Simon, *Public Relations: Concepts and Practices,* Second Edition
Simon, *Publicity and Public Relations Worktext,* Fifth Edition
Smeyak, *Broadcast News Writing,* Second Edition
Tan, *Mass Communication Theories and Research*
Zeigler & Howard, *Broadcast Advertising: A Comprehensive Working Textbook*
Zeigler & Johnson, *Creative Strategy and Tactics in Advertising*

OTHER BOOKS IN THE GRID SERIES IN ADVERTISING AND JOURNALISM

Francois, *Mass Media Law and Regulation,* Third Edition

BROADCAST NEWS WRITING

Second Edition

G. Paul Smeyak
University of Florida

Grid Publishing, Inc., Columbus, Ohio

2950 North High Street
P.O. Box 14466
Columbus, Ohio 43214-0466

Printed in the United States.

1 2 3 4 ☒ 6 5 4 3

Library of Congress Cataloging in Publication Data

Smeyak, G. Paul.
Broadcast news writing.

(Grid series in advertising and journalism)
Includes bibliographical references.
1. Broadcast journalism—Authorship. I. Title.
II. Series.
PN4784.B75S6 1983 808.06607 82-9293
ISBN 0-88244-255-4 (pbk.) AACR2

CONTENTS

INTRODUCTION viii

ACKNOWLEDGMENTS xi

1 STYLE 1

Page Format
Names and Titles
Punctuation
Abbreviations
Numbers and Statistics
Hyphenation
Contractions
Pronunciation Guide
Editing Copy
Quiz
Exercises
Endnote

2 GRAMMAR 29

Word Choice
Foreign Words and Phrases
Slang
Complexity
Verbal Overkill
Tongue Twisters
Quotations
Sources and Attributions
Clauses
Misplaced Modifiers
Transitions
Color
Tenses
Write Positive
Pronouns
Quiz
Exercises
Assignments
Endnotes

3 LEADS AND ORGANIZATION 65

Lead Elements
Lead Types
Localizing
Rewriting and Updating
Organization
Quiz
Exercises

Assignments
Endnotes

4 INTERVIEWS, LEAD-INS, TAG LINES 93

Interview Procedures
Editing Procedures
Lead-ins
Bridges
Tag Lines
Quiz
Exercises
Assignments

5 WRITING NEWS FOR CABLE AND TELEVISION 115

Script Format
Still Visuals
Moving Visuals
Quiz
Exercises
Assignments
Endnotes

6 NEWS JUDGMENTS 157

What is News
Elements of News
Real Time Coverage
Ethical Judgements
Quiz
Exercises
Assignments
Endnotes

7 NEWS SOURCES 175

News Wire Services
Network Services
Future File
Investigative Reporting
Public Service Monitors
News Beats
Subscriptions
Telephones
Public Relations Departments
Competition
Stringers
Quiz
Exercises
Assignments
Endnotes

8 NEWS ORGANIZATION, FORMATS AND FORMULAS 203

Program Consultants
Radio News
Music Formats and News Targeting

Radio News Formats
Television and Cable News
Newscast Formats
News Sets
News Producers
Television News Formula
Quiz
Exercises
Assignments
Endnotes

9 LEGAL JUDGMENTS 237

First Amendment
Political Broadcasting
The Fairness Doctrine
Personal Attack
Telephone Recording
News Staging
Defamation
Invasion of Privacy
Obscenity and Indecent Language
Free Press-Fair Trial
Privilege
Freedom of Information
Quiz
Exercises
Assignments
Table of Cases

APPENDIX A 269

Glossary of Terms

APPENDIX B 275

Common Writing Errors

APPENDIX C 277

The Radio Code

APPENDIX D 279

The Television Code

APPENDIX E 281

Standards for Cameras in the Courtroom, Florida

APPENDIX F 284

Statements of Principles of the Bench-Bar-Press of the State of Kansas

INDEX 293

INTRODUCTION

It is hard to believe that many of the early radio and television news pioneers are still alive. That is some indication of how quickly broadcasting and cable have developed into major news forces. The short history of broadcast journalism is fascinating reading and should be required of anyone interested in news and the development of the electronic media.

Almost from the start, news has been an important part of radio and television programming. The 1916 radio experiments by Lee DeForest in New York involved broadcasting the results of the Wilson-Hughes presidential elections. Four years later, two stations went on the air and to this day historians debate which was the first commercial operation. However, it is interesting to note that both stations carried news or election results as part of their inaugural broadcasts. 8MK, owned by the *Detroit News*, carried Michigan and national election results in August 1920. The election information came from 8MK's parent newspaper and a wire service. In November, KDKA, Pittsburgh, Pennsylvania, went on the air with an inaugural broadcast of music and the Harding-Cox election results gleaned from the *Pittsburgh Post*.

Although a few radio stations started news operations in the early 1920s, broadcast journalism was going through a novelty stage and it was not widely accepted until the 1930s. Many early radio stations did not offer news programming, and those stations that did try to provide news got most of their news from local newspapers, with or without the consent of the local newspaper editor. The few radio stations that did set up news departments hired their announcer-reporter-writers from the newspaper ranks. Newspaper writers like Lowell Thomas and H. V. Kaltenborn became early stars of broadcast journalism with their doomsday-like deliveries. Radio journalism in the 1920s and 1930s, such as it was, was stylistically an extension of newspaper journalism. Early radio news was written for the eye not the ear; it was meant to be read in a newspaper, not read aloud or heard over the air.

In the 1930s, the *March of Time*, which dramatized news, became a popular program and indicated the public's appetite for "actualities" and live news reports. However, it took the war in Europe to bring radio news to the threshold of respectability. In 1938, CBS radio's Director of Public Affairs, Paul White, devised our modern day news format. White conceived the first World News Roundup, which was a news program with live telephone or wireless reports from European correspondents in London, Rome, Vienna and Berlin. A news-hungry American public listened intently to voices of reporters in Europe telling America that the world was going mad.

Paul White's World News Roundup format is still in use. It has gone full circle. Initially there was no easy way to record news reports or interviews for replay in newscasts, and everything had to be live. Eventually, audio tape, film and video tape were developed and this allowed inexpensive recordings of good quality which could be replayed in many newscasts. The development of recording technology eliminated live reports in all but the most newsworthy events. Television also found live reports from areas outside the United States impossible until the development of communications satellites in the 1960s. Now, with modestly priced portable equipment available to most local radio and television stations, live coverage is quite common. The networks and local stations cover live events as a matter of routine. Paul White's World News Roundup format remains basically the same; the technology has dramatically improved since the 1938 European crises and World War II.

Many of broadcast journalism's major talents got their start in news during the European crises and World War II. Charles Collingwood, Edward R. Murrow and Edward L. Shirer were prominent radio correspondents. Other journalists such as Walter Cronkite, Harry Reasoner, Howard K. Smith and Eric Sevareid worked for newspapers or press wire services during this time. These men would later transfer their journalistic skills to radio and television. The reporting and writing skills of these men contributed to the strength of the early broadcast journalism. Some of these people had the "air presence" that led to fame and huge salaries, but they were news writers/reporters first and announcers second.

Things have not changed all that much since World War II. News directors in radio, television and cable still want people on staff who are good writer-reporters. Surveys by various colleges of journalism or professional news organizations still rank writing as the major skill desired by news directors. Assuredly a good voice and air presence are important for cable, television and radio reporters, but those must be coupled with solid reporting and writing skills. There are, unfortunately, news announcers who have virtually no editorial skills or judgments. These people rely on others to provide them with news copy, and they have no marketable news abilities other than good voices and pretty faces.

This text is designed for use by people who want to get into electronic journalism and become proficient writer-reporters. Broadcast journalism students come primarily from two disciplines: radio-television and journalism. Students from either background can use this text because it deals with the central aspects of good journalism--writing and reporting. Along with your instructor's help, guidance and comments, this book will lead you into news writing for cable, radio and television. The emphasis is on writing and reporting, although some law and broadcast technology is included. While the technology of radio, television, and cable is obviously important, this text deals with technology only as it affects the writer and writing judgments. There are two reasons for keeping technology in this text to a minimum; technology changes rapidly and radio, television, and cable production cannot be learned from a textbook or series of pictures.

As a method of instruction, broadcast news stories are examined in four parts: leads, organization, grammar, and style. Experienced newswriters, who write by instinct, might cringe at this learning device, but it does help novice newswriters examine the four important story elements and put them together in an acceptable writing style.

Fill out the quizzes at the ends of chapters. These will help you keep up with concepts and important elements of each chapter. However, the thing that will really help you and turn you into a good writer is writing. The more you write the better you will become. The agony of writing your first news story will soon give way to an accomplished writing style only if you write stories every day. Write stories and take them to teachers or professionals for a critique. No matter how busy people are, they will generally take a few minutes out to read your stories and offer constructive comments.

The first three chapters deal with leads, organization, grammar, and style in a sequence that easily and logically leads news students into writing their first stories. Chapter 1 deals with writing style. Style generally refers to the whole writing process and, in that broad meaning, most of this textbook deals with writing style. In the narrow view, the first chapter deals with the style of editing, punctuation, and the mechanics of getting a broadcast news story on paper. Chapter 2 deals with the oral grammatical style used by broadcast news writers. This chapter stresses conversational writing and deals with common writing problems and pitfalls. Chapter 2 also deals with colorful writing techniques that "liven" up a news story. Chapter 3 covers the various types of leads and how to select the information to put in broadcast news leads. Organization is also included in this chapter because the news lead and story organization are impossible to separate.

After reading and discussing the first three chapters, broadcast journalism students should have the information and skills to start writing news stories. Only constant writing and instructor criticism and evaluation will lead to the development of a good writing style. It is often interesting to have students keep a stringbook of their stories in chronological order. At the end of the semester the improvement is obvious and a big ego boost to the overworked student and professor.

Chapter 4 brings the newswriter into contact with the technological and aesthetic demands of radio. Radio listeners expect to hear the sounds of news events and newsmakers. Since few radio stations can afford specialization in the newsroom, writers must be able to interview as well as write scripts for the actuality story or voicer.

Chapter 5 deals with the complexities of television news writing and the production process which affects news content and story organization. Television is visual and the writer must learn to work skillfully with video tape and film. This chapter relies heavily on the interviewing, editing and writing concepts learned in Chapter 4.

Once the writer feels secure with the writing process, Chapters 6 and 7 provide the information necessary for the writer to become a news evaluator and news gatherer. Chapter 6 defines news and the elements that make a news story interesting to local news audiences. Chapter 7 discusses the sources of news. This chapter also evaluates the strengths and weaknesses of various news sources, such as the wire services, public relations firms and the networks. Chapter 7 also looks at the way potential news stories are organized in a "future file" which is the appointment calendar for the news department.

Chapter 8 discusses the impact of program consultants on radio and television news and tries to present a balanced view of this controversial issue. The program consultants have had a significant impact on news organization, story content, formats, and formulas. The broadcast newswriter must be aware of this issue and have a knowledge of newscast structure and various news philosophies.

Chapter 9 presents legal problems and issues that news people must deal with on a daily basis. News, by its very nature, deals with controversy and places news people in positions where they must make legal judgments which affect the station, themselves, and the person involved in the newsworthy event. News people must not only know their rights but how and why the law protects people involved in politics, trials, and controversial issues.

ACKNOWLEDGMENTS

A lot of people directly or indirectly contributed to this book. Throughout my years in radio and television news I learned a lot from many people who were kind enough to take a moment to show me something. If they read this book and see something vaguely familiar, it could be that I have unknowingly appropriated their words or ideas.

Many people directly contributed to this book by allowing me to use photographs or providing me with information.

A number of people also directly helped me in the production of Broadcast News Writing. They are Al Raye, Delberta Morgan, Ed Wells, Gary Mason and Helen Powers.

Paul Smeyak

Gainesville, Florida

1

STYLE

The news stories that newspaper and magazine journalists write are published and seen by thousands of people who buy newspapers and magazines. News scripts that broadcast journalists write are seldom seen by anyone outside of radio, television, or cable stations. News scripts, in broadcasting, are kept inside the station and used by news and production people in presenting news. The broadcast audience hears what is read and, in the case of television and cable, sees the slides or video that accompany the news script.

Broadcast news script must accomplish two objectives. First, scripts must carry news content written in a simple, *oral* style which will interest and appeal to the audience listening or watching. The oral or *conversational* writing style that broadcast journalists use allows newscasters to read scripts fluently without stumbling, disturbing the timing or confusing production staffs. Second, scripts must contain production directions so that news content can be presented on the air without technical or production errors. Production directions on the script allow producers, directors and broadcast technicians to integrate news stories into highly complex radio, cable or television production processes. The writing and mechanical styles that you will learn to use are designed to accomplish both of these important objectives. See examples 1-1 and 1-2.

PAGE FORMAT

Many news departments have policies which forbid news writers from using anything but standard 8 1/2 by 11 typing paper for news scripts. Half sheets and scraps can get lost, be easily thrown away or slide out of a stack of news scripts. These losses always occur at the worst possible moments. More than a few radio and television newscasters have found at the end of a newscast, to their horror, that they've mislaid or lost the weather forecast or last story because it was on a small piece of paper. It is hard enough to keep track of standard size sheets of paper in newsrooms, which tend to be messy, and any practice which reduces the chance of error should be followed.

Type only on one side of the page. If stories you are working on run longer than one page, go to a second or third page instead of typing on the reverse side. This is standard practice in print and electronic journalism.

EXAMPLE 1-1

SAMPLE RADIO NEWS SCRIPT

Condominium Accident
6-20 Noon News
Pell

THREE LOCAL CONSTRUCTION WORKERS HAVE BEEN SERIOUSLY INJURED IN A CONDOMINIUM ACCIDENT SOUTH OF HOUSTON. FIRST REPORTS FROM THE SCENE INDICATE THAT A CRANE CARRYING A LARGE BUCKET OF CONCRETE TIPPED OVER ONTO THE TOP FLOOR WHERE THE THREE MEN WERE WORKING. EMERGENCY MEDICAL TECHNICIAN FLOYD WILSON WAS WITH THE FIRST RESCUE SQUAD ON THE SCENE AND HE TELLS US WHAT HE SAW...

Tape cart: :34 seconds

O/C.. "Transported them to Mercy Hospital."

A MERCY HOSPITAL SPOKESWOMAN SAYS THE THREE MEN ARE BEING TREATED AT THIS MOMENT.

Tape cart: :18 seconds

O/C.. "are listed in critical condition."

FEDERAL OCCUPATIONAL SAFETY AND HEALTH ADMINISTRATION INVESTIGATORS ARE AT THE CONDOMINIUM CONSTRUCTION SITE NOW TO DETERMINE THE CAUSE OF THE ACCIDENT.

-30-

EXAMPLE 1-2

SAMPLE TELEVISION/CABLE NEWS SCRIPT

CONDO ACCIDENT
6-20   6 PM NEWS
PELL-FIELD

VIDEO	
Anncr/slide #127	THREE LOCAL CONSTRUCTION WORKERS ARE IN CRITICAL CONDITION AT MERCY HOSPITAL AT THIS HOUR. THE MEN WERE INJURED IN A CONSTRUCTION ACCIDENT AT THE SPARROW CONDOMINIUM SITE SOUTH OF HOUSTON. EYEWITNESS NEWS REPORTER BILL FIELD REPORTS....
V-cass	time....1:37 O/C....standard out cue.
Fonts: :10 Bill Field Reporting :28 Floyd Wilson Medical Technician 1:12 Jean Hoffman Mercy Hospital Spokeswoman	

Set your typewriter margins to allow one inch on both sides of the page for radio news scripts. For a typewriter using pica type, set the paper guide at 0 and your margins at 10 and 75. When you start typing, allow one inch of unused space at the top of the page and leave two inches at the bottom of the page. These margins at the sides, top and bottom will help keep the copy from being crammed onto pages; leave space for corrections and give news announcers space to hold pages without obscuring words.

One inch margins in radio will also allow you to time news copy accurately without using a stop watch. The average announcer (you should time yourself for accuracy), reading 150 to 160 words per minute, reads 15 to 16 full lines of copy in one minute. With one inch margins, a 15 line story will take one minute to read; 8 lines would take 30 seconds and four lines would take 15 seconds. So, if your news editor tells you to write a 20 second story, you can estimate the number of lines with a good degree of accuracy.

In the upper right or left hand corner of the first page of every script, one inch down from the top, *slug* your news story. The slug contains a brief description of the news story, date, time of day and name of the newswriter. If another person is involved with the news story, that person's name should also be added to the slug.

CONDO ACCIDENT-PAGE 1
6-20 6 PM
PELL-FIELD

If the story runs onto a second page, a partial slug should be typed at the top of the second page along with a page number. This way, if pages one and two get separated out from each other, they can be quickly found and brought together.

PAGE 2, CONDO ACCIDENT

Now, someone in a hurry does not have to read the entire story to know the topic, how old the story is, and with whom to check if there are any questions. There will not be any mistakes as to the order of pages.

In some instances, where slugs have been left off news scripts, news stories several days old have accidentally been aired because no date was included in the body of the stories and newsreaders were not familiar with the news events. Newscasters have also deleted important stories from their newscast because something in the unslugged story did not appear correct and they did not know with whom to check out the facts. Rather than make a serious error, they correctly held the news story off the air.

A word of warning about those two-page stories. Often, two-page stories get out of order or one of the pages disappears. If stories run more than one page, you should carefully and clearly mark the page numbers at the top of each page for radio. Television writers use unit numbers and page numbers which will be explained in Chapter 5. When news announcers go through their copy before a newscast, one thing they should check carefully is that page two is present and following page one. Single page stories in radio do not have to be marked.

News scripts should be well spaced and easy to read. Double space your news copy unless otherwise instructed. However, some news announcers prefer triple spaced copy because it is easier to read and they are less likely to stumble or lose their place. Most newsroom typewriters use pica sized type because it is larger than elite type and easier to read.

PICA SIZED TYPE IS BETTER SPACED AND EASIER TO READ

ELITE SIZED TYPE IS SMALLER AND HARDER TO READ

Many news departments have a policy that the news copy is typed in *UPPER CASE* and the production directions on the script are typed in *lower case*. Using UPPER and lower case clearly sets off the news script from the production directions reducing the possibility of error. Newscasters know that everything in UPPER CASE is content and to be read on the air while production people know that words in lower case are production directions. Typing news copy in UPPER CASE also conforms with the writing style of the broadcast wires of the major press wire services. A small but growing number of news directors and announcers are trying to reverse the policy of content being typed in UPPER CASE and directions in lower case. They insist, and research backs them up, that it is easier for announcers to read news copy which utilizes both UPPER and lower case. Capitalized proper names and the beginning and ends of sentences are easier for announcers to see if traditional writing style is used.

Most good news operations have policies banning the use of Associated Press, United Press International or Reuters wire copy on the air unless there is an emergency. In certain instances, however, there may not be time to rewrite a late-breaking news story or bulletin and the announcer will have to read wire copy. Most news announcers, by the way, also carry extra wire copy into the studio to be used as filler material in case they have mistimed their news or, for some reason, have to fill extra time. If newscasters have to use wire copy, which is usually cut smaller than 8 1/2" x 11", it should be neatly trimmed and stapled on standard size sheets of paper. The copy size will match all of the other copy and there will be less of a chance the wire copy will get lost or mislaid. See example 1-3.

In most instances, only one news story should be typed or, in the case of wire copy, stapled on a page. The general rule is one story goes on one page no matter how short the story. The only exception to this rule is if you are typing out a series of headlines which will be read as one story or if two or more related stories are combined into one major or long story.

Although many news organizations do not have policies regarding *end signs*, it is good policy to indicate the end of every story by using a traditional end sign. At the end of your news scripts, skip a few spaces and at center page type or write one of the following end signs and circle it:

If you are working on stories which run more than one page, at the end of page one indicate there is a second page by typing MORE or by drawing a heavy arrow.

MORE

See example 1-4 for the correct radio news format.

EXAMPLE 1-3

THIS BULLETIN WAS JUST RECEIVED IN THE WRUF NEWSROOM

FLASH

(ROME, ITALY) - THE POPE HAS BEEN SHOT. WHILE RIDING IN AN OPEN LIMOUSINE, POPE JOHN PAUL THE SECOND WAS SHOT AT LEAST ONCE AND POSSIBLY TWICE. HE WAS RUSHED TO A NEARBY HOSPITAL FOR TREATMENT.

RU42 _____CDT

AT THIS MOMENT THERE IS NO FURTHER INFORMATION ON THE POPE'S CONDITION. TO REPEAT THIS BULLETIN. (Repeat)

WRUF NEWSPEOPLE ARE STANDING BY TO RELAY ALL INFORMATION ON THE POPE TO YOU AS SOON AS IT BECOMES AVAILABLE...BACK TO REGULAR PROGRAMMING.

EXAMPLE 1-4

RADIO PAGE FORMAT EXAMPLE

MURDER AT GAS STATION
10/5 6AM
SOFIA

TUCSON POLICE SAY THEY HAVE NO GOOD LEADS IN THE MURDER OF AN ALL NIGHT GAS STATION ATTENDANT.

POLICE FOUND THE BODY OF 19-YEAR-OLD WILLIE ROTH LOCKED IN THE STATION RESTROOM EARLY THIS MORNING. ROTH HAD BEEN SHOT TO DEATH.

A CUSTOMER BECAME SUSPICIOUS AND CALLED POLICE WHEN HE COULD NOT FIND ANYONE AT THE OPEN GAS STATION ON THE CITY'S SOUTH SIDE.

POLICE SAY THEY HAVE NO APPARENT MOTIVE BECAUSE NO MONEY OR MERCHANDISE IS MISSING. DETECTIVES THEORIZE THAT A CUSTOMER MAY HAVE SCARED OFF THE MURDERER BEFORE HE HAD TIME TO TAKE ANYTHING FROM THE STATION.

-30-

NAMES AND TITLES

There is an old saying that names makes the news. This is true to a certain extent but, in some instances, names confuse the news.

Broadcast news writers should almost never start off stories with unknown names because the listener's attention may not be totally on the newscast. Radio is considered a background medium, and listeners may be driving, doing housework, talking, reading or doing a multitude of other activities. Unknown names may be missed by listeners if such names lead off stories or appear in lead sentences. You should *set up* or give meaning to names before they are used in stories. The best way to set up names is to give job titles or reasons why the people are in the news. For example:

A CHICAGO POLICEMAN SAVED THREE CHILDREN FROM A BURNING APARTMENT THIS MORNING. THE PATROLMAN...FRANK SILVIO...SPOTTED SMOKE SEEPING FROM THE THIRD FLOOR WINDOWS OF A BROWNSTONE APARTMENT AT 32711 SHERATON DRIVE.

The writer has set up the officer's name by indicating in the lead sentence that Silvio is a police officer and he is in the news because he saved the lives of three Chicago children. Not only has the name been set up in the lead but the lead verbally cues Chicagoans that this is a story about their city and some people who live there.

Names that are widely known can be used to lead off a story, but you should be sure your listeners will instantly recognize the names. Names familiar to you may be unknown to your listeners. Remember, working in news brings you into contact with many people, and it is your job to know them and what they do. The average person will not have your knowledge of names or events. You will become familiar with a number of people who wield great power but who stay behind the scene and may be unknown except to a small group of insiders. For example, a governor's chief administrative assistant may virtually be unknown outside the state house. However, this person's actions will literally affect everyone in the state. The names Haldeman and Erlichman were not known to many people in Washington, and their government jobs seemed innocuous until reporters digging into the Watergate scandal exposed their power and influence on the Presidency.

Widely known names in one region may be unknown names in another city or region. For example:

CLEVELAND MAYOR GEORGE VOINOVICH THREW HIS WEIGHT BEHIND THE CRITICISED REGIONAL TRANSIT AUTHORITY. AT AN AFTERNOON NEWS CONFERENCE... VOINOVICH SAID IMPROVING THE SYSTEM WOULD BENEFIT EVERYONE IN THE METROPOLITAN AREA.

Mayor Voinovich and the Regional Transit Authority are widely recognized in Cleveland, Ohio, and the above lead sentence would be acceptable in Cleveland. People living in Columbus, Dayton or Cincinnati, Ohio, less than two hundred miles away, might not know or care about Mayor Voinovich or the Regional Transit Authority.

As a newswriter, you should always think in terms of who you are writing for and with whom you are trying to communicate. You should ask yourself what has meaning for your local viewer or listener.

This brings up the question of just how important are names in a particular news story. Again, the key to your decision is what is important to your local audience. Read the following lead and second sentence:

A ONE CAR ACCIDENT IN THE EAST BOUND LANE OF SANTA MONICA FREEWAY LESS THAN AN HOUR AGO KILLED TWO PEOPLE. THE VICTIMS HAVE BEEN IDENTIFIED AS SUSAN AND WILLIAM BRYANT OF 3615 MAYFAIR STREET, CEDAR RAPIDS, IOWA....

Written for a Santa Monica audience, this story contains useless information. The names and addresses of the victims really have no meaning for people living in Santa Monica, California. It would be sufficient for the newswriter to say that a couple from Cedar Rapids, Iowa, were killed in a one car accident.

This same story written for a Cedar Rapids audience, however, might appear:

A CEDAR RAPIDS COUPLE VACATIONING IN SANTA MONICA, CALIFORNIA, WERE KILLED IN A ONE CAR ACCIDENT. THE VICTIMS, SUSAN AND WILLIAM BRYANT OF 3615 MAYFAIR STREET....

In some news stories, the names of people are not nearly so important as the person's actions or job. In the following examples, note that the persons' job title or actions are the important story elements. Names are left out but this omission does not detract from the stories:

CLEVELAND'S MAYOR IS BACKING A CONTROVERSIAL REGIONAL TRANSIT AUTHORITY PLAN FOR HIS CITY AND THE SURROUNDING SUBURBAN AREAS. HE SAYS THE CITY CANNOT CONTINUE TO PROSPER WITHOUT A REGIONAL TRANSPORTATION SYSTEM THAT CROSSES MUNICIPAL BOUNDARIES.

Or,

ONE OF THE SURVIVORS OF YESTERDAY'S PLANE CRASH NEAR FORT WORTH, TEXAS, SAYS THERE WAS AN EXPLOSION MOMENTS BEFORE THE CRASH.

Or,

CANADA'S INTERIOR MINISTER SAYS OIL EXPORTS TO THE UNITED STATES WILL BE CUT BY THIRTY PERCENT IN DECEMBER.

Deleting names in the above three story examples has not significantly reduced the information in each story. As a newswriter, you must determine if your news listeners or viewers really need to know the names of Cleveland's mayor, Canada's interior minister or survivors of a Texas plane crash. In many instances, especially when news events deal with foreign names, including those names in stories, can be confusing for both the newsreader and the news listener. Do not include foreign names in stories unless names are well known or, for some reason, inclusion of names is important to story content.

Broadcast journalists also handle names differently than newspaper writers who include the first name, last name, and middle initial, if appropriate, in first references. A newspaper journalist might write:

RONALD REAGAN, PRESIDENT OF THE UNITED STATES

FIDEL CASTRO, PRESIDENT OF CUBA

MENACHEM BEGIN, PRIME MINISTER OF ISRAEL

DONALD REGAN, SECRETARY OF THE TREASURY

FRANCOIS MITTERAND, PRESIDENT OF FRANCE

Broadcast news writers try to simplify their writing style by leaving out unnecessary words and commas that make news copy hard to read. Middle names and initials are deleted unless the last name is common and there could be confusion. The only other exception to this is when middle names and initials are integral parts of the person's name such as J. R. Ewing; B. B. King; Martin Luther King, Junior; G. Gordon Liddy; J. Walter Thompson or H. G. Wells.

Commas also break the news reader's rhythm or pacing, and this can be avoided by placing title or job position before the person's name.

Broadcast journalists might write:

PRESIDENT REAGAN

CUBAN PRESIDENT CASTRO

ISRAELI PRIME MINISTER BEGIN

TREASURY SECRETARY REGAN

FRENCH PRESIDENT MITTERAND

As you might have noticed, broadcast newswriters also simplify or shorten titles if it can be done without losing meaning. Juxtaposing a few words can help simplify a complex title or statement. Instead of writing:

DICK HESTER, GAINESVILLE DEPUTY MANAGER FOR UTILITIES

Write:

CITY UTILITIES MANAGER DICK HESTER

The only thing we have lost by simplifying names and titles is complexity. Story content remains the same, but we have performed an editing function designed to make our news stories easier to understand and easier to read.

In some news stories, a person's party affiliation or organizational membership is an important factor and should be stressed in the news copy. For example:

REPUBLICAN PRESIDENT REAGAN TOLD DEMOCRATIC HOUSE MEMBERS TO STOP BLOCKING HIS 1983 BUDGET WHICH CALLS FOR FURTHER SOCIAL SPENDING CUTS. THE PRESIDENT TOLD THE DEMOCRATS THEY ARE DEFYING THE WILL OF THE AMERICAN PUBLIC.

Party member ship needed to be stressed in the news copy because the conflict between a Republican President and a Democratically controlled House of Representatives is important in understanding the story.

Whenever names are used in connection with crimes, controversies, legal actions or moral issues, be extra careful to avoid possible name confusion. This is where it is *not correct* to simplify names, and you should include first names and middle initials. For example:

POLICE CHARGED 19-YEAR-OLD WILLIAM CHARLES JONES OF 2133 ATLANTIC AVENUE IN MIAMI WITH POSSESSION OF...

The above example of a name used in connection with a crime or possible crime should eliminate any confusion about which William Jones was charged by police. He is 19 years old, has a middle name of Charles and lives at 2133 Atlantic Avenue in Miami. In this instance, any other William Jones in Miami should not suffer embarrassment because the news writer was careful to clearly identify the person in the news story.

Some confusion occurs when news writers use the titles *doctor* and *professor*. When referring to a physician, surgeon or someone with a medical degree licensed to practice medicine, refer to that person in your news story as doctor. When referring to a person who has a Ph.D. or Doctorate of Philosophy, refer to that person as professor. For example:

A PHILADELPHIA PATHOLOGIST, DOCTOR MICHAEL SMITH HAS BEEN ELECTED CHAIRMAN OF THE PENNSYLVANIA AMERICAN MEDICAL ASSOCIATION.

A UNIVERSITY OF OKLAHOMA EDUCATOR HAS BEEN APPOINTED TO AN IMPORTANT POST IN THE DEPARTMENT OF HEALTH, EDUCATION AND WELFARE. PROFESSOR WILLIAM MARKET...

It is common journalistic practice not to repeat titles after the first reference in a story. For example:

SECRETARY OF STATE HAIG MET WITH CHINESE LEADERS FOR MORE THAN FOUR HOURS TODAY. HAIG CHARACTERIZED THE TALKS AS FRANK AND CONSTRUCTIVE...

One exception to this rule is when referring to the President of the United States. The policy in most news departments is to use the title in all references to the President and never refer to the President only by his last name. For example:

PRESIDENT REAGAN MET WITH CONGRESSIONAL LEADERS AND TRIED TO PERSUADE THEM TO MOVE QUICKLY ON HIS TAX CUT PROPOSALS. AFTER THE MEETING...PRESIDENT REAGAN TOLD NEWSPEOPLE THAT...

Another exception is when referring to members of the clergy in a news story. Continue to use a clergy title in all references even though there are subtle differences in the first and succeeding references. For Roman Catholic and Eastern Orthodox clergy on the first reference use:

THE REVEREND WILLIAM SIMMONS

In later references, use:

FATHER SIMMONS

For Jewish clergy on the first reference, use:

RABBI WILLIAM GIMAN

In later references, use:

RABBI GIMAN

For Protestant clergy on the first reference, use:

THE REVEREND MATTHEW WILLIAMS

In later references, use:

THE REVEREND WILLIAMS

Many news departments are doing away with the use of Mr., Mrs., Miss, or Ms. in news stories. No title is used in the first reference, and Mr., Mrs., or Miss is only used in following references if titles are needed to distinguish between people with the same last name.

A CEDAR RAPIDS, IOWA, COUPLE WERE KILLED IN A CAR ACCIDENT IN CALIFORNIA. THE VICTIMS HAVE BEEN IDENTIFIED AS WILLIAM AND SUSAN BRYANT OF 3615 MAYFAIR STREET. MR. BRYANT WAS KILLED INSTANTLY. MRS. BRYANT WAS TAKEN TO A SAN FERNANDO HOSPITAL WHERE SHE DIED SEVERAL HOURS AFTER THE ACCIDENT.

PUNCTUATION

The punctuation style that broadcast journalists use is dictated by news department policies or the demands of newsreaders who may request that their copy be written or punctuated in a specific manner. Since newsreaders have the ultimate responsibility for making sure that the news story reads well and sounds good on the air, you should write and punctuate your copy as they request.

Rules for punctuation in broadcasting are somewhat relaxed. Punctuation serves only to help news announcers read and interpret the script on the air. To avoid confusion, use only hyphens, commas, periods, three dashes or three dots. Many newswriters use three dashes---or three dots...to indicate pauses or to offset words and phrases that need emphasis.

THE PRESIDENT...IN HIS STATE OF THE NATION ADDRESS TO CONGRESS...

SAYS THAT THE MOOD OF THE COUNTRY HAS CHANGED. HE SAYS---CONGRESS MUST

BEAR SOME OF THE BURDEN FOR INFLATION.

The rationale for using three dots or dashes is that announcers can easily see when natural breath pauses can be taken and where to add emphasis or inflect to offset phrases.

Three dots...should never be used by broadcast newswriters to indicate that material has been deleted from quotes. This practice is acceptable in newspaper journalism or term papers where the person reading the material can see and understand what is being done. The broadcast listener cannot see the three dots and this would only confuse the newsreader.

MEANWHILE...IN IRELAND...I-R-A LEADERS SAY THAT PRIME MINISTER

THATCHER'S VISIT WILL CAUSE MORE VIOLENCE.

Hyphens or periods are commonly used to indicate to announcers that letters or number groupings should be read individually. For example:

CLARENCE SMYTHE...THAT'S SPELLED S-M-Y-T-H-E

THAT TELEPHONE NUMBER IS 3-7-7---2-1-1-2

ABBREVIATIONS

The best advice about abbreviations in broadcast news copy is to avoid them. If you use abbreviations in your news copy, you should be prepared for the day when a newsreader will inadvertently read the abbreviated form on the air. If you write A-F-L in your news copy, you should expect the news announcer to read "A-F-L" and not "AMERICAN FEDERATION OF LABOR." The following abbreviations are widely known and can be used in abbreviated form.

U-S-S-R	P-M	U-S	I-R-A
MR.	A-M	A-F-L	Y-M-C-A
F-B-I	C-I-A	MRS.	N-A-A-C-P
G-O-P	U. S.	MS.	Y-W-C-A
I-O-U	DR.	U-N	P-F-C

Other abbreviations, not as widely known, should only be used after the complete name is used in the first reference.

THE UNITED AUTO WORKERS HAS REJECTED THE LATEST CONTRACT OFFER BY

THE THREE MAJOR AUTOMAKERS. A U-A-W SPOKESPERSON SAYS...

You should be conservative when using abbreviations, and if you have doubts about audience recognition of an abbreviation do not use it. You should always strive for clear news copy which will be easily understood by listeners.

Some abbreviations have, over time, become so common that they have become words and they are understood by most people. These abbreviations should not be hyphenated because they are read as words and not spelled out by newsreaders. Some examples are:

NATO = North Atlantic Treaty Organization

NASA = National Aeronautics and Space Administration

CORE = Congress of Racial Equality

SEATO = Southeast Asia Treaty Organization

UNICEF = United Nations International Children's Emergency Fund

UNESCO = United Nations Educational, Scientific and Cultural Organization

The names of countries or states should never be abbreviated. The only exceptions to this are the U-S and the U-S-S-R.

Military and police ranks or titles of officials should not be abbreviated. The only exception is for the military rank of Private First Class, P-F-C.

The days of the week and months should also be written out as you want them read on the air. You should write March, not Mar.; Tuesday, not Tues.

The following abbreviations should *never* be used in a broadcast news script.

PROF.	ATT.	D.A.	C-S-T
DOA	DIR.	A-D-W	BLVD.
DWI	DEM	E-S-T	AVE.
RD.	ST.	P-S-T	RR

NUMBERS AND STATISTICS

Each of us lives in a world filled with numbers and statistics. From five digit zip codes to nine digit social security numbers, we are bombarded with telephone numbers; stock quotations; ball scores; credit card numbers; warranty numbers; death tolls and even numbers to wait in line for service.

Statistics and numbers have become an important part of our lives and this reliance on numbers has carried over into news. On holiday weekends, newswriters talk about highway death tolls surpassing the five hundred mark. The United States GNP (gross national product) approaches a trillion dollars; inflation rates and interest rates are double digit and defense weapons systems cost billions of dollars.

We are overwhelmed by numbers. The overload is so great that many people automatically tune out numbers and statistics or they no longer try to understand their meaning. The job of the newswriter is to determine which numbers and statistics will have interest and meaning for listeners and then present the numbers in an understandable manner. There is no hard and fast rule on how many numbers could or should be used in news stories, but the general rule is that the more numbers you use the more complex news stories become. Unless news stories deal with stock quotations, election results or sports scores, you should not use more than three or four numbers or statistics in one story. Television newswriters often try to simplify the presentations of numbers or statistics by using a character generator to graphically display numerical information. See chapter 5.

Three or four digit numbers can create problems for newsreaders. Your job is to help announcers avoid stumbling and confusion, and you should follow these rules for numbers.

Write out numbers one through eleven

Use numerals for numbers 12 through 999

Use numerals for sports scores, times and dates

After 999, write out thousand, million, billion and trillion

Following these rules, the numbers:

4,015	would be	four-thousand-15
300,000	would be	300-thousand
12,500	would be	12-thousand-500
1,100	would be	one-thousand-100
	or	eleven-hundred

It is easier for announcers to read aloud the numbers written in broadcast style. The reason is that it is easier for someone to read words than it is for them to look at a series of numerals and quickly translate the zeros into hundreds, thousands, millions or billions.

If a sentence starts off with a number, the general rule is to write the number out.

For clarity, all numbers should be rounded off unless the use of exact numbers is necessary, such as in stock quotations, ball scores or close election results.

4,015	would be	FOUR-THOUSAND
	or	SLIGHTLY MORE THAN FOUR THOUSAND
	or	JUST OVER FOUR THOUSAND

News listeners realize that some liberties are taken by newswriters, who round off numbers and statistics if it does not affect story content. Most news stories will not be affected by rounding off numbers, but it does take a certain amount of news judgment to determine when this can be done.

Instead of writing A HUNDRED or A THOUSAND, most news writers will write ONE HUNDRED or ONE THOUSAND. In oral communication, the "A" could be mistaken for "eight."

Numerals should be used for ages, dates and addresses. Ages should always go before the person's name, unlike newspaper writing style.

THE 19-YEAR-OLD VICTIM WAS KILLED ON AUGUST 12TH.

HE LIVED AT 332-15 SOUTH BOULEVARD IN FORT WAYNE.

You should add *st.*, *rd.*, *nd.*, and *th.* to anything rank ordered or days of the month. Most announcers will add them anyway because it is easier to say AUGUST 12TH or the 12TH OF AUGUST than it is to say AUGUST 12.

Do not use symbols in news copy. Instead of using @, #, $, %, ¢, &, *, + or =, write out what the symbols mean. As with writing out numbers, it is easier to read EACH, NUMBER, DOLLAR, PERCENT, CENTS, AND, PLUS or EQUALS rather than try to mentally translate what the symbols mean into words during a pressure situation while on the air.

$27.12	would be	27 DOLLARS AND 12 CENTS
	or	MORE THAN 27 DOLLARS
72%	would be	72 PERCENT
#13	would be	ITEM NUMBER 13
$.15 @	would be	15 CENTS EACH

Fractions should be written out, and when working with decimal points, write out the decimal point.

1/4	would be	one-fourth
2/3	would be	two-thirds
12.6 billion	would be	12-point-six-billion

Your job as a newswriter is not just to present information and numbers, it is also to convey what the numbers mean in easily understood concepts. Average people do not know what a trillion dollar GNP is, let alone how it relates to their daily activities on the job or at home. For example:

THE TAMPA SCHOOL BOARD WANTS AREA VOTERS TO DECIDE ON A PROPOSED

TEN MILL TAX LEVY FOR SCHOOL OPERATIONS EXPENSES.

Or:

GOVERNMENT ECONOMISTS ARE PREDICTING THAT THE GROSS NATIONAL

PRODUCT WILL GO DOWN THIS QUARTER...FOR THE SECOND CONSECUTIVE QUARTER.

The news stories talking about a ten-mill tax levy and a gross national product are important stories. They will have meaning for many people if we present the information in an understandable manner. A lot of people might ask themselves what is a mill or the gross national product? What does it mean to me? How much is ten mills, and what would an additional ten-mill tax do to my property tax bill? These are questions that we should answer in our news stories. A good idea is to add explanatory phrases or reference points to help listeners understand complex economic terms, numbers or statistics. Translating what numbers mean can be done easily, and it adds a lot to news stories. Without newswriters' translating and synthesizing, much of the news will have very little meaning for average news listeners. Explanatory sentences are needed in both stories.

THE TAMPA SCHOOL BOARD WANTS AREA VOTERS TO DECIDE ON A PROPOSED TEN MILL TAX LEVY FOR SCHOOL OPERATING EXPENSES. A MILL IS ONE-TENTH OF A PENNY AND WOULD ADD 20-DOLLARS YEARLY TO THE PROPERTY TAX ON A 45-THOUSAND DOLLAR HOME.

Or:

GOVERNMENT ECONOMISTS ARE PREDICTING THAT THE GROSS NATIONAL PRODUCT WILL GO DOWN THIS QUARTER...FOR THE SECOND CONSECUTIVE QUARTER. THE GROSS NATIONAL PRODUCT IS THE TOTAL VALUE OF OUR NATION'S ANNUAL OUTPUT OF GOODS AND SERVICES. THIS MEANS, AS A NATION, WE ARE PRODUCING LESS THAN WE DID LAST YEAR.

Here are some examples of the need for reference points or explanatory sentences.

THE SENATE VOTED TO RAISE THE NATIONAL DEBT CEILING TO 935 BILLION DOLLARS. THAT'S A DEBT OF NEARLY 15-HUNDRED DOLLARS FOR EVERY MAN, WOMAN, AND CHILD IN AMERICA.

Or:

WITH 149 OUT OF 302 PRECINCTS REPORTING...BOB WILLIAMSON LEADS JOHN FRANKEN IN THE MAYOR'S RACE WITH 24,332 VOTES TO 23,401.

SO...WITH NEARLY HALF THE PRECINCTS REPORTING...WILLIAMSON HOLDS A NARROW ONE-THOUSAND VOTE LEAD OVER HIS OPPONENT.

You should always search for ways to make numbers, statistics or complex economic terms relevant to news listeners. The ability to translate complex information into meaningful stories is one important characteristic of good newswriters.

HYPHENATION

Broadcast newswriters should never split or hyphenate words at the end of sentences. If you start a word on one line and see that it will not fit, the word should be completely marked out and the whole word typed on the next line. Sentences should never be continued from one page to another page. It is bad enough to lose page two of the news story, but to lose page two in mid-sentence is catastrophic. If two pages are used for a news story, end page one with a complete sentence or, better yet, a paragraph.

While it is absolutely forbidden to split words between lines or pages, some words are easier to read if they are hyphenated. The general rule is to hyphenate all words with the prefixes SEMI, CO, ANTI and NON. For example:

SEMI-CONDUCTOR

ANTI-ESTABLISHMENT

CO-DEFENDANT

NON-AGGRESSION

Even if words are not normally hyphenated, this is one of those areas where literary grammatical style gives way to broadcast news style.

Numbers should also be hyphenated. This will visually cue news readers not to pause or to read numbers or letters as written. For example:

SEVEN-YEAR-OLD

SIX-POINT-THREE BILLION

F-B-I

24-15 SOUTH ORCHARD AVENUE

CONTRACTIONS

In everyday conversation, the average person automatically contracts pronouns and verbs. In English classes, however, we are taught to write in a formal literary grammatical style where contractions are seldom used. Broadcast writing style, which is designed to be read aloud and heard by news listeners, uses contractions to sound conversational and natural. Our broadcast writing style should try to approximate normal conversations and this includes using contractions. For example:

THE PRESIDENT SAYS *HE'LL* MEET WITH CANADIAN LEADERS TO DISCUSS OIL IMPORTS.

Or:

UNITED AUTO WORKERS LEADERS SAY *THEY'LL* RECOMMEND ACCEPTING THE LATEST CONTRACT OFFER FROM CHRYSLER.

Contractions used in the two examples make the news stories easier to read aloud for news announcers. They are conversational and natural sounding. Use the following contractions in your news writing.

HE IS to HE'S

HE WILL to HE'LL

HE WOULD to HE'D

DO NOT to DON'T

DOES NOT to DOESN'T

IS NOT to ISN'T

ARE NOT to AREN'T

WILL NOT to WON'T

WOULD NOT to WOULDN'T

THEY ARE to THEY'RE

THEY WILL to THEY'LL

HAS NOT to HASN'T

It will should not be contracted to *it'll* because the contractions sound awkward when read aloud.

There are times when you will intentionally not contract words in news stories to add emphasis or make a point. Murphy Martin, former ABC newsman, seldom contracted pronouns and verbs in stories of major importance where he wanted to add extra emphasis. Not contracting makes stories sound formal and strong. For example:

THE PRESIDENT SAYS *HE WILL* MEET WITH MEXICAN PRESIDENT JOSE LOPEZ PORTILLO AND DISCUSS THE PROBLEM OF ILLEGAL ALIENS.

Or:

UNITED AUTO WORKERS LEADERS SAY *THEY WILL* RECOMMEND ACCEPTING THE LATEST CONTRACT OFFER FROM CHRYSLER.

Not contracting HE WILL and THEY WILL adds power to the stories because it forces announcers to emphasize that contractions were not used. News listeners may not consciously recognize that pronouns and verbs were not contracted but the formality of the story will have an impact.

PRONUNCIATION GUIDE

Nothing hurts news credibility or sounds more amateurish than newsreaders stumbling over pronunciation or glibly mispronouncing local names or words. Newswriters and announcers should never assume they know the correct pronunciations of new, difficult or foreign names or phrases.

The trickiest words are proper names that have several different pronunciations. These words lie in wait for novice writers or announcers who think if that's the way it's pronounced in France that's the way it's pronounced in Kentucky. An example is the city VERSAILLES (VER-SIGH), France, where a famous treaty between the Allies and

Germany was signed in 1919. However, in Kentucky, the community's name is VERSAILLES which is pronounced VER-SAY-LES. Another example is Lima (Lee-magh), Peru and Lima (ligh-magh), Ohio. The people in Ligh-Magh, Ohio, were quite upset when Walter Cronkite talked about tornadoes that struck the central Ohio city of Lee-Magh-Ohio. It was bad enough to suffer the tornado damage, but it was added insult when the name of the city was mispronounced on network television.

Another name that has caught many unwary newsreaders is the pronunciation of that Michigan city, Sault Saint Marie. The correct pronunciation is SAULT (SOO) SAINT MARIE and not SAULT (SALT) SAINT MARIE.

We have Americanized many foreign phrases and words and they can cause pronunciation problems for newsreaders. It is obvious that newsreaders have primary responsibility for pronunciations, but you can help with difficult words and phrases by writing things phonetically. United Press International and the Associated Press transmit phonetic pronunciation guides daily, and you can use these guides when writing stories with difficult names and phrases. You should also become sensitive to local names and places and quickly learn correct pronunciations of prominent people, local landmarks and streets. Don't ever be afraid of asking others about pronunciations, and if no one in the newsroom knows the correct pronunciation, telephone someone who does. Don't ever feel that you are admitting ignorance by telephoning someone to ask the correct pronunciation of their name or to get any other fact in the news story correct. The real sin would be to end up with mispronunciations or fact errors. Local telephone operators are also good sources for the pronunciation of community names.

Newswriters should phonetically write out unfamiliar or difficult words and, if possible, verbally coach newsreaders with correct pronunciations.

The Associated Press phonetic pronunciation guide is a handy thing to know.[1]

AH-like the "a" in arm

A-like the "a" in apple

EH-like the "ai" in air

AY-like the "a" in ace

E-like the "e" in bed

EE-like the "ee" in feel

I-like the "i" in pin

Y-like the "i" in time

OH-like the "O" in go

OO-like the "oo" in food

UH-like the "u" in puff

KH-a guttural sound

ZH-like the "s" in vision

J-like the "j" in Job

EDITING COPY

One of the hardest things for novice broadcast writers to do is proofread news stories, edit copy and correct mistakes. This final step in writing is extremely important because this is where you will catch style and fact errors and prepare the stories for announcers to present on the air. This is your last opportunity to mold your works of art and turn in good stories instead of average stories.

One good piece of advice is for you to read stories out loud, although you should have been doing this as you wrote. If you read the stories aloud, you should find rough spots, long sentences, alliterations, tongue twisters and bad phrasing. Rough spots and other problems can be corrected before stories are handed in to editors or newsreaders. Reading stories silently or subvocalizing will not accomplish the same result as reading the stories aloud. Even experienced writers in major newsrooms read their copy aloud while they make final edits and corrections.

The first editing job you should do is read stories questioning facts, spelling, grammar, punctuation, and logic. Did you say what you wanted to say? Is what you said logical and understandable to others who do not have your factual knowledge of events? If three people were injured in a car accident and two people were taken to the hospital, what happened to the third?

After you read stories aloud, determine whether the stories make sense the first time they are read or whether you have to reread them for understanding. If you have doubts, ask someone in the newsroom to read your stories. Remember, the listener gets only one chance to hear and understand the news stories you just wrote. Look for minor details and read stories with a questioning mind that accepts nothing at face value. Other things that should be checked are possible defamation or unclear attributions. No word should be split from one line to another, and no sentences should be continued from page one to page two. Stories should have end marks, and each page of multi-page stories should have page numbers.

Delete the word *that* in as many instances as possible. Many times *that* is an unnecessary word that adds harshness to news copy. "That" is a legitimate word for clarification but, in many instances, is overused and can be deleted without affecting meaning.

Do not use literary or newspaper copy editor's symbols to make corrections. These symbols cannot be easily understood and quickly translated by newscasters reading copy in front of microphones or cameras. For example, try to read the following sentence aloud.

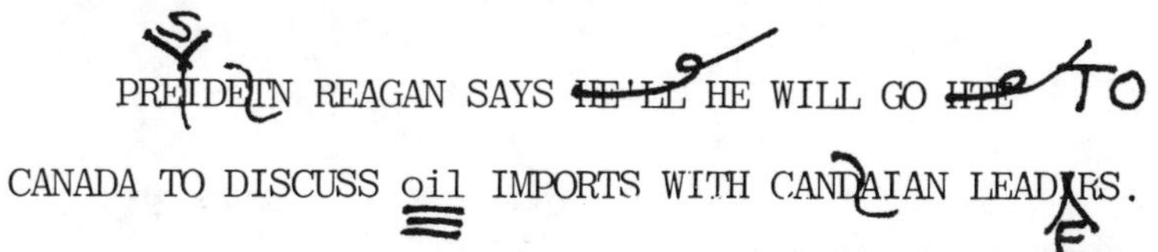

Reading the above sentence aloud is very difficult because the proofreader's symbols confuse and interfere with content. Broadcast newswriters use heavy pencils or flow pens for corrections, so that errors are completely blocked out. If letters are transposed or spelling errors made, the words should be completely taken out and corrections printed above in neat block letters. Read aloud the following sentence.

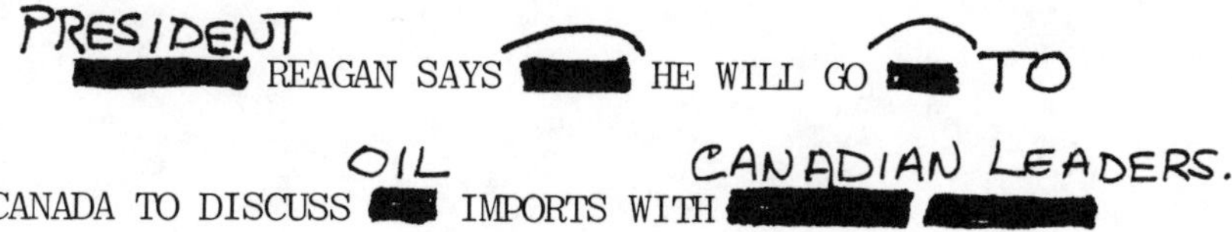

Now, mistakes do not show through copy to confuse newsreaders, and broadcast corrections make the story possible to read without hesitation or stumbling.

Avoid making copy corrections that leave news stories looking like a roller coaster.

THE TRANSIT IS TO...

The copy is extremely difficult to read even if corrections are made neatly in broadcast style. The newswriters should take out whole lines or retype the stories.

Limited amounts of material can be inserted without making copy unintelligible. Write or type information neatly and directly above the place where the insert is to take place.

THE REGIONAL AUTHORITY IS GOING TO...

If, after all editing and corrections are completed, stories are hard to read or messy, then stories should be retyped. Messy copy is hard to read on the air and can create problems for announcers. Always hand in clean copy.

QUIZ

1. If you set your typewriter paper at 0, your typewriter margins for a pica typewriter should be set at____________________________.

2. An eight-line radio news story with one-inch margins would take a news announcer approximately how long to read?____________________________

3. A story slug should contain what elements?

4. What are two standard end signs for news copy?

5. What are the rules for determining whether to write out a number or use the numeral?

6. Write the following in broadcast writing style:

   1/3 ____

   7 ____

   17 ____

   3,012 ______________________________________

   $19.14 ______________________________________

   They will ____________________________________

   It will ______________________________________

7. How would you write the first and second references for the following people: Mr. Richard Wilson (Attorney-at-Law), Lloyd Milan, Mayor, Gainesville, Georgia.

First reference:

Second reference:

8. What are the rules for using Mr., Mrs., Miss and Ms.?

EXERCISE I

1. Change the following sentences to conform with the broadcast news writing style:

   a. He was the coworker

   b. Edward I. Koch, Mayor, New York City

   c. Ralph Jones, 16, 3415 East Memphis Road

   d. John Wilson, President of the fireman's Union Local Twenty, told reporters he will recommend that his union accept the contract offer by management.

   e. Julian Bond, Atlanta, Georgia Mayor; met with council members to discuss $23,116,211.43 city budget. The budget discussions will be #4 on the agenda.

EXERCISE II

Carefully read the following news story. At each point where you find a style error, number the error and on this page write the corresponding number and indicate the correction needed.

The first error has already been marked on the story and the correction given on this page.

1. Incomplete slug. Does not contain story summary such as "Huber on zoning."

Smeyak
10-3

Ralph Huber, Urbana City Councilman, says he is going to lead a fight to overturn recent zoning commission rulings. Mr. Huber says he things the zoning commission has over-stepped its bound when it rezoneeed a residential area for light industry.

Mr. Huber told reporters today that certain members of the zoning commission might benifit financailly from rezoning the 4rd St. Area just south of Miles Blvd.

Mr. Huber met with area residents yesterday who are forming a group to fight the recent zoning decisions. The residents have collected some $3112.00 to hire an attorney to fight present eh their case.

ENDNOTE

1. *AP Broadcast News Handbook* (New York: Associated Press, 1982) p. 230.

2

GRAMMAR

The oral grammatical style of broadcast news writing stresses clarity, simplicity and informality; the same elements found in everyday conversational speech. Newswriters are *conversationally* telling listeners or viewers what happened during the day, not pontificating about world events. Sometime we get carried away with our own importance as newspeople and forget that our job is not to talk down to our listeners but to talk with them conversationally about events that affect their lives. Our writing style must be conversational and reflect the way we speak.

Your words, ideas, sentences and stories must be understood by children, laborers, recent immigrants to the United States, professional people, college graduates and grade school dropouts. Listeners are not homogeneous and you are talking to people who have differing backgrounds, educational experiences, and life-styles. A simplified writing style enlarges the potential audience while complexity reduces the number of people who can understand what you are saying. News consumers must be able to hear broadcast news stories once and be able to understand. Unlike newspapers, which can be read and reread, broadcast news stories are *transitory;* they go by listeners once and they must be understood that first time. There are no second chances for broadcast news listeners, who cannot request a repeat of stories when they do not understand what you were trying to say. If stories are complex or hard to understand with stuffy or imprecise language, the writer has failed to do his or her job.

Broadcast newswriters should say what is meant *simply* and *clearly* using simple words, simple sentences and simple ideas.

WORD CHOICE

The smallest unit that we work with is the word, and good newswriters are very careful in their word choice.[1] Words do not only tell news listeners what happened; words carry a meaning and power all their own. Some words have a connotative meaning which may be more powerful than the denotative meaning. A good example is the word *propaganda*, which originally denoted spreading the Christian faith and is the name of an organization in the Roman Catholic church which has jurisdiction over missionary work. Consider the denotative meaning of *propaganda* which has come to connote spreading false information and rumors to injure and confuse. *Gay* is another word which has a connotative meaning much different from its denotative meaning. *Gay* now implies homosexuality or bisexuality instead of happily excited.

The writer's motto should be *eschew obfuscation*. Eschew obfuscation is a fancy and complex way of saying avoid confusion. If the word choice is between a simple basic word and a larger more complex word, always strive for simplicity. Large complex words are understood by a small audience while one-syllable simple words are understood by nearly everyone.

Instead of	Use:
initial	first
prior to	before
conflagration	fire
procure	get
encounter	meet
objective	aim or goal
sufficient	enough
explicit	plain or clear
modify	change
utilize	use
initiate	start or begin

In most instances, newswriters should use the same words in their news stories that are used in everyday conversation, except for slang and jargon. The following two examples are instances when a newswriter forgot about simplicity and clarity. Both examples occurred in the same sports story:

EPITOME OF GOOD BALL PLAYING

PLETHORA OF TRADES

Epitome and *plethora*! How many listeners really understood what that sports writer was trying to say?

Some language critics say that Americans are losing their ability to speak and write. These critics point to our reliance on jargon and cliches. Cliches are like jokes and the first time is the best. Repeated exposure leads to a lessening of impact. You should avoid using cliches in news copy because it builds reliance on other people's words and ideas. You should write simply and directly using your own writing style and words. If you use other people's ideas and words you will never develop your own distinctive writing style.

A list of cliches could be endless and constantly changing but in just a few radio newscasts the following cliches were heard:

DEALT A BLOW (a crushing blow is the epitome)

DARING ESCAPE (aren't they all daring?)

RAGING FIRE (they all rage)

ANOTHER ROUND OF TALKS (why round?)

OIL RICH MIDDLE EAST (they also have a lot of sand)

BAD WEATHER PLAGUED (doesn't it always plague?)

ON A MORE PLEASANT NOTE (overused)

HERE IN THIS COUNTRY (overused)

GRINDING HEAD-ON COLLISION (overused)

FOREIGN WORDS AND PHRASES

Broadcast writers should avoid using foreign words and phrases unless the words or phrases are so widely known that they are used in everyday conversation. Coup, junta, en route,ex officio, boutique and in absentia have become commonly used in newswriting but many people probably still do not understand what they mean. Even though these words have become *Americanized* and incorporated into our language, many news listeners will not understand them. Test yourself, without consulting your dictionary, and write out the meaning for the following words:

coup

junta

en route

ex officio

boutique

in absentia

coup de grace

de facto

persona non grata

ad hoc

All of the above words are frequently used by network or local broadcast newswriters.

Be cautious when dealing with medical, legal or scientific terms. Many medical, scientific and legal terms are rooted in Latin and should be treated as foreign words and phrases. *Ex Parte* communications, *Writs of Mandamus* or *Certiorari* are common legal words understood by attorneys, but these phrases are not widely understood by laypeople or those not familiar with the legal profession. Medical and scientific terms such as *osmosis, carcinoma, femoral artery, femur* and *thorax* also need to be brought to the level of the audience. We are talking about the diffusion of fluids, cancer, the artery in the thigh, thighbone and chest.

SLANG

Most broadcast news operations forbid the use of slang or jargon. Slang and jargon are like foreign words and phrases because they are the language of special groups or small segments of society. However, some radio and television stations, trying to target their news to specialized audiences, may use slang or jargon which is commonly used by those audiences in an effort to attract that listenership.

Most newswriters avoid slang and write that people are *robbed* not *ripped off*. A person is arrested for possession of amphetamines or drugs not *uppers* and *downers*. It is marijuana not *grass* or *pot*.

Most broadcast journalists tend to be relatively young and able to understand the mores and jargon of various groups in our society, such as the drug culture or certain ethnic groups or gangs. In a television news series dealing with the drug culture, a reporter once referred to the increasing drug habit among middle class children of "sniffing coke." This is a common phrase among many people who work with young people or who are aware of drug jargon. However, one well-educated woman who heard the series later confessed that she missed the whole meaning of the story. She could not understand what thrill anyone would get from sniffing a Coca-Cola through a straw into his or her nose. She heard the phrase "sniffing coke" and completely misunderstood the drug jargon. In an effort to understand, she related the phrase to things she thought she understood. The lesson is simply that jargon and slang are not understood, or easily misunderstood, by many people.

COMPLEXITY

Complexity in broadcast and cable journalism can be reduced by writing simple declarative sentences. The Associated Press calls declarative sentences the "basic ingredient" for anyone who writes news.[2] Simple declarative sentences are short, direct, and make simple understandable statements about something. For example:

MEMPHIS POLICE CHARGE TWO MEN WITH THE ARMED ROBBERY OF A DOWNTOWN SAVINGS AND LOAN ASSOCIATION.

CITY COMMISSIONERS AGREE TO EXPAND THE CHARLESTON BUS SYSTEM INTO THE COUNTY SUBURBAN AREAS.

NEW MEXICO STATE POLICE HAVE SET UP ROAD BLOCKS TO ENFORCE A QUARANTINE ON CALIFORNIA FRUIT AND VEGETABLES.

Good writing is simple writing. To communicate we must be understood and simplicity, brevity and clarity are the keys to understanding. For example, much of the Bible is written at the grade school level of understanding, and it is one of the most widely read and sold books in the world. There are only 69 words in the Ten Commandments, which are written in simple declarative sentences. The beautiful and lyrical 23rd Psalm contains only 118 words. In comparison, our city traffic, health, parking and zoning codes take thousands of words to explain, and we are forced to hire attorneys to interpret their meaning, which is often disputed by other attorneys.

The newswriters should say what they mean to say--using simple words, simple sentences and simple ideas. Complex sentences are just that--complex. A good rule of thumb is one sentence equals one idea. It is also common for broadcast and cable newswriters to use sentence fragments or incomplete sentences. Under normal circumstances a sentence fragment would not be acceptable writing, but since electronic journalists try to mimic normal conversation this is acceptable.

The grammatical differences between newspaper and electronic journalism is narrowing. Twenty years ago most newspaper writers slavishly followed an inverted pyramid writing style that utilized long, complex sentences and forced all five Ws into the lead. The inverted pyramid writing style is still common, but many newspaper writers are now using a broadcast or narrative approach to writing. An example of the inverted pyramid style:

President Reagan, Defense Secretary Weinberger, and Secretary of State Haig met yesterday at the President's western ranch to discuss underground deployment of the MX missile, which is termed "vital to the security of the United States and her allies."

Haig and Weinberger agreed the MX missile should be buried in underground silos in Idaho and Nevada, but other presidential advisors, arguing for above ground deployment say, above ground, the missiles can be moved from one location to another to confuse and deter enemies of the United States.

Reading the above newspaper style story aloud and trying to interpret for audiences would be very hard for newsreaders because of the phrasing and long sentences. News announcers could not read the story without running out of breath and pausing in mid-sentence.

The same story, in our broadcast conversational style, might be written:

PRESIDENT REAGAN HAS YET TO MAKE UP HIS MIND ON HOW HE WILL DEPLOY THE MX MISSILE, WHICH HE CONSIDERS VITAL TO AMERICA'S SECURITY.

HE'S GETTING CONFLICTING ADVICE FROM HIS TOP ADVISORS AND POLITICAL FRIENDS.

YESTERDAY, SECRETARY OF DEFENSE WEINBERGER AND SECRETARY OF STATE HAIG MET WITH THE PRESIDENT AT HIS WESTERN RANCH IN CALIFORNIA. BOTH HAIG AND WEINBERGER WANT THE MX MISSILE BURIED UNDERGROUND IN IDAHO AND NEVADA.

OTHER ADVISORS FAVOR PUTTING THE MX MISSILE ABOVE GROUND. THEY FEEL IF IT CAN BE MOVED TO DIFFERENT LOCATIONS IT WILL CONFUSE POTENTIAL ENEMIES.

Has there been a loss of meaning in the broadcast news story? There has been a reduction of complexity! The newspaper story is 88 words long, contains eight commas and two long sentences. The broadcast rewrite is longer with 93 words but it has only two commas in six sentences. The sentences in the broadcast story are much shorter and easier to understand than the newspaper sentences. Although some short sentences can be terribly complex, the general feeling is that short sentences, containing one simple idea, are easier to read and understand. Short sentences, however, are not an absolute guarantee stories will be understood. The sentences must have continuity and logically build from idea to idea.

Short sentences, while preferred in broadcast news copy, can make stories sound choppy and abrupt. A series of short sentences read aloud creates a jagged cadence that makes listening a chore. Alternating long and short sentences creates a flow or rhythm--a rhythm that makes reading easier for newscasters and listening more pleasant for news listeners.

The MX missile story is an example of building a nice story rhythm through sentence length. The story contains alternating longer and shorter sentences. The sentences in the broadcast story are, in order, 24, 11, 20, 14, 9 and 15 words long.

Short sentences also carry greater impact and power than longer sentences. Extremely short sentences or sentence fragments have the ability to punctuate and indicate finality. For example:

THERE IS A MAJOR FOREIGN POLICY SHIFT IN THE WORKS AS SECRETARY OF STATE HAIG IS TRYING TO CONVINCE PRESIDENT REAGAN TO ESTABLISH FORMAL DIPLOMATIC RELATIONS WITH NORTH KOREA.

THE PRESIDENT MAY AGREE.

The sentences contrast. The lead sentence is long and has a leisurely flow while sentence two is short and abrupt. The simplicity and shortness of sentence two adds power; it also decisively ends the story.

Another method of creating continuity or flow from one sentence to another is to start sentences with *and* and *but*. These two words provide a bridge between sentences; connecting ideas. For example:

LIBYAN JET FIGHTERS FIRED AIR-TO-AIR HEAT SEEKING MISSILES AT U. S. PLANES OFF THE LIBYAN COAST IN INTERNATIONAL WATERS.

AMERICAN PILOTS EASILY OUTRAN THE SOVIET MADE MISSILES AND LANDED SAFELY ON THEIR CARRIER.

BUT DESPITE THE INCIDENT...U.S. OFFICIALS SAY THE NAVAL EXERCISES WILL CONTINUE AND THEY HOPE FOR LIBYAN RESTRAINT IN THE FUTURE.

AND FOLLOWING THE U. S. PUBLIC STATEMENT...LIBYAN OFFICIALS SAID THE NAVAL EXERCISES ARE A VIOLATION OF THEIR TERRITORIAL WATERS.

The use of *but* and *and* to start off a sentence is generally not considered good practice in formal writing. However, starting sentences with *but* and *and* is quite common in everyday language usage; especially conversational language.

VERBAL OVERKILL

Novice broadcast newswriters should try to develop a sparse writing style devoid of cliches, meaningless phrases and over-modifications. Once this sparse, clear writing style is mastered then you can try to develop your own distinctive creative writing style that reflects your own use of language and sentence structure. However, this sparse style that you should first develop will be the backbone of your daily writing.

Overwriting is one of the fastest ways to confuse stories and your audience. Confusion aside, broadcast newswriters have limited time in which to tell stories and economy of words and sentences is important. The average five-minute radio newscast, minus time for the open, close, and commercial break, contains fewer than 500 words. A normal 30-minute newscast, minus open, close, and eight commercial minutes contains less than 3,000 words. Words and time are important commodities for electronic journalists and overwriting is a sure sign of a beginner.

The first thing to remember is that all stories can be cut or edited down. The first editing process takes place when writers decide which facts are important and must be included in news scripts. Other facts or interesting sidebars that do not fit in with the story must be left out or saved for follow-up stories. The editing of facts takes place prior to and during the writing process. This is a part of the journalistic process that is most criticized by media observers or people who are involved in the news story. There is not enough time in newscasts to include all the facts, nuances or feelings that people involved in news stories think are important. The news process involves editing by trained writers/editors who must make decisions about facts to be included and elements to be left out of news scripts. This is news judgment which takes years of news experience to develop and even highly skilled writers and editors make mistakes or show their copy to others to get second or third opinions. This is an area where there are few absolute instances of white or black and most judgments are shades of gray.

Adverbs and adjectives should be omitted from your news copy unless they are necessary to clarify the words they modify. An adjective usually modifies a noun or pronoun. The purpose of adjectives is to make the meaning of the pronoun more definite. An adjective answers the questions what kind, which one, or how many.

THE SUSPECTS

THE ROBBERY SUSPECTS

THE THREE ROBBERY SUSPECTS

THE THREE NEW ORLEANS ROBBERY SUSPECTS

The three New Orleans robbery suspects is an overmodified sentence. There are three adjectives modifying the noun *suspects*. This type of overmodified phrase can turn into a tongue twister for newscasters and the phrase should be rewritten. If all the adjectives are needed, the sentence should be written:

THE THREE ROBBERY SUSPECTS FROM NEW ORLEANS.

Splitting up the adjectives with prepositions breaks the sentence rhythm, making it easier to read aloud.

Adverbs modify verbs, adjectives or other adverbs. Adverbs answer where, when, how, and to what extent. These are all vital elements of news stories which should answer the five Ws of what, where, when, who, or why. However, adverbs can be overused and turn sparse, simple stories into long, wordy stories. For example, how important are the following adverbs to understanding?

HE WAS *EXTREMELY* NICE

IT WAS AN *UNUSUALLY* GOOD CAR

THE ROOM WAS *SPOTLESSLY* CLEAN

HE WAS *TOO* LATE

HE WAS *VERY* TIRED

Granted, in some circumstances, these adverbs would be necessary or nice to use because they add dimensions of understanding. However, we generally overuse adverbs. If you want to say more than:

HIS PERFORMANCE WAS BAD

by adding the adverb unusually:

HIS PERFORMANCE WAS UNUSUALLY BAD

Why not say:

IT WAS HIS WORST PERFORMANCE

We try to use adverbs when we are already dealing with superlative words.

SHE WAS EXCELLENT

We try to go beyond this simple, straightforward sentence by adding adverbs. Do we really add meaning with more adverbs or are we overwriting because we are afraid that our simple words will not convey our meaning? We try to go beyond our meaning with:

SHE WAS *EXTREMELY* EXCELLENT

SHE WAS *VERY* EXCELLENT

SHE WAS *REALLY* EXCELLENT

Part of what we face is that we live in a society where advertising writers try to convince us that their product is better than excellent. We feel that we have to compete with more adverbs, more puffery and more superlatives to help news listeners understand what we are trying to say. If your writing is simple and sparse, when you do use adverbs they will stand out and add the strength you want.

A good way to avoid using adverbs and overwriting is to describe what happened. Instead of saying she was extremely excellent, very excellent, or really excellent, describe the incident that led you to make the statement.

THE USUALLY RESTRAINED NEW YORK THEATER CRITICS GAVE HER A STANDING OVATION, FORCING HER TO COME BACK FOR ELEVEN CURTAIN CALLS.

Another example of summarizing instead of describing would be:

THE FIREMEN WERE TERRIBLY TIRED AFTER FIGHTING THE GASOLINE FIRE.

Why not describe the physical circumstances indicating the degree of exhaustion?

IN 100 DEGREE TEMPERATURES, THE FIREMEN COLLAPSED ON THE GROUND TOO EXHAUSTED TO REMOVE THEIR HOT, HEAVY PROTECTIVE CLOTHING.

The power of description outweighs overworked adverbs. This is something that great broadcast writers learned or knew instinctively. Edward R. Murrow had an uncanny eye for seeing and a simple descriptive writing style to convey the emotion of what he saw as a journalist. If you find your stories overmodified, recast your sentences to describe what occurred. This will usually lead to more interesting stories because description of events has great emotional impact.

Much of our overwriting involves cliches or phrases that fill too much space for the amount of meaning conveyed. For example, have you heard of getting a *general consensus*? *General consensus* is redundant. A consensus means getting general assent or agreement and the word general is not needed. The problem is that we have heard so many people use the phrase *general consensus* that we have incorporated it into our vocabulary without really examining the phrase for meaning. Or, how about *true facts*? Have you ever heard of *true facts*? Facts cannot be false because a fact is true. Some other cliches or phrases that should not be in our vocabulary are:

Instead of:	Use:
in advance of	before
at this point in time	now
stems from the fact	because
due to the fact that	because or due to
in order to	to
take action	act
owing to	because

A full list of cliches could probably fill much of this book. Listing cliches is less important than sensitizing you to their misuse.

Other words that should not be used by broadcast news writers are *latter*, *formerly* and *respectively*. The use of these words can only occur in stories following a series of names, places, or things. They call on news listeners to relate to something previously mentioned and this leads to confusion and misunderstanding.

Two other commonly misused words are *literally* and *figuratively*. Many times writers say something literally happened but they really intended to say something figuratively occurred. Remember, the literal meaning is the exact meaning.

FIREMEN WERE LITERALLY DEAD AFTER FIGHTING THE THREE ALARM FIRE FOR EIGHTEEN HOURS.

Were the firemen really dead? Saying the firemen were literally dead means they are not living. Literally dead cannot mean tired or exhausted.

UNION OFFICIALS WERE LITERALLY LEAPING FOR JOY AFTER GETTING A TWENTY PERCENT PAY RAISE FOR AEROSPACE WORKERS.

Were the union officials really leaping for joy or were they merely excited about their accomplishments and did the writer try to metaphorically describe their emotions? Be exact in your writing and remember that literal means factual.

UNION OFFICIALS WERE HAPPY ENOUGH TO BE LEAPING FOR JOY AFTER GETTING A TWENTY PERCENT RAISE FOR AEROSPACE WORKERS.

Use figuratively and literally sparingly because these words are often misused and they have lost their original impact.

That and *those* are restrictive words that can help you practice word economy. Some stories, like space shots or trials, receive so much news attention that you can assume nearly everyone knows of the event. Use of that and those assumes the audience has prior knowledge of the story. For example:

THOSE TWO RUSSIAN COSMONAUTS CIRCLING THE EARTH ARE CONDUCTING EXPERIMENTS ON THEIR SOYUZ SPACE CRAFT TODAY.

Or:

COAST GUARD SEARCH TEAMS FOUND THE WRECKAGE OF *THAT* FREIGHTER LOST IN LAKE SUPERIOR LAST WEEK.

Or:

THE SURVIVORS OF *THAT* EAST GERMAN TRAIN WRECK HAVE BEEN TAKEN TO HOSPITALS IN EAST BERLIN.

In each of the above examples, news writers are assuming that news listeners have prior knowledge of the events. If, however, you have doubts about the audience's knowledge of the story, you should give the complete background to the story.

TONGUE TWISTERS

There are certain words, sounds and phrases that are hard for announcers and newscasters to read aloud without stumbling or slurring. Nearly every announcer has a few particular words or sounds they avoid but there are certain tongue twisters that pose nearly universal problems and should be avoided.

Two of the most common speech problems are the *slushy S* and *whistling S*. A quick survey of your broadcast news class will indicate that a surprising number of people have S problems. To find out if you do, read the following aloud in front of someone with a good ear for speech patterns or speech deviations.

THE SECOND QUARTER BUSINESS STATISTICS SHOW LEADING ECONOMIC INDICATORS FORECAST A BUSINESS SLUMP IN THE COMING YEAR. THE ADMINISTRATION WAS SEEKING SUPPORT TO AVOID AN ECONOMIC SLUMP BY REDUCING INTEREST RATES ON MORTGAGES AND BUSINESS LOANS.

Even if you do not have S problems, many people do and this means you should avoid writing sentences or phrases where sibilants or S's run together and create problems. Instead of writing:

Business Statistics

Business Slump

Businesses

Was seeking support

You should write around sibilants and avoid S's.

Business reports

Business downturn

Business firms or organizations

Was looking for help

Also avoid writing plural or possessive endings to proper names already ending with an S. Adding that possessive or plural ending can create awkward phrasing.

The Harrises were going

Harris's farm

Howard Hughes's hotel

Instead, rewrite the phrase to avoid the extra S.

The Harris family was going

The Harris farm

The Hughes hotel

Sibilants or S's are not the only problem you should be aware of as broadcast or cable news writers. Consonants can also force announcers to either slur phrases or overemphasize to avoid running words together. You should avoid word combinations where the last letter of one word is the same or has the same sound as the first letter in the next word. For example:

OAK CLIFF	FINE NUMBER
RED DEER	BANK CARD
PETER ABBOT	RIVER RUN

If newscasters are not careful, these word combinations will come out sounding like one word; OAKLIFF, REDEER, FINEUMBERS, PETERRABBOT (as in Easter Bunny fame), BANKARD and RIVERUN.

There are also certain words or phrases that can become problems for newscasters. In most instances, these words and phrases contain several consonants or sounds with the same value. For example:

RURAL

ALUMINUM

MAYORALITY

The similar consonants or sibilants come so close together that awkward vocal patterns are created. You can write around these problems if you see them developing ahead of time. This is the best reason for vocalizing or reading aloud stories as you write and finally reading stories aloud as a final check before giving them to newscasters. More than one announcer has stumbled over the following phrases:

MAYORALITY RACE

RAILROAD WORK RULES DISPUTE

REGIONAL RURAL REHABILITATION PROGRAM

Most tongue twisters can be straightened out by rearranging the sentences and adding a word or two.

THE MAYOR'S RACE

THE RAILROAD LABOR-MANAGEMENT DISPUTE OVER WORK RULES

THE PROGRAM FOR REHABILITATING RURAL AREAS

Straightening out those tongue twisters takes an extra word or two but this is minor compared with the problems tongue twisters or awkward phrases can create. The rules regarding word economy are waived in the case of tongue twisters. A few extra words are preferable to verbal stumbles by newscasters.

Tongue twisters can also be created by running names and titles together. For example:

SOUTH DAKOTA DEMOCRATIC SENATOR GEORGE MC GOVERN

OHIO REPUBLICAN GOVERNOR JAMES RHODES

FORMER DEMOCRATIC PRESIDENTIAL CANDIDATE AND

WISCONSIN SENATOR EUGENE MC CARTHY

Other phrases may have awkward rhythms or cadences that throw off a newscaster's delivery. For example:

UNIVERSITY OF IOWA FRESHMEN STUDENT ENROLLMENT

SPECIAL INVESTIGATIVE UNIT CHIEF'S DESK

Again, the only way around these awkward phrases is to see them coming and write around them by adding a preposition.

FRESHMEN ENROLLMENT AT THE UNIVERSITY OF IOWA

REPUBLICAN GOVERNOR JAMES RHODES OF OHIO

DEMOCRATIC SENATOR GEORGE MC GOVERN OF SOUTH DAKOTA

QUOTATIONS

Newswriters should approach quotes and quotations in the same manner they approach the use of numbers and statistics. An editorial judgment must be made to determine how important quotations will be to stories and what type of impact quotes will have on news listeners or viewers. Quotes can be an important aspect of stories by lending authority and credibility. However, do not use quotes from newsmakers just to add quotes to your stories. Many times you, as a newswriter, will be able to paraphrase what individuals say and make stories more concise and understandable.

Smoothness or story rhythm is an important aspect of newswriting because the way stories are written affects how stories will be read aloud by newscasters. For example:

AT HIS NEWS CONFERENCE...THE PRESIDENT SAID...QUOTE...I WILL GO TO LEBANON AND ISRAEL IF IT WILL BRING ABOUT PEACE IN THE MIDEAST...UNQUOTE.

The above sentence is choppy and newscasters reading this story as written would pause four times, breaking the sentence flow. The story would be easier to read aloud and have a better flow if the newswriter paraphrased what the president said at the news conference.

AT HIS NEWS CONFERENCE...THE PRESIDENT SAID HE'D GO TO LEBANON AND ISRAEL IF IT WOULD BRING PEACE TO THE MIDEAST.

In most news stories, writers should avoid using *quote* and *unquote* in scripts. This breaks the flow of news stories and creates a choppy effect when newscasters, to add emphasis, pause before and after the words *quote* and *unquote*. If someone must be quoted directly, phrases can be used which indicate that it is a direct quote. Some commonly used phrases are:

AS THE PRESIDENT SAID...

THE PRESIDENT SAID...AND WE QUOTE HIM...

IN HIS/HER WORDS

AS HE/SHE PUT IT...

THE PRESIDENT TOLD NEWSPEOPLE...

The only time that you should resort to using quote and unquote in news scripts is when wording is critical or questionable. There are instances when newswriters want listeners to clearly understand that what is being said are direct quotes because the ideas are extremely controversial, the quote contains profanity, or there is a critical need to present exact quotes. In most instances, it is not necessary to add unquote at the end of statements. Your writing and the newscaster's reading abilities will make it obvious when the quotes are over. For example:

THE YOUNG NAVAL OFFICER SAID...QUOTE..."DAMN THE TORPEDOES, FULL SPEED AHEAD."

THE PRESIDENT SAID...AND WE QUOTE HIM..."THIS LATEST PROVOCATION MEANS WAR."

Most newscasters make it obvious when they are directly quoting someone by pauses and voice inflection. News listeners know exactly when Peter Jennings, Dan Rather or Roger Mudd are quoting someone without actually hearing them say *quote* or *unquote*.

When it is necessary to use quotes in stories, newswriters should avoid using lengthy quotations if possible. Long quotes are hard to deal with for newswriters and newscasters. News listeners will also have trouble following what is or is not being quoted. To avoid those problems, most newswriters will mix direct quotes and paraphrases. For example:

PRESIDENT REAGAN TOLD HIS CABINET THEY WOULD...IN HIS WORDS... "HAVE TO BITE THE BULLET AND TRIM THE FEDERAL BUDGET BY SIXTEEN BILLION DOLLARS MORE." THE PRESIDENT SAID REVENUE PROJECTIONS INDICATE A DEFICIT BEYOND WHAT WAS ORIGINALLY PLANNED FOR. THE PRESIDENT TOLD CABINET MEMBERS..."WE MUST TRIM ALL UNNECESSARY FEDERAL SPENDING."

If lengthy quotes have to be used in news stories, you should break up the quotes with qualifying phrases or rename sources to reestablish who is saying what.

A few phrases that let news listeners know the story is still using direct quotes are:

THE MAYOR WENT ON TO SAY...

SHE CONTINUED...

SHE ADDED THIS WARNING...

THE MAYOR CONCLUDED BY SAYING

In most news events when important statements have been made, statements will have been recorded on film, video, or audiotape. There normally will not be a need to quote directly because stories will contain soundbites of newsmakers. However, there are still those times when cameras or audio recorders are not present and newswriters will have to recreate what was said by using direct quotes or paraphrasing quotes.

SOURCES AND ATTRIBUTION

Now that you know the rules for quoting, you must determine what and when to quote and how to attribute statements to sources.

Generally, broadcast newswriters attribute less than their newspaper counterparts. Source attribution adds words to stories and, in some instances, makes stories harder to read aloud and understand. Attributing too many statements in stories will interfere with story flow and confuse listeners or viewers.

The standard rule is to attribute controversial, profane or critical statements when there might be confusion as to who made the statements or when credibility is needed. Source credibility carries over into news stories and the stronger the source the more impact the content or quote will have. For example, note the increasing strength of the following sentences:

WEAK: A LARGE BUDGET DEFICIT COULD MEAN A HIKE IN PERSONAL INCOME TAXES.

WEAK: A SUBCOMMITTEE MEMBER SAID A LARGE BUDGET DEFICIT COULD LEAD TO A HIKE IN PERSONAL INCOME TAXES.

STRONG: WAYS AND MEANS COMMITTEE CHAIRMAN DAN ROSTENKOWSKI SAID A LARGE DEFICIT COULD LEAD TO A HIKE IN PERSONAL INCOME TAXES.

POWERFUL: PRESIDENT REAGAN WARNED CONGRESS THAT A LARGE BUDGET DEFICIT COULD LEAD TO A HIKE IN PERSONAL INCOME TAXES.

As sources increase in prominence and credibility, quotes and stories become more powerful or believable.

There are some general rules for source attributions and quoting.

Do not lead off news stories with quotations followed by source attributions. This is confusing for news listeners, although, leading off with quotes is common newspaper practice where readers can see the quotation marks and understand what is being done. This also sets up situations where attributions are dangling at the ends of the sentences and they are awkward for announcers to read. For example:

"WAR BETWEEN IRAN AND IRAQ IS IMMINENT"...ACCORDING TO IRAQ PRESIDENT HUSSEIN. IRAN'S MILITARY FORCES ARE ON ALERT.

As long as news consumers can see the script the meaning of the story is quite clear. The Iraq President is saying "War between Iran and Iraq is imminent." The newswriter has also found out that Iran's military forces are on alert. The first statement is clearly attributed to Iraq's President, but announcers may not be able to verbally convey that the second statement should not be attributed to President Hussein.

Announcers have to pause twice in these two sentences. The first pause is between the quote and the dangling attribution. The second pause comes at the end of the first sentence following the dangling attribution. The dangling attribution leaves doubt as to which statement is being attributed to the source. If newswriters and announcers are not careful, news listeners may hear:

WAR BETWEEN IRAN AND IRAQ IS IMMINENT. ACCORDING TO IRAQ PRESIDENT HUSSEIN, "IRAN'S MILITARY FORCES ARE ON ALERT."

The meaning of the story has changed because listeners do not understand that the powerful statement about war being imminent was made by the President of Iraq. The impact of the story has been altered significantly. The dangling attribution can leave doubt as to which statement is being attributed to the source.

The best way to avoid all of this confusion created by dangling attributions is to put attributions before the quotes. This will be clear for news listeners and it fits our conversational writing style. In normal conversation if you told a friend that someone said something, you would undoubtedly lead off with the source and then give the statement. For example:

THE BOSS JUST SAID WE ARE GOING TO START WORKING AT NIGHT.

Or:

THE PRESIDENT OF IRAQ SAID WAR BETWEEN IRAQ AND IRAN IS IMMINENT.

Or:

SENATOR HOWARD BAKER SAYS HE'S GOING TO RUN FOR RE-ELECTION.

Or:

NEW YORK MAYOR KOCH SAYS THE CITY IS IN GOOD ECONOMIC CONDITION.

You should also avoid placing attributions in the middle of sentences or phrases. By identifying sources mid-sentence, newscasters are forced to pause or inflect in two places to indicate material is being quoted. For example:

"THE WAY TO CONSERVE OUR WATER SUPPLY" SAYS NEVADA GOVERNOR ROBERT LIST..."IS TO REDUCE WASTEFUL PRACTICES."

It is better to lead off with attributions:

NEVADA GOVERNOR ROBERT LIST SAYS "THE WAY TO CONSERVE OUR WATER SUPPLY IS TO REDUCE WASTEFUL PRACTICES."

Delaying attributions to second sentences can be done occasionally as a writing device but only if first sentences are not profane, controversial or critical. If first sentences are clear and not emotional, then writers can use this device to good advantage occasionally. For example:

"I'LL NEVER EAT FISH AGAIN." THAT'S WHAT UNIVERSITY OF MAINE FRESHMAN SUE LYONS SAID AFTER WINNING HER SORORITY GOLD FISH SWALLOWING CONTEST.

Delaying attributions to second sentences can help newswriters cut down the number of attributions needed in a story. Be careful, though, that delayed attributions are done only with reputable sources. There are also some news stories where attributions can be deleted. For example, the following sentence contains an attribution but it is not really needed.

A STATE DEPARTMENT SPOKESMAN, WILLIAM CASSMAN, SAYS SECRETARY OF STATE HAIG WILL SPEAK WITH EUROPEAN LEADERS ABOUT DEPLOYMENT OF THE NEUTRON BOMB.

The attribution is not needed because the announcement is not controversial. This routine story could be cut down considerably if the attribution is deleted.

SECRETARY OF STATE HAIG WILL SPEAK WITH EUROPEAN LEADERS ABOUT DEPLOYMENT OF THE NEUTRON BOMB.

Deleting the source attribution has not perceptibly affected the story's impact.

In some instances, especially in foreign news items, it is less important to name sources than it is to give the sources' titles and official positions. Foreign names will probably have little meaning to local audiences but official positions indicate the importance or strength of sources. For example:

THE RUMANIAN COMMUNIST PARTY LEADER TOLD WESTERN NEWSPEOPLE

HIS COUNTRY WANTS CLOSER ECONOMIC TIES WITH THE WEST.

The Rumanian leader's name, even if newscasters could pronounce it, would probably have very little meaning to news listeners in the United States, Canada or New Zealand. Including foreign names actually complicates many stories.

In longer stories, where source attributions may be used three or four times to remind listeners who is being quoted, some variety is desired after the primary attributions are made. You should be careful to make sure that after the primary attribution, each subsequent reference to the source is clear. The following example is not clear:

THE CHAIRMAN OF THE ST. LOUIS REGIONAL TRANSIT AUTHORITY SAYS

HE IS GRATEFUL AND RELIEVED THAT THE R-T-A PROPOSAL WAS APPROVED BY

THE VOTERS. WILLIAM JONES SAYS NOW R-T-A CAN MOVE AHEAD.

The question is whether or not the chairman of the St. Louis Regional Transit Authority and William Jones are one and the same person. That is not clear in the story because the primary attribution is not clearly linked to the name in the second sentence. The way the above story is written, William Jones could be an RTA supervisor or the contractor bidding on the RTA extension. The following story provides the necessary link by adding one word.

THE CHAIRMAN OF THE ST. LOUIS REGIONAL TRANSIT AUTHORITY SAYS

HE IS GRATEFUL AND RELIEVED THAT THE R-T-A PROPOSAL WAS APPROVED BY

THE VOTERS.

CHAIRMAN WILLIAM JONES SAYS NOW R-T-A CAN MOVE AHEAD.

Now there is a clear link between the primary and secondary attribution because we added the word "chairman" to the second sentence. There is no doubt that William Jones is also the chairman of the RTA and he made both statements. In other attributions in the same story we could just say "Jones" or "the RTA chairman" as alternative attributions.

Secondary attributions can be important methods of adding information to news stories. For example:

THE U. S. ATTORNEY GENERAL GEORGE FRIEND TOLD A SENATE CRIME

COMMITTEE THAT WE NEED A BETTER APPROACH TO HANDLING THE CRIMINAL

AND THE VICTIM OF CRIME.

IN HIS TESTIMONY...THE FORMER GEORGETOWN LAW SCHOOL PRCFESSOR

WARNED THE SENATORS THAT OUR CRIMINAL SYSTEM GIVES MORE PROTECTION

TO THE CRIMINAL THAN THE VICTIM. FRIEND...WHO HAS CHAMPIONED CIVIL

LIBERTIES CASES...TOLD THE COMMITTEE...

Not only have we gained variety in attributions, but we have also used secondary attributions to give listeners additional information about George Friend's background and credentials.

Be careful when using personal pronouns as secondary attributions. People listening to news stories may not be able to connect who HE, SHE, or THEY might be. If more than one person is named in a story, you should avoid using personal pronouns because it will not be clear to whom the pronoun refers. It is best to be specific and instead of using personal pronouns, re-establish the source's identity. Repeat primary attributions, if necessary, to avoid confusion.

CLAUSES

Another difference between newspaper and broadcast writing style is in the use of clauses. The Associated Press warns its broadcast writers that "clauses can create problems and for that reason should be avoided."[2] Clauses can create confusion but we cannot allow our writing to become sterile and totally avoid the use of clauses. The Associated Press is warning its newswriters that clauses increase the complexity of a sentence and can indicate the writer is trying to include too much information into one sentence. Either the sentence structure needs revision or the long, complex sentence needs to be rewritten as two sentences.

The only absolute rule with clauses is that they should never separate subjects and verbs or source attributions and quotes. This is where clauses become troublemakers and create confusion. For example:

> SECRETARY OF STATE HAIG, HAGGARD FROM LONG NEGOTIATIONS WITH SOVIET LEADER BREZHNEV, TOLD NEWSPEOPLE HE IS HAPPY WITH THE NEW ARMS LIMITATION AGREEMENT.

By the time newscasters get through reading the above sentence, news listeners may be confused as to who was haggard and who was happy over the agreement. The sentence could have been written:

> AFTER LONG HOURS OF NEGOTIATIONS WITH SOVIET LEADER BREZHNEV, SECRETARY OF STATE HAIG SAID HE IS HAPPY WITH THE NEW ARMS LIMITATION AGREEMENT. HAIG APPEARED HAGGARD...

The best writing pattern to follow is simple declarative sentences with subject-verb-object orders. This is a straightforward sentence structure that reduces mystery or confusion.

Do not totally rule out using clauses, but be careful when you do use clauses. Normal sentence structure has dependent clauses following independent clauses. Independent clauses can stand alone, while dependent clauses need to be attached to other clauses. For example:

(Independent clause)
HOUSE AND SENATE LEADERS FAILED TO REACH A COMPROMISE

(Dependent clause)
ON THE SOCIAL SECURITY PLAN DESPITE PRESSURE FROM THE WHITE

HOUSE.

Dependent clauses placed before independent clauses can occasionally be confusing or hard for newscasters to correctly interpret. But this type of inverted pattern can build suspense or bring about an emotional punch. For example:

(Dependent clause)
DESPITE PRESSURE FROM THE WHITE HOUSE...HOUSE AND SENATE

(Independent clause)
LEADERS FAILED TO REACH A COMPROMISE ON THE SOCIAL SECURITY PLAN.

In this particular instance, with the dependent clause in front of the independent clause, the sentence is not confusing and inverting the normal pattern enhances the sentence.

It is common practice to use prepositional phrases to locate where the story took place as a transitional device. This practice, though, as with any writing device, can become monotonous and should not be overused. Some common transitional devices are:

IN PHOENIX, ARIZONA...THREE MEN WERE ARRESTED

IN WASHINGTON, D.C. ...THE NATIONAL FEDERATION OF

AT A ROCHESTER NEW YORK STADIUM...PROTESTORS BLOCKED

As you become a skilled writer, you will not use transitional prepositional phrases often. There are better ways of writing transitions and avoiding this type of cliche.

MISPLACED MODIFIERS

Misplaced modifiers occur in complex sentences. In most instances, writers have included all necessary information but the information is poorly organized. Modifying phrases or words are out of place and the entire meaning of the sentence is changed. Many news listeners may not catch misplaced modifiers because their minds subconsciously make the corrections.

Misplaced modifiers can easily be found and corrected if writers carefully proofread news stories of have someone else read their stories as a double check. In each of the following examples (unfortunately taken from news scripts) try to find the errors before moving on to the corrected sentences:

WRONG: AUTHOR TRUMAN CAPOTE SPOKE ON THE AUTHOR'S LIFE IN

HOCH AUDITORIUM

While Truman Capote spoke on the author's life, I am sure he did not mean the author's life in Hoch Auditorium. The sentence should probably have been written:

CORRECT: MORE THAN EIGHT-HUNDRED STUDENTS IN HOCH AUDITORIUM HEARD WRITER TRUMAN CAPOTE SPEAK ON THE AUTHOR'S LIFE.

Another example of a misplaced modifying phrase:

WRONG: THE PRESIDENT CRITICIZED CONGRESS FOR ITS DELAY IN ACTING ON HIS ECONOMIC AND ENERGY PLANS BEFORE THE MARYLAND LEGISLATURE.

The President's economic and energy plans are not before the Maryland Legislature. The President spoke before the Maryland Legislature and took that opportunity to criticize the U. S. Congress for failing to act on his programs. The sentence should have been written:

CORRECT: SPEAKING BEFORE THE MARYLAND LEGISLATURE... THE PRESIDENT CRITICIZED CONGRESS FOR ITS DELAY IN ACTING ON HIS ECONOMIC AND ENERGY PLANS.

Because of the sensitive nature of some news stories, newswriters have developed a writing style which allows them to write about certain events without placing guilt or defaming individuals. Some novice newswriters do not understand precisely what they are trying to do or say and they make mistakes. For example, people charged with crimes are not necessarily criminals. People are suspects until courts decide the issues. *Alleged* and *reportedly* are used in news stories where newswriters want to make sure that people understand that while police have charged someone with a crime there is still doubt about guilt. For example:

POLICE SAY THE SUSPECT REPORTEDLY...

However, these qualifying words unfortunately are often misused, sometimes with tragic-comic results. The following misplaced words were heard in local newscasts.

CHARGES WERE FILED AGAINST THE ALLEGED MAN

THE REPORTED SUSPECT

Important words were misused and story content was significantly altered.

In each of the above examples, newswriters failed to say what they wanted to say. The information is incorrectly presented because modifying words or phrases are in the wrong place. Carefully reading over your copy will help you eliminate some of the problems of misplaced words or modifying phrases. Testing might include reading sentences aloud in three or four different ways to see how sentences sound and fit together.

TRANSITIONS

Transitions are those words and phrases used by writers to get from one story to another or from one aspect of a story to another. Some transitions have been overused and have become cliches. For example:

HERE AT HOME

HERE IN THIS COUNTRY

MEANTIME

IN OTHER RELATED DEVELOPMENTS

INCIDENTALLY

Transitions, if properly used, can take a number of related elements of a story and deftly tie them together. See Example 2-1.

The first part of the "Sadat assassination" story deals with events occurring in Egypt. Starting with the fifth paragraph, other related elements of the story are brought in with the paragraph describing Prime Minister Begin's reaction to the assassination. Paragraph six related U. S. official comments and paragraph seven covers Libyan reaction to President Sadat's death.

In Example 2-1, a number of related aspects of the Sadat assassination are pulled together in one story. In each one of the paragraphs, location references are given to alert listeners about transitions from one aspect of the story to another. These types of transitions are more subtle than utilizing overworked cliches.

COLOR

More people in the United States get their news from radio, television, and cable than any other news source. While newspaper and news magazine readership is on the decline, the audiences for broadcast and cable news continue to grow. Television networks are planning major expansions in their news programming. ABC started the popular "NIGHTLINE" during the Iranian hostage crisis. ABC executives found such a large audience wanting news at that late hour that even when the crisis was resolved "NIGHTLINE" remained in place. Cable News Network (CNN) started a 24-hour television news service. NBC executives announced plans to expand their early evening news to one hour, although both CBS and ABC executives had discussed similar expansions for several years. People like to view television news and listen to radio news. Unlike print journalism, radio and television news is immediate and personal. News consumers become involved in broadcast news stories: feeling the grief of older couples defrauded out of their life savings, the tragedy of hurricanes, or the exhilaration of winning football teams. Much of this vicarious involvement is created through the use of interviews, actualities, and live reports. But some of this involvement is created through a personal writing approach developed by broadcast and cable journalists reporting news in conversational, colorful language. Colorful language is not dwelling on sensational aspects of news; it is finding inherent drama in news events and not getting between it and news consumers.

News scripts are always being handed back to newswriters with comments of "it's full, it needs to be livened up" or "it needs some life, rewrite it." Editors or newscasters handing back stories may not be able to describe exactly what is wrong, but they know the stories can be better and should be better than they are. Adding

EXAMPLE 2-1

SADAT
ASSASSINATION
3:00 p.m. news
9-7

EGYPT'S PRESIDENT ANWAR EL-SADAT IS DEAD, THE VICTIM OF AN ASSASSINATION THIS MORNING WHILE HE REVIEWED A MILITARY PARADE IN CAIRO.

FOR SEVERAL HOURS NEWS OF HIS DEATH WAS WITHHELD BY THE EGYPTIAN GOVERNMENT...APPARENTLY TO GIVE THEM TIME TO PLAN STRATEGY.

THE MAN IN CHARGE OF EGYPT AT THIS TIME IS SADAT'S VICE PRESIDENT... HOSNI MUBARAK. MUBARAK IS BELIEVED TO BE A STRONG SUPPORTER OF SADAT'S INTERNATIONAL POLICIES BUT LITTLE ABOUT THE VICE PRESIDENT IS KNOWN OUTSIDE OF EGYPT.

THE CITY OF CAIRO AND THE WHOLE OF EGYPT IS QUIET. ONE WESTERN DIPLOMAT LIKENED THE MOOD TO ONE OF SUBDUED SHOCK.

ONE OF SADAT'S CLOSE FRIENDS...ISRAELI PRIME MINISTER BEGIN EXPRESSED DEEP SORROW UPON LEARNING OF THE DEATH OF SADAT...A MAN WHO HELPED BRING PEACE BETWEEN ISRAEL AND EGYPT...A PEACE THAT PARTIALLY HINGED ON THE RELATIONSHIP AND TRUST BETWEEN BEGIN AND THE DEAD EGYPTIAN PRESIDENT.

THERE IS SOME SPECUALTION IN THE UNITED STATES THAT THE ASSASSIN'S BULLETS THAT KILLED SADAT MAY HAVE ALSO DEEPLY WOUNDED THE PEACE PROSPECTS BETWEEN ISRAEL AND EGYPT. U. S. OFFICIALS ARE CAUTIOUS ABOUT PREDICTING EGYPT'S COURSE OF ACTION UNDER AN UNKNOWN LEADERSHIP.

ONE OF SADAT'S BITTEREST ENEMIES IN THE MID-EAST...LIBYAN LEADER MAUMMAR QADDAFI HAS PROCLAIMED A DAY OF REJOICING IN LIBYA TO CELEBRATE SADAT'S DEATH.

30

color can turn average stories into good stories that have greater meaning for the people who will hear them. In all probability, the writer's talents or writing style did not live up to the event's possibilities. Maybe the writer sat down and quickly knocked out stories without thinking about the meaning of the stories or the impact they would have on people listening to news. The newswriter failed to find the inherent drama in news events and develop it through colorful language. The writer may have written stories in past tense, used passive words or stressed the negative instead of positive aspects. These types of stories will not get audience involvement because the writer personally failed to get involved with the stories. The writer did not find or understand the importance of the news events and quite obviously could not convey something he or she did not feel.

TENSE

When we talk with friends we usually talk about things that have just happened and we tell our stories in present or present perfect tense. Newspaper and wire service copy is usually written in past tense, but broadcast news is written in a conversational style that, if possible, should use present or present perfect tense. Present tense says something *is happening* now, while present perfect tense says something *has just happened*. Immediacy becomes part of the story because we are talking about something that is happening or has just happened. Immediacy is a key element of broadcast news and listeners are impressed with the urgency of something happening now. For example:

PRESIDENT REAGAN *IS* MEETING WITH SECRETARIES OF DEFENSE AND STATE OVER DEPLOYMENT OF THE MX MISSILE AND THE B-ONE BOMBER. MR. REAGAN *IS* EXPECTED TO ANNOUNCE THIS AFTERNOON A SCALED DOWN PLAN FOR THE MX DEPLOYMENT AND A LIMITED BUILDING PROGRAM FOR THE B-ONE BOMBER.

The lead sentence is written in present tense, stressing what *is* going on at this moment which is, the President is holding meetings with top advisors. *IS* stresses that the action is taking place at that moment. The use of present or present perfect tense usually eliminates the need for words like "today," "at this moment," "this morning" or "this afternoon." This does not mean that you should always avoid the use of "today" or the other time phrases. The present tense can only be effectively used in stories that are ongoing or have just happened.

The second sentence in the above story switches to the future tense--what Mr. Reagan is expected to do in the future. The use of future tense in newswriting is not unusual, but predicting future actions should be based on solid information.

Parts of this story, however, may need to be placed in time perspective for news listeners. News is an ongoing process, and it is not unusual to use present, future and past tense in the same story. For example:

PRESIDENT REAGAN IS MEETING WITH SECRETARIES OF DEFENSE AND STATE OVER DEPLOYMENT OF THE MX MISSILE AND THE B-ONE BOMBER. MR. REAGAN IS EXPECTED TO ANNOUNCE THIS AFTERNOON A SCALED DOWN PLAN FOR THE MX

DEPLOYMENT AND A LIMITED BUILDING PROGRAM FOR THE B-ONE BOMBER.

THREE YEARS AGO, PRESIDENT CARTER SCRAPPED THE B-ONE BOMBER AND THE MX MISSILE PROGRAMS BECAUSE OF COST.

Parts of the above story need to be placed in time perspective for news listeners. It is important for news consumers to understand that various MX and B-1 proposals have been around for years and previous presidents have considered them.

The use of *today* seems to be a concern for novice news writers. Some ways to eliminate today from news stories are to use other time references. For example:

LESS THAN AN HOUR AGO, A SMALL CESSNA 150 CRASHED AT THE LITTLE ROCK AIRPORT.

SHORTLY BEFORE EIGHT THIS MORNING, ONE PERSON WAS KILLED AND TWO OTHERS WERE INJURED...

Or:

RIGHT NOW, CITY COMMISSIONERS ARE DELIBERATING THE FATE OF THE CITY'S MASS TRANSIT SYSTEM...

Or:

DALLAS POLICE...*AT THIS MOMENT*...ARE AT THE SCENE OF A...

Some novice newswriters, carried away with the immediacy of broadcast news, try to add color to their stories by cheating on updates. They try to force old stories into present or present perfect tense and leave out needed time references such as *yesterday* or *last week*. They forget that not every story happened today and that old news is still newsworthy under certain circumstances. Do not lie about time elements. Old news stories, if they are being updated or reported for the first time, may have as much interest or immediacy as something happening at that moment. Don't cheat on time elements because it is factually wrong and, invariably, someone will catch your "error." The following is an old story reported a week after the event.

LAST WEEK A SMALL PRIVATE PLANE TOOK OFF FROM WEST PALM BEACH AIRPORT FOR THE SHORT HOP OVER TO THE BAHAMAS. THE PLANE NEVER ARRIVED. TODAY...A SMALL BAHAMIAN FISHING BOAT PLUCKED 28-YEAR-OLD RALPH ZYMEK OUT OF THE OCEAN BADLY SUNBURNED AND INCOHERENT. HE SURVIVED A WEEK AT SEA...WITHOUT WATER...AND BADLY CUT FROM THE CRASH. HE'S ALIVE IN A MIAMI HOSPITAL TELLING COAST GUARD OFFICIALS HOW HE SURVIVED.

Although the plane crash took place more than a week before the story is reported, the time element actually enhances the impact of the story. The use of "last week" does not diminish the news or human interest value of what took place. Because of the unusual aspects of the story, the use of past tense and present tense fits together in logical order. The story is clear and news listeners will understand the time element which is an important part of the news story.

Some stories have to be written in the present tense. For example, when someone gives his/her opinion past tense does not fit. For example:

FLORIDA GOVERNOR BOB GRAHAM *SAID* TODAY HE THOUGHT THAT THE FEDERAL GOVERNMENT MUST BEAR A GREATER SHARE OF THE HAITIAN REFUGEE COSTS.

Written in the past tense, this news story stresses what Bob Graham thought in the past. Does he still feel the same way and would he say the same thing again? Unless you have contrary information, you should assume that Governor Graham's attitudes have not changed and the reference to what he thinks should be in the present tense even if the story is hours or days old.

FLORIDA GOVERNOR BOB GRAHAM *SAYS* THE FEDERAL GOVERNMENT MUST BEAR A GREATER SHARE OF THE HAITIAN REFUGEE COSTS.

THE GOVERNOR SPOKE AT A KIWANIS LUNCHEON IN MIAMI... THE AREA WHICH HAS SEEN THE GREATEST INFLUX OF HAITIAN AND CUBAN REFUGEES IN THE PAST 18-MONTHS.

Now the story has life. Governor Bob Graham still believes in what he says about refugee costs even though he made the statement hours ago. When the statement was made, though, needs clarification through a time reference in the second sentence. By writing the story in the present tense and eliminating time references the writer is able to cut four words out of the lead sentence, and the shorter sentence is easier to read.

In the reverse, some stories must be written in the past tense to make sense. The news item may be dated and the use of present or present perfect tense may sound awkward and create confusion. For example:

ONE MAN *IS* KILLED IN A ONE CAR ACCIDENT IN DOWNTOWN BALTIMORE *LAST NIGHT*.

Even though broadcast newswriters mix tenses in stories, the above example is ridiculous. The words *is* and *last night* in the story conflict. The story occurred last night--far enough in the past so that past tense is natural and phrasing the story in the present or present perfect tense makes the story sound awkward.

ONE MAN *WAS* KILLED IN A ONE CAR ACCIDENT IN DOWNTOWN BALTIMORE *LAST NIGHT*.

The point to remember when dealing with tenses is to make stories sound natural. If stories are dated, then use past tense to describe what happened instead of trying to force stories to sound fresh by using present or present perfect tense. In many instances, however, simply updating leads can allow you to use present or present perfect tense in leads to emphasize the freshest element of stories. The use of present and present perfect tense in lead sentences will be discussed in Chapter 3.

ACTIVE VOICE

One good way to make vital stories sound boring is to write in the passive voice instead of the active voice. Passive voice slows down news stories and de-emphasizes the natural excitement and action in news. Stories written in passive voice have subjects being acted upon. Some passive voice examples:

THE VICTIM'S CAR WAS STRUCK BY A TRAIN...

REDUCING SERVICES TO THE COUNTY WAS DISCUSSED AT LAST NIGHT'S REGIONAL TRANSIT BOARD MEETING...

THE TWO SUSPECTS WERE CHARGED WITH MURDER...

The same information is in each of the above sentences, but the presentation of the information downplays the natural exictement in each of the news stories.

The key to writing in the active voice, in most instances, is word order. The subject must control the action rather than being on the receiving end. The same sentences written in active voice have a much different feel.

THE TRAIN STRUCK THE VICTIM'S CAR.

THE REGIONAL TRANSIT BOARD IS DEBATING WHETHER OR NOT TO REDUCE BUS SERVICE TO THE COUNTY.

TWO SUSPECTS FACE MURDER CHARGES.

The same facts and basic wording are present but the sentences are rewritten to stress the action-oriented active voice. Another aspect of writing in the active voice is present in the Regional Transit Authority story. Boards, commissions, authorities, panels and councils do not meet to discuss--THEY DISCUSS, ACT, DEBATE or DECIDE. How boring it is to talk about the meeting when the real action item is what they met about and how they handled the topics. The use of active voice and present perfect tense can take a day-old commission meeting and stress the action elements. For example:

THE COUNTY COMMISSION *HAS REJECTED* PLANS TO RENOVATE THE OLD SEAGLE BUILDING. *YESTERDAY*, COMMISSIONERS HEARD ARGUMENTS...

Or:

THE SCHOOL BOARD *HAS VOTED* TO CLOSE A PREDOMINANTLY BLACK

SCHOOL IGNORING ARGUMENTS FROM AREA RESIDENTS. ANGRY BLACK RESIDENTS

TOLD THE SCHOOL BOARD MEMBERS *LAST NIGHT* THAT...

Don't write about school board or commission meetings, write about what school boards or commissions do during meetings and stories will stress active elements.

ACTIVE VERBS

Using forceful or active verbs is also a way of adding color to news stories. Active verbs describe rather than merely relay facts. For example:

THE MAYOR *WENT* INTO THE COUNCIL ROOM FOR HIS MEETING WITH

THE POLICE CHIEF.

The verb *went* certainly set the tone of the above story. How much different this story would be if the neutral verb was replaced with something more descriptive, like *strolled*.

THE MAYOR *STROLLED* INTO THE COUNCIL ROOM FOR HIS MEETING

WITH THE POLICE CHIEF.

What does *strolled* indicate to you about the mayor or his attitude as he went to meet the police chief? *Strolled* has given the story a whole new feeling that will be conveyed to the news listeners. *Strolled* indicates a casual approach as compared with *strode*.

THE MAYOR *STRODE* INTO THE COUNCIL CHAMBERS FOR HIS MEETING

WITH THE POLICE CHIEF.

Now the mayor's actions take on a purposeful aura. *Strode* changes the feeling of the story. The Mayor is now forceful and businesslike.

Everytime you choose a verb, make sure the verb describes exactly what happened. Verbs add color and action to stories, but the wrong verb choice changes the meaning of stories.

Some active or forceful verbs have been overworked and have become cliches. Beginning writers always have firemen *rushing* or *racing* to the scenes of whatever disasters may have occurred. *Crash* is another overworked verb. Why does it always have to be a two car *crash?* Why not a two car accident? Does the car always have to crash into the utility pole or another car. Why not *struck* or *hit*? Admittedly, *raced* and *crashed* are active verbs that add color and excitement to news stories, and announcers are able to read these two words with a great deal of emphasis. But, they are overworked and should be used sparingly only when other active verbs do not adequately fit the situation.

Said is another verb that poses problems for novice newswriters. *Said* (or the present tense *says*) is a neutral verb commonly used to set up quotes or paraphrased information. Beginning writers run into problems when they think they've used *said* too often in the same story and they start to use synonyms. Synonyms for *said* do not always carry the same connotative meaning. For example:

THE MAYOR *DISCLOSED*

THE MAYOR *VOWED*

THE MAYOR *DECLARED*

THE MAYOR *REPORTED*

THE MAYOR *TOLD*

THE MAYOR *STATED*

THE MAYOR *PROMISED*

Each of the synonyms for *said* changes the meaning of stories. *Disclosed* implies that information has been kept secret. *Vowed, promised, stated,* and *declared* add force to statements that *said* and *told* do not convey. *Reported* implies a formality of preparation and delivery. For example:

SECRETARY OF STATE HAIG *REPORTED* TO THE SENATE FOREIGN RELATIONS COMMITTEE ON LIBYAN INVOLVEMENT IN THE ASSASSINATION OF EGYPTIAN PRESIDENT ANWAR SADAT.

The use of *added* and *went on to say* as synonyms for *said* is a common practice for broadcast newswriters but, in most instances, it is wrong. These synonyms imply statements were afterthoughts and of lesser importance. If it is an afterthought and of lesser importance, why bother to report the statement?

PRESIDENT REAGAN SAYS U-S TROOPS WILL NEVER BE USED IN THE SUDAN. *HE ADDED* THAT A SENATE VOTE PROHIBITING MILITARY AID TO SUDAN WAS AVOIDING OUR RESPONSIBILITY TO THE CAUSE OF MIDEAST PEACE.

A better use of *added* would be:

THE STATE HEALTH DIRECTOR REPORTED TO A HOUSE LEGISLATIVE COMMITTEE THAT HEALTH VIOLATIONS WERE FOUND IN FORTY-THREE PERCENT OF THE STATE'S ELDERLY CARE CENTERS.

LATER IN THE MEETING STATE HEALTH DIRECTOR WHITE *ADDED* THAT NEARLY HALF OF THOSE VIOLATIONS WERE MINOR AND EASILY CORRECTED.

In this example, *added* does not make the second statement an afterthought. The second sentence expands and clarifies the first statement.

WRITE POSITIVE

In many news stories writers face choices of whether or not to write stories in a positive or negative manner. Writing positive is another way of adding color to news stories. You stress the positive aspects of stories--what people intend to do rather than what they plan not to do. It is a matter of describing a half-filled water glass as either half-empty or half-full. Most of us, except the eternal pessimist, are attuned to the positive role rather than the negative. We tend to view the positive role as forceful and dynamic while we see the negative position as obstructionist.

First, some negative examples:

PRESIDENT REAGAN SAYS HE WILL NOT SIGN INTO LAW A BLOATED FEDERAL BUDGET...

Or

SECRETARY OF STATE HAIG SAYS HE DOES NOT SEE ANY NEED FOR ESTABLISHING FULL DIPLOMATIC RELATIONS WITH IRAN UNTIL THERE IS A STABLE GOVERNMENT IN CONTROL OF THE COUNTRY.

Or:

TEXAS GOVERNOR WILLIAM CLEMENTS SAYS HE WILL NOT ATTEND AN AUSTIN POLITICAL FUND RAISING DINNER BECAUSE OF AN IMPORTANT GOVERNORS' CONFERENCE.

Now, the stories are rewritten in a positive voice:

PRESIDENT REAGAN SAYS HE WILL VETO A BLOATED FEDERAL BUDGET BILL...

Or:

SECRETARY OF STATE HAIG SAYS WHEN THERE IS A STABLE GOVERNMENT IN CONTROL OF IRAN WE WILL ESTABLISH FULL DIPLOMATIC RELATIONS WITH THAT COUNTRY.

Or:

TEXAS GOVERNOR WILLIAM CLEMENTS SAYS HE WILL ATTEND AN IMPORTANT GOVERNOR'S CONFERENCE AND WILL MISS AN AUSTIN POLITICAL FUND RAISING DINNER.

The President, Secretary of State, and Texas Governor have been cast in forceful roles by changing negatively written stories into positive stories. These men now seem to be in control of events rather than reacting to forces outside their control.

The vast majority of news listeners will not realize what we have done, but we will have avoided a negative story and added color to our writing style.

It's obvious that you cannot change the negative aspects of every story. In some instances, a positively phrased sentence would be confusing.

THE MAYOR TOLD CITY COUNCIL *HE WILL REFUSE TO OPPOSE* ATTEMPTS

BY THE CITY WORKERS TO CHANGE THE CITY BARGAINING STATUS.

He will refuse to oppose is wordy and obscures the meaning of the story. Written in the negative, the meaning of the sentence is immediately clear.

THE MAYOR TOLD CITY COUNCIL *HE WILL NOT OPPOSE* ATTEMPTS

BY CITY WORKERS TO CHANGE THE CITY BARGAINING STATUS.

Above all else, our writing must be clear. Positively phrased statements are preferred but your goal should be clarity of writing style. Colorful language without understanding is useless.

PRONOUNS

Listener involvement in your news stories can also be increased by the use of the pronouns, *we*, *our*, *us*, and *you*. For example:

WELL, CITY COUNCIL VOTED TO RAISE *OUR* TAXES AGAIN.

Or:

MORE BAD WEATHER IN STORE FOR *US* TONIGHT.

Or:

WE'RE GOING TO BE PAYING MORE TAXES IF SENATOR TOM

BILLINGS HAS HIS WAY.

Or:

IF *YOU'RE* DRIVING A LARGE CAR...*YOU* MAY BE PAYING MORE

GASOLINE TAXES NEXT YEAR.

Use of pronouns personalizes the news and binds the news listeners/viewers to news stories. When newscasters use pronouns, news listeners are being told that we are all in this together. Newscasters are placing themselves in the same situation and on the same level as news listeners by saying we are all going to be affected by whatever happens.

A subtle barrier of formality is placed between newscasters and news listeners when *our*, *we*, *us*, and *you* are omitted from the news script.

CITY COUNCIL VOTED TO RAISE TAXES AGAIN.

Or:

MORE BAD WEATHER IN STORE FOR THE REGION TONIGHT.

Or:

TAXES WILL BE GOING UP IF SENATOR TOM BILLINGS HAS HIS WAY.

Or:

LARGE CAR OWNERS MAY BE PAYING MORE GASOLINE TAXES NEXT YEAR.

The more traditional writing style allows newscasters to remain detached from the news. They retain an objective image and many newspeople feel this is the proper role for newscasters and news departments. So, while the use of *our*, *us*, *we*, and *you* can increase listener involvement, some newspeople feel it imperils the traditional neutrality of newscasters. There is some feeling that if newscasters indicate they are also involved and affected by news events, their objectivity can be questioned.

During the Vietnam conflict, some news departments banned the use of *us*, *we*, and *our* in Vietnam-related stories because there was such a deep emotional division over the war. These news departments wanted to avoid accusations that they favored either side.

QUIZ

1. Give an example of what is meant by the term "dangling attribution."

____

____

2. In a broadcast news story, how would you use the words "former" and "latter?" Why?

____

____

____

3. How would you delineate the differences between a story written in active voice and a story written in passive voice?

____

____

____

4. Good broadcast news writing is ____________________ writing.

5. Clauses can create problems. To avoid problems with clauses, what order should you normally follow?

____

____

____

6. What is meant by connotative meaning of a word?

____

____

7. What are the broadcast writing rules for using slang or jargon?

____

____

____

8. What are the rules for using "quote" and "unquote" in news copy?

9. Newspaper reporters follow an inverted pyramid writing style that places the five Ws in the lead. Broadcast reporters try to follow what style?

10. For current or breaking news stories, what verb tense is desirable for broadcast news stories?

EXERCISES

Rewrite the following sentences so they conform to broadcast writing styles.

1. "RIOTS IN GDANSK, POLAND, WILL CONTINUE AS LONG AS THERE ARE FOOD SHORTAGES AND MARTIAL LAW," ACCORDING TO UNDERSECRETARY OF STATE WILLIAM CASSMAN.

   ____

   ____

   ____

   ____

2. AN F-A-A INVESTIGATOR HAS SAID THE INVESTIGATION WILL START TOMORROW.

   ____

   ____

   ____

3. SIDNEY WAITE, HOUSE COMMITTEE CHAIRMAN, CRITICISED COMMITTEE MEMBERS FOR NOT ATTENDING AN IMPORTANT LEGISLATIVE SESSION BEFORE THE NATIONAL PRESS CLUB.

   ____

   ____

   ____

   ____

4. THE CITY COMMISSION MET LAST NIGHT AND COMMISSIONERS CONSIDERED ANNEXING THE WESTMORELAND SUBDIVISION.

   ____

   ____

   ____

ASSIGNMENTS

1. Determine which two or three radio stations in your community have the best radio news operations. Record a local newscast from each station and, in writing, analyze the stations' news writing styles. Which station has the best writing style?

2. Clip out five local news stories from your newspaper and re-write them, changing grammar, attributions, quotations, verb tense, and voice to conform to broadcast writing style. Hand in the rewritten copy to your instructor with the newspaper articles clipped to the copy.

3. On a cassette tape, record yourself reading wire copy and the following statement to determine if you have voice or articulation problems. Listen to the tape with someone skilled in announcing or speech analysis.

THE SECOND QUARTER BUSINESS STATISTICS SHOW LEADING ECONOMIC INDICATORS FORECAST A BUSINESS SLUMP IN THE COMING YEAR. THE ADMINISTRATION WAS SEEKING SUPPORT TO AVOID AN ECONOMIC SLUMP BY REDUCING INTEREST RATES ON MORTGAGES AND BUSINESS LOANS.

ENDNOTES

1. Appendix B contains a list of common word choice and writing errors.

2. *AP Broadcast News Handbook*, p. 18.

3

LEADS AND ORGANIZATION

LEAD ELEMENTS

The lead of any news story is generally considered to be the first sentence, although this is not always true. Sometimes, leads consist of the first several sentences or phrases of stories. An example of a two sentence lead was used by Gary Nunn of NBC news.

IT IS OFFICIAL. PRESIDENT SADAT OF EGYPT IS DEAD.[1]

Two sentence leads are unusual. However, Nunn was relying on the fact that the Sadat assassination story had been running continuously on all radio and television networks for several hours prior to his newscast. During the live network news coverage, few newspeople were willing to come out and say officially that Sadat was dead until a government statement was released in Cairo.

Leads or first sentences of news stories are expected to *catch* and *maintain* listener attention and summarize stories or some important aspect of the stories. Newspaper journalists have developed a highly structured approach for leads and story organizations. Newspaper leads contain all of the basic elements of news stories: Who, What, Why, When, Where, and How. Stories are organized like an inverted pyramid.

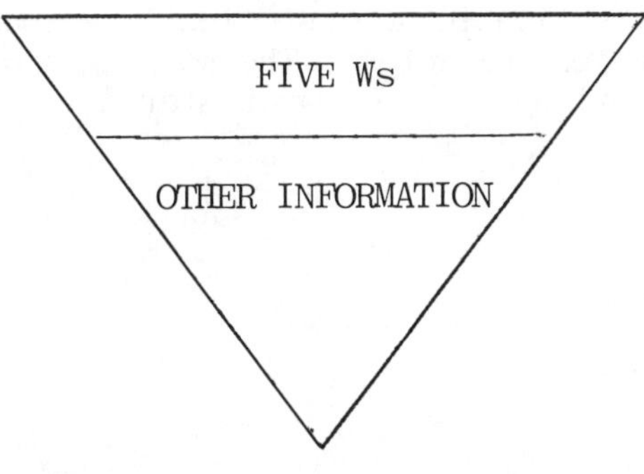

All of the important facts, the five Ws, are contained in lead sentences. Other facts, less important or explaining leads, are presented in order of descending importance which, if diagrammed, look like the inverted pyramid above. Newspaper readers, in a hurry, could read the lead sentences and know the essence of the stories. Newspaper editors, faced with trying to fit long stories into small spaces, could cut the last paragraphs of stories without losing essential information.

A newspaper story written in inverted pyramid style might look like the following example:

> Elizabeth S. Benton, 26, 2214 SW 23rd Avenue, Delaware, Ohio, underwent surgery this morning at Doctor's Hospital for injuries sustained in a one car accident on Morse Road at 11:05 p.m. last night.
>
> Benton is reported in stable condition by a hospital spokesperson. She was admitted in serious condition with extensive head and chest injuries.
>
> Columbus police report that Benton, who was driving eastbound on Morse Road, apparently lost control of her car. Her car jumped the center median strip, swerved into the westbound lane and struck a concrete bridge abutment.

This highly structured approach to newspaper writing has been giving way to a narrative organization and writing style. Some newspaper editors and reporters feel that the inverted pyramid organization shoves too many facts at readers in too short a time. They feel that a narrative writing style parcels out facts in a natural, conversational manner that leads to greater comprehension.

Broadcast newswriters have been using a narrative organization and writing style for more than forty years. Newspaper style leads containing the five Ws and an inverted pyramid will not work in cable, radio and television. Announcers find that they cannot easily read newspaper style copy because it is choppy instead of conversational. News listeners are overwhelmed by newspaper leads which pack too many facts into one sentence. Broadcast news listeners cannot go back and reread unclear lead sentences as they might do with newspapers. The Associated Press has good advice for broadcast writers to "let Who, What, When, Where and Why come naturally in your story. Let one thought flow into the next."[2] This advice reinforces the broadcast narrative writing style.

Broadcast leads are not like newspaper headlines, although they may serve the same general purpose. Newspaper headlines are designed to catch the readers' attention and focus that attention to news stories. Newspaper headlines convey the meaning of stories in a few general words. The wording and size of letters indicates the perceived importance of newspaper stories. Newspaper headlines might read:

> Graft A Way of Life
>
> Accident Kills Three
>
> Drug Ring Exposed
>
> Dog Bites Child

Newspaper headlines are seldom complete sentences; they are usually short phrases designed to focus reader attention to main stories. Broadcast leads, on the other hand, are sentences or phrases that have a natural flow and read well. For example:

FEDERAL INVESTIGATORS SAY THAT AS MANY AS SIXTY PERCENT OF OKLAHOMA COUNTY OFFICIALS, PAST AND PRESENT, TOOK KICKBACKS AND GRAFT.

Or:

THREE PEOPLE WERE KILLED EARLY THIS MORNING IN A TWO CAR ACCIDENT ON THE INNERBELT.

Or:

A WELL-ORGANIZED DRUG RING, WHICH OWNED AIRPORTS AND SMALL REGIONAL AIRLINES IN FLORIDA AND FIVE MIDWESTERN STATES, HAS BEEN BROKEN BY FEDERAL AGENTS.

Or:

A FIVE-YEAR-OLD DENTON GIRL FACES A PAINFUL SERIES OF RABIES SHOTS UNLESS AUTHORITIES FIND THE DOG THAT BIT HER.

Broadcast news leads may summarize or emphasize one or more aspects of stories, but broadcast leads will seldom be as detailed or explicit as newspaper leads. Instead of the five Ws inserted into the newspaper leads, broadcast leads may emphasize either *who*, *what*, *when*, or *where*. The *how* and *why* of news events will probably be the body of the news stories.

WHERE will probably be an important aspect of most local, state or regional leads. Locating where stories take place can direct audience attention to local or regional stories of interest and it can serve as a transition from one story to another. For example:

(where)
IN EL PASO, POLICE ARRESTED FIVE PEOPLE AND CHARGED THEM WITH TRANSPORTING ILLEGAL ALIENS INTO THE UNITED STATES.

Or:

(where)
IN SOUTH BOSTON...OPPONENTS TO SCHOOL BUSING SAY THEY PLAN ON GOING TO COURT...

Or:

(where)
HERE IN SALT LAKE CITY, LEADERS OF THE MORMON CHURCH ANNOUNCED THEY...

Locating where stories take place with prepositional phrases is a good writing device to use occasionally. However, there are less obvious ways of locating where stories take place by simply incorporating where into the what of the stories.

EL PASO POLICE ARRESTED FIVE PEOPLE AND CHARGED THEM WITH TRANSPORTING ILLEGAL ALIENS INTO THE UNITED STATES.

Or:

SCHOOL BUSING OPPONENTS IN SOUTH BOSTON SAY THEY ARE GOING TO COURT...

Or:

MORMON CHURCH LEADERS IN SALT LAKE CITY SAY THEY...

WHERE should be included in almost every lead. This is especially true when you consider that a lot of radio listening is done in cars. Many travelers are not sure what radio station they are tuned into or where the station is located.

The only time WHERE will not be an important part of leads is when widely known national or international people or organizations are the primary emphasis. For example:

(what)
THE U. S. OLYMPIC BOYCOTT WAS THE MAJOR TOPIC AT THE ANNUAL INTERNATIONAL OLYMPIC COMMITTEE MEETING. I-O-C CHAIRMAN, LORD KILLANAN OF IRELAND, REBUKED U. S. ...

Or:

(who) (what)
PRESIDENT REAGAN TOLD THIRD WORLD LEADERS THAT A TRANSFER OF WEALTH FROM RICH TO POOR IS NOT THE SOLUTION TO WORLD HUNGER. AT THE THIRD WORLD CONFERENCE IN CANCUN, MEXICO...

In the above examples, WHERE became a secondary element of the stories and was placed in the second or third sentences. WHAT and WHO were the important lead elements.

International organizations such as the United Nations or the Olympic Committee are not associated with particular countries and WHERE may not be an important aspect of the stories, in comparison with WHAT and WHO. Some national or international figures, such as actors, athletes or politicians, are so mobile that WHERE can safely be de-emphasized. WHERE remains a part of the news stories but it does not have to be part of the leads.

WHEN may be taken care of by the way leads are written. If leads are in the present or present perfect tense, WHEN is assumed to be now. WHEN, as was discussed in earlier chapters, is also a way of judging the newsworthiness of many stories, and the use of time references can indicate the freshness or immediacy of stories. Network newswriters, because of national and international time differences, will often specify WHEN in leads by referring to today or yesterday. The following leads are examples:

PALESTINIAN AUTONOMY TALKS BETWEEN ISRAEL AND EGYPT RESUME TODAY IN TEL AVIV.[3]

Or:

THE AWACS ARGUMENT CONTINUED ON THE HILL TODAY WHEN SECRETARY OF STATE HAIG SAID IT WOULD BE...[4]

Or:

THIS JUST IN, POLICE AND UNDERGROUND MOSLEM GROUPS FOUGHT A SERIES OF GUN BATTLES IN SEVERAL PARTS OF CAIRO TODAY.[5]

Or:

DOCTORS TODAY REPORT THE FIRST AMERICAN TEST ON HUMANS OF A NEW ARTIFICIAL BLOOD.[6]

WHAT is obviously going to be the key element in virtually all broadcast news leads. WHAT emphasizes the hard news angle of stories. For example:

(who)
THE SIERRA CLUB, WHICH CONCENTRATES ITS EFFORTS ON PROTECTING

(what)
THE ENVIRONMENT, IS FORMING A POLITICAL ACTION COMMITTEE.[7]

Or:

(who)
LIBYA'S LEADER MOAMMAR QADDAFI SAYS HE BELIEVES THE U. S.

(what)
IS PLANNING WAR AGAINST LIBYA.[8]

Or:

(who)
POLISH TROOPS FANNED OUT THROUGHOUT WARSAW TO HELP DISTRIBUTE

FOOD AND QUOTE..."QUELL LOCAL DISTURBANCES."[9]

Before you get into the various types of leads, there are some do's and don'ts that will help your writing. As you have been advised, do not start off leads with names unless those names are widely known. Prepare news listeners for names by setting up names with job titles or reasons for the people being in the news.

Instead of:

ANN SMITH, A UNIVERSITY OF KANSAS SOPHOMORE, IS THE NEW MISS KANSAS. MISS SMITH WAS SELECTED FOR THE HONOR OVER FOUR OTHER SEMI-FINALISTS LAST NIGHT IN WICHITA. MISS SMITH LIVES IN TOPEKA...

Write:

A UNIVERSITY OF KANSAS STUDENT IS THE NEW MISS KANSAS. ANN SMITH FROM TOPEKA WAS SELECTED AS THE STATE'S REIGNING BEAUTY OVER FOUR OTHER SEMI-FINALISTS IN WICHITA LAST NIGHT.

While it is not always possible, try to avoid starting leads with numbers. Many times a lead can be recast to avoid the first word being a number. Also avoid starting leads with dependent clauses. Inverting the normal sentence structure should seldom be done in leads, even though it is commonly done in the body of stories.

LEAD TYPES

There are four basic types of leads used by broadcast newswriters. They are *throw away* or *warm up* leads, *soft* or *feature* leads, *hard news* leads and *comprehensive* or *umbrella* leads.

A great number of factors affect the writer's decision on what type of lead to use in a particular story. The announcer's ability to read certain types of news copy is very important for the writer to consider. The writer's ability to write certain types of stories, the story content, the audience, and the impact of the story are also factors that must be weighed in the decision. For example, Harry Reasoner of CBS News has the ability to read tongue-in-cheek types of leads and convey the subtle humor of certain types of situations. Other newsreaders do not have this ability and this affects the selection of leads and the style of writing. Another example would be that in hard news stories that are breaking at that moment feature leads would not be appropriate.

THROW AWAY LEADS

Throw away or warm-up leads, much like newspaper headlines, are designed to catch news listeners' attention with general summations of stories. Information presented in the throw away leads will be repeated later in the news copy. For example:

A MEMPHIS MAN IS DEAD AND POLICE ARE SEARCHING FOR THE HIT AND RUN DRIVER WHO KILLED HIM. EARLIER TODAY, RICHARD WILLIAMS OF 345 ABALONE DRIVE WAS STRUCK BY A CAR AND KILLED AS HE WALKED ACROSS THE STREET IN FRONT OF HIS HOME. ACCORDING TO WITNESSES THE CAR THAT STRUCK HIM DID NOT EVEN SLOW DOWN.

POLICE ARE NOW SEARCHING FOR THE DRIVER OF THE CAR. WITNESSES SAY THE DRIVER WAS YOUNG...BETWEEN THE AGES OF 16 AND 22. POLICE HAVE A DETAILED DESCRIPTION OF THE CAR AND DRIVER BUT NO ONE WAS ABLE TO GET THE CAR'S LICENSE NUMBER.

Everything mentioned in the lead is repeated and amplified in the body of the story which relays the specifics. The repetition is not really noticed because the wording is different and detail is added. In general terms, the throw away lead cues the listener to expect a story about a car fatality in Memphis. It warns listeners interested in news about the Memphis area that this story may be of concern to them.

Throw away leads, to a certain extent, are based on the broadcast news formula developed in the late 1930s by Paul White, the first news director of CBS radio. White's formula is:

> Tell them what you're going to tell them.
>
> Tell them.
>
> Tell them what you've just told them.

It is not necessary to be as redundant in your writing as the Paul White formula indicates, but throw away leads demand some redundancy between the lead and the body of stories.

The reasoning behind the Paul White formula was that people, used to reading newspapers, needed a great deal of repetition to understand radio news. That thinking was based on faulty or limited information about the human mind and the amount of information that the human mind can process and remember. At one time, motion picture makers feared making movies longer than one reel, or twenty minutes, because the generally accepted feeling was that people would not sit and watch something longer. Television program executives in the early days of TV also felt that any program longer than half an hour was too long to maintain audience attention. This type of thinking has changed because of research into human perception and the viewing/listening habits of people using radio and television.

Research has also shown that entertainment and news programming do not always get the listener's or viewer's total attention. Radio listening is primarily a background diversion and our attention to what is being broadcast varies with what we are doing and what is presented on radio. Television news may also have to compete with family conversations, meals, or trips to lavatories or kitchens. Throw away leads are designed to cue listeners, who are not paying total attention, that stories may be of special interest. Throw away leads can be transitions from inattention to full attention on radio or television news stories. Like headlines, throw away leads prepare listeners or viewers for information in the body of the story.

Throw away leads are neither used by all broadcast or cable newswriters nor required in all news departments. Some writers and editors feel that throw away leads are wasted sentences and those people really interested in news will be listening intently. No matter what philosophy you choose to follow, it is wise to be a little redundant in your newswriting. Repeating names or locations adds only a second or two to stories and it may clear up some confusion.

HARD NEWS LEADS

First reports of breaking stories or important news updates will almost always have hard news leads. Hard news leads stress the immediacy of news and information in leads, unlike throw away leads, is important to understand and remember because it will not be repeated. If news listeners missed the following lead, much of the story's news value and impact would have been missed:

A FIRE BOMB RIPPED THROUGH THE EGYPTIAN GOVERNMENT TOURIST OFFICE THIS MORNING IN NEW YORK CITY. POLICE SAY THE OFFICES WERE HEAVILY DAMAGED EVEN THOUGH ONLY ONE OF THE TWO BOMBS THROWN INTO THE BUILDING EXPLODED. A MAN WHO IDENTIFIED HIMSELF AS BELONGING TO THE JEWISH DEFENSE LEAGUE CLAIMED RESPONSIBILITY FOR THE BOMBING TO PROTEST THE CAMP DAVID PEACE ACCORDS.[10]

The lead contains extremely valuable information on which the rest of the news story is based. In the lead are the only references to the fire bomb, New York City, and the target of the bombing, which was the Egyptian Government tourist office.

The same is true in this ABC radio news story:

WELL, THE HOUSE OPENS DEBATE ON A BILL THAT WOULD LET NUCLEAR POWER PLANTS BEGIN OPERATION AT FULL CAPACITY BEFORE PUBLIC HEARINGS ON PLANT SAFETY ARE COMPLETED. OPPONENTS SAY THE MEASURE COULD ALLOW SOME UNSAFE PLANTS TO OPEN.[11]

If news listeners missed the lead in the nuclear power story the second sentence makes absolutely no sense.

Hard news leads, such as the ones used above, rely on timely information which will decrease in value as time passes. Hard news is a perishable commodity and time decreases the importance of news events. Hard news leads stress the news that is going on at that moment or has just happened.

Other hard news lead examples are:

THE WHITE HOUSE TODAY SHOWED OFF AWACS SUPPORT OF MORE THAN A DOZEN DEFENSE EXPERTS FROM PREVIOUS ADMINISTRATIONS.[12]

Or:

A BEIRUT NEWSPAPER QUOTES PRESIDENT REAGAN AS SAYING THE P-L-O SHOULD BE INCLUDED IN THE MIDDLE EAST PEACE TALKS ONCE THE P-L-O RECOGNIZES ISRAEL'S RIGHT TO EXIST.[13]

Or:

CONSUMER FOOD NEWS SAYS WE'RE GOING TO HAVE A GOOD SUPPLY OF TURKEYS FOR THIS THANKSGIVING.[14]

All of the above leads are clear, concise and contain information important in understanding the body of each news story. Throw away leads could easily be added to each story, but this would add an extra sentence to each story. In a ten story radio newscast, those extra sentences could take up as much as 30 seconds, which is enough time for one additional story.

SOFT NEWS LEADS

Soft news or feature leads are appropriate for feature stories or hard news stories where feature angles are emphasized. Unlike hard news stories, feature stories and leads do not necessarily emphasize the timeliness of news stories. For example, the assassination of Egyptian President Anwar Sadat is hard news. A background piece giving an analysis of the mideast without Sadat is interesting but could be held for several days without the value of the story decreasing. See Example 3-1.

This type of story could have run anytime during the week after Egyptian President Sadat was assassinated because it tried to analyze the situation. Other stories more closely related to the assassination and subsequent transfer of political power in Egypt were hard news and could not be held because the passage of time decreased their importance.

Some writers or reporters tend to use soft news or feature leads even for some hard news stories. Soft or feature leads allow writers to be creative and express their own writing styles. David Brinkley, Harry Reasoner, Eric Sevareid and Charles Kuralt are famous for feature leads which fit their interpretive styles of reporting and unique ways of looking at news events. A puckish humor, ascerbic wit or tongue-in-cheek view of the world creep into these feature leads as the writers try to deal with nuances or add perspective to facts. Featurish leads, in many instances, fit into the think pieces or interpretive stories that are news but not necessarily hard news, although the stories may be related to hard news events. Many writers who use soft news leads want to deal with the lasting meaning of stories, not just the transient facts, which become old as soon as newscasts are over. They are trying to step outside the immediacy of situations and add perspective to stories by going one step further.

As an example, former CBS newsman Roger Mudd led to an Eric Sevareid commentary on astrology with the following feature lead:

ALMOST FOUR CENTURIES AGO, THE BARD WROTE, THE FAULT DEAR BRUTUS IS NOT IN THE STARS BUT IN OURSELVES. THAT WE ARE UNDERLINGS. NOW A GROUP OF DISTINGUISHED SCIENTISTS HAVE VOICED THE SAME CONCLUSION.

ERIC SEVAREID COMMENTS...[15]

Sevareid's commentary was based on a report by distinguished scientists who concluded that astrology, the belief that stars affect our lives, was not valid. The scientific report provided Sevareid the justification for a discussion on man, destiny, and responsibility. The scientific report was the news peg on which Sevareid hung his commentary. The hard news value of the report was minimal but Sevareid tried to look beyond scientific conclusions to a philosophical truth.

Feature or soft news leads do not have to be used only on historical or philosophical stories. Feature leads can be used to add humor or color to hard news stories. For example, if local police started a crackdown on marijuana use in public, the hard news lead might be:

GAINESVILLE AND UNIVERSITY OF FLORIDA POLICE ARE GOING TO

EXAMPLE 3-1

Mideast Analysis
10/1
Clayton

ANWAR SADAT IS DEAD. THE VICTIM OF ASSASSINS. HE WAS A MAN OF COURAGE...OF VISION. HE WAS A STABILIZING POLITICAL INFLUENCE IN A GEOGRAPHIC AREA KNOWN FOR VAST OIL RESERVES BUT LITTLE POLITICAL STABILITY.

SADAT BROKE WITH THE LONG STANDING ARAB VIEW TOWARD ISRAEL WHEN HE SIGNED THE CAMP DAVID PEACE ACCORDS BRINGING PEACE BETWEEN EGYPT AND ISRAEL.

WITH THE STROKE OF HIS PEN HE BROUGHT LIMITED PEACE...BUT HE ALSO CREATED THE SITUATION WHICH BROUGHT ABOUT HIS DEATH. IN HIS COUNTRY HE GAVE THE MOSLEM FUNDAMENTALISTS ONE MORE REASON TO HATE HIM. THAT HATE LED A BAND OF FANATICS TO JUMP OUT OF A MILITARY PARADE VEHICLE AND MURDER THE PRESIDENT OF EGYPT.

SADAT IS THE SECOND PRO WESTERN LEADER TO FALL BECAUSE OF MOSLEM FUNDAMENTALISTS. THE SHAH OF IRAN WAS THE FIRST VICTIM OF THIS OLD FORCE THAT IS DEMANDING A RETURN TO THE OLD RELIGIOUS WAYS.

A THOUGHT MUST BE RUNNING THROUGH THE MINDS OF ARAB LEADERS IN SAUDI ARABIA, EGYPT, JORDAN, IRAQ, AND SYRIA THAT THEIR MOST POWERFUL ENEMIES MAY ALREADY BE INSIDE THEIR RESPECTIVE COUNTRIES. THE ISRAELI THREAT THAT MANY OF THESE ARAB LEADERS PERCEIVE IS ACTUALLY LESS THAN THE THREAT OF THEIR RELIGIOUS COUNTRYMEN.

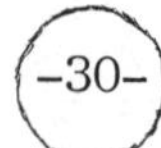

STRICTLY ENFORCE DRUG ORDINANCES. THE GOAL IS TO KEEP PUBLIC MARIJUANA USE DOWN AT FLORIDA FOOTBALL GAMES. FOOTBALL PATRONS HAVE COMPLAINED ABOUT WIDESPREAD MARIJUANA SMOKING IN THE STANDS DURING GAMES.

The same story, using a soft or feature lead, might be written:

CAMPUS SIGNS SAYING "KEEP OFF THE GRASS" ARE TAKING ON NEW MEANING FOR UNIVERSITY OF FLORIDA STUDENTS. COMPLAINTS FROM FOOTBALL PATRONS ABOUT WIDESPREAD MARIJUANA SMOKING IN THE STANDS DURING GAMES HAVE PROMPTED POLICE TO SAY THEY ARE GOING TO GET TOUGH WITH PUBLIC POT SMOKERS.

Some stories virtually cry out for a feature lead or unique treatment. However, it takes news experience and maturation to know when this can safely be done and accepted by listeners. There are examples of feature leads that have offended or alienated listeners because the leads or story treatments appeared to attack moral or religious tenets. A good idea when you are writing leads which might offend some listeners is to ask your news editor or producer to read the stories carefully and give advice.

COMPREHENSIVE LEADS

Comprehensive or umbrella leads are used to tie two or more related stories together. Sometimes stories may not be directly related until newswriters decide they should be pulled together to show relationships or to save time by compacting several events into one story. Newswriters need to find some common elements to tie stories together and these elements can be geography, people, similar events or one event that has several different angles. See Examples 3-2 and 3-3.

Comprehensive leads are very much like throw away leads because they usually do not get into specifics. Leads must remain general and elements mentioned in leads are covered in greater detail in the bodies of stories. The advantage of comprehensive or umbrella leads is that they allow newswriters to add perspective to stories. By pulling related events together in one story, listeners are better able to understand some complex relationships. If each of the events in Example 3-3, the Economy Wrap-up story, were treated as separate stories some listeners might not realize how a decline in housing could affect the jobless rate.

Newswriters should always be aware of the possible editorial aspects of using a comprehensive or umbrella lead. By juxtaposing story elements or by determining which aspects of stories should be included (or not included), social or political biases can be brought into stories. It is virtually impossible to divorce yourself from the editorial process because no one can be totally neutral, but there is a line that must divide newswriters from editorial writers. That line, unfortunately, is not fixed. Careful news judgment must be used to make sure that you remain a newswriter, if that is your job.

EXAMPLE 3-2

ANTI-NUCLEAR DEMONSTRATIONS
MICHAELS-HARRISON
6-17, 6:00 P.M.

THERE WERE ANTI-NUCLEAR DEMONSTRATIONS THROUGHOUT EUROPE TODAY.

GERMAN AND BELGIAN NUCLEAR OPPONENTS MARCHED PEACEFULLY THROUGH THEIR RESPECTIVE CAPITALS HOPING TO FORCE THEIR GOVERNMENTS NOT TO DEPLOY NATO NUCLEAR WEAPONS.

IN SWEDEN, HOWEVER, THE ANTI-NUCLEAR DEMONSTRATIONS WERE AIMED AT THE SOVIET UNION, WHICH VIOLATED SWEDISH TERRITORIAL WATERS WITH A NUCLEAR ARMED SUBMARINE. SWEDISH MILITARY OFFICIALS HAVE CONFIRMED THAT THE SOVIET SUBMARINE BEACHED IN RESTRICTED WATERS PROBABLY HAS NUCLEAR TIPPED TORPEDOES ON BOARD. TRACES OF NUCLEAR MATERIAL WERE DETECTED ON THE SUBMARINE.

###

EXAMPLE 3-3

ECONOMY WRAP-UP
NOVELL-CLAYTON
11-4, Noon news

THE NATION'S ECONOMY DOMINATES THE NEWS TODAY. FOR A THIRD QUARTER IN A ROW...LEADING ECONOMIC INDICATORS HAVE DECLINED AND ECONOMISTS SAY THE NATION IS NOW IN A RECESSION.

THAT NEWS IS NOT A SURPRISE TO PEOPLE IN THE HOUSING INDUSTRY. THE NATIONAL CONTRACTOR'S ASSOCIATION RELEASED FIGURES SHOWING HOUSING STARTS ARE DOWN MORE THAN 20 PERCENT OVER THIS PERIOD LAST YEAR.

THE ONLY THINGS GOING UP APPEAR TO BE THE JOBLESS AND INTEREST RATES.

THE DEPARTMENT OF LABOR SAYS THAT THE JOBLESS RATE HAS GONE UP MORE THAN ONE PERCENT THIS QUARTER DUE, IN PART, TO A DECLINE IN THE HOUSING INDUSTRY. THAT MEANS THAT 350,000 MORE AMERICANS LOST THEIR JOBS OR WERE LAID OFF IN THE PAST THREE MONTHS.

AND THE FEDERAL RESERVE BOARD SAYS INTEREST RATES WILL REMAIN HIGH UNTIL INFLATION REMAINS UNDER CONTROL.

LOCALIZING

Sociologists and cultural critics say that Americans are people without roots who move frequently and travel extensively around the country. One quick look at a map shows a complex network of high speed interstate highways and the nation is serviced by many major airlines, bus companies and car rental agencies. Despite our need or desire to travel, most of us live in a very small part of this world. Excluding those who travel for a living or commute long distances, we live, work, and play within fifty miles of our homes. An occasional ski trip, vacation or visit back home to see our parents expands our circle of living temporarily, but our daily reality and interests are within that fifty-mile circle. What happens outside that circle may be interesting but unless it touches our lives it has little lasting meaning. A Soviet-United States grain deal, signed in Washington, has little meaning to the average non-farming American until bread prices at local markets go up. Suddenly, the grain deal has saliency; it means something to your pocketbook. A chemical industry found guilty of dumping hazardous waste into a stream two hundred miles away has little direct meaning unless your community drinking water comes from the same stream. Suddenly that event has direct meaning to you and your family.

There are certain interests, such as sports or business news, which transcend our natural interest in things that happen closest to us. But, for the most part, proximity, the nearness to news events, is one of the guidelines you can use to determine what might interest people in your listening or viewing area. Generally, the closer the news events the more interest people exhibit. Even inside that fifty-mile circle, something that happens on your own block has more saliency than something that happens on the other side of town.

Localizing news stories is capitalizing on the natural interest people have in what happens closest to them or those they know. Most news services cannot localize their news stories because they cater to national or regional audiences. For example, the national wire service reports of a news event involving a significant number of injuries or deaths must be written from a national angle and carry a national lead.

A CHARTERED JET CARRYING VACATIONING SCHOOL TEACHERS TO HAWAII CRASHED ON TAKEOFF FROM CHICAGO'S O'HARE AIRPORT TODAY KILLING ALL ON BOARD. AN AIRLINE SPOKESPERSON SAYS THE PLANE CARRIED 88 PASSENGERS AND A CREW OF SIX. A FEDERAL AVIATION SPOKESPERSON SAYS THE CAUSE OF THE CRASH IS NOT KNOWN BUT THE FLIGHT RECORDER WAS RECOVERED INTACT FROM THE WRECKAGE. A FULL INVESTIGATION INTO THE CRASH WILL BE CONDUCTED BY F-A-A INVESTIGATORS WHO ARE ALREADY AT THE SCENE.

In Chicago, this story would be considered local but in other areas of the country this would be considered a national news story unless there was some local angle. After initial reports, press wire services would transmit a casualty list released by the airlines. However, quick thinking local reporters might call local school principals or administrators to find out if any local teachers might have been on the chartered flight. If wire services listed local people or reporters turned up local names, the story should be rewritten to localize the lead and integrate the local angle into the story. For example:

TWO DENVER HIGH SCHOOL TEACHERS ARE REPORTED TO HAVE BEEN ON

A JET PLANE THAT CRASHED AT CHICAGO'S O'HARE AIRPORT... KILLING ALL ON BOARD.

THE TEACHERS ARE IDENTIFIED AS 43 YEAR OLD MRS. WILLIAM SIMMONS AND 51 YEAR OLD NANCY MORELAND. BOTH WOMEN TAUGHT AT ROOSEVELT HIGH SCHOOL.

THE JET WAS CHARTERED BY A TEACHERS ORGANIZATION TO TAKE 88 TEACHERS TO HAWAII FOR A TWO WEEK VACATION. ALL 88 PASSENGERS AND THE CREW OF SIX WERE KILLED IN THE CRASH WHICH IS BEING INVESTIGATED BY THE FEDERAL AVIATION AGENCY.

The first story, with a national lead and no mention of a local angle, would probably have minor interest for Denver residents. It would be just another plane crash; tragic, of course, but a thousand miles away and of no real concern. The second story probably would have a fairly strong impact in the Denver community. If both women had taught in Denver for any length of time, they probably had hundreds of friends and had taught several thousand students. This story would obviously affect those who knew the two teachers, and it would interest many Denver residents who did not know the teachers personally.

REWRITING AND UPDATING

Few things will tell listeners or viewers more about news organizations than hearing the same story throughout the day without the story being rewritten or updated. A person driving to work in the morning may hear a story about a traffic accident, fire or political event. If that person hears the identical radio story at night, that station's news credibility will suffer. Hearing the same stories over and over again without being updated or rewritten tells listeners that the news staff is lazy, sloppy, or not very aggressive. People interested in news will probably start looking for another radio station which meets their needs.

Failure to rewrite or update is most obvious in radio where radio newscasts are frequently aired. The general rule is to update leads or stories as often as possible by finding the freshest or newest angles. Without an updated lead, a traffic accident story can sound old within two or three hours. For example, the first reports of a morning rush hour traffic accident may stress the traffic situation for other drivers going to work.

ATLANTA POLICE REPORT A SERIOUS TRAFFIC ACCIDENT AT THE INTERSECTION OF SOUTHBOUND INTERSTATE 75 AND INTERSTATE 275. POLICE SAY A SEMI-TRACTOR TRAILER TRUCK AND TWO CARS COLLIDED LESS THAN AN HOUR AGO TYING ALL THREE LANES OF TRAFFIC LEADING INTO ATLANTA FROM THE NORTHERN SUBURBS. AMBULANCES HAVE TAKEN THREE PEOPLE TO AREA HOSPITALS BUT DETAILS ARE SKETCHY AT THIS

TIME. POLICE ARE ADVISING ALL MOTORISTS TO AVOID USING I-75 SOUTHBOUND INTO ATLANTA DURING THE MORNING RUSH HOURS.

Within thirty minutes, more information might be available on the accident or the people injured. To run the same story again without updating would be foolish because many people who heard the first report might still be listening to your newscasts waiting for updated information. The second story might have a whole new approach.

AT LEAST ONE PERSON IS DEAD IN A TRUCK-CAR ACCIDENT THAT HAS COMPLETELY BLOCKED INTERSTATE 75 SOUTHBOUND LANES NORTH OF ATLANTA. POLICE SAY THAT A SEMI-TRACTOR TRAILER AND TWO CARS COLLIDED AT THE INTERSECTION OF I-75 AND THE I-275 OUTERBELT. THE I-275 OUTERBELT IS OPEN BUT TRAFFIC IN THE AREA IS DOWN TO ONE LANE.

AMBULANCES TOOK THREE PEOPLE TO AREA HOSPITALS AND ONE UNIDENTIFIED PERSON WAS PRONOUNCED DEAD AT THE SCENE OF THE ACCIDENT.

POLICE ARE ADVISING MOTORISTS IN THE NORTHERN SUBURBS TO USE ALTERNATIVE ROUTES TO GET TO WORK.

The updated lead should always stress the newest information available. The writer should look for what *IS* going on right at that moment so the lead can be written in present or present perfect tense. Finding out what is happening at that moment changes the lead and the rest of the story will be reorganized around your new lead.

For novice newswriters, unsure of police, accident, fire, court or governmental procedures, updating story leads can be confusing and time consuming. Knowledge of police, fire and government procedures is extremely important because many public news events follow typical patterns. Newswriters must realize that the original news story is just the start of the news process. Like one pebble starting a rock slide, the original news event can generate a number of related events that can be used as news updates or new leads. For experienced writers, updating may not involve more than knowledge of police procedures and quick rewrites to change story leads. The original news story will stress what took place. For example:

ONE PERSON IS DEAD AND THREE INJURED PEDESTRIANS WERE TAKEN TO A DOWNTOWN BUFFALO HOSPITAL SHORTLY BEFORE 8:00 THIS MORNING.

Experienced writers looking for updates know that police, especially in fatal accidents, will reconstruct accidents to pinpoint causes. Even without any new information, writers know that accident investigation teams will go immediately to accident scenes and start their investigations. The next story on the accident would stress the newest information or what *IS* going on at that moment. For example:

POLICE ACCIDENT INVESTIGATORS ARE AT THE SCENE OF THIS MORNING'S FATAL ACCIDENT THAT KILLED THE DRIVER OF A CAR AND SENT THREE INJURED PEDESTRIANS TO AREA HOSPITALS.

Once the hospital had a chance to examine and process the victims injured in the accident, the story rewrite and lead could emphasize the victims' conditions and names, if names have been released by police or hospital officials.

THOSE THREE PEDESTRIANS RUN DOWN BY AN OUT OF CONTROL CAR THIS MORNING IN BUFFALO ARE REPORTED IN CRITICAL CONDITION AT BUFFALO MEMORIAL HOSPITAL. THE DRIVER OF THE CAR WAS PRONOUNCED DEAD AT THE SCENE OF THE ACCIDENT...AN APPARENT HEART ATTACK VICTIM.

In this particular instance, a fairly routine traffic accident story in a major city, the story probably would not be pursued after the first day unless something new or unique occurred to keep the story important. A new or major development might be the official accident report listing the driver's cause of death or one of the victims' dying.

So far, all of the rewriting and lead updating has come from available information generated by the original news event. This is the type of updating that does not require innovative or aggressive news reporting. Some stories, though, may not generate their own updates as neatly as accident or fire stories. For example, what will you do if the Defense Department announces the closing of a local military ordinance depot and ammunition arsenal in your area? Your station will obviously carry the initial announcement of the story transmitted by the wire service. Now you will be faced with updating what is obviously a major story for the people in your community. How do you go about the process?

This story, because of its broad impact, might be approached in a number of different ways. One suggestion would be to look at the story from your own immediate needs and also as a long term event. For example:

1. Immediate needs

   Update for next newscasts

2. Long term

   Stories which will be generated over period of time until depot is closed

IMMEDIATE NEEDS

Obviously, the most immediate need is to deal with this story for your next scheduled newscast. The most immediate thing that you can do is contact your local Congressional representative and senator. They must have comments on the depot closing, and they might be able to tell you why the decision was made. Other questions that you should try to answer are what will be the immediate impact on the community and will the arsenal be closed immediately or will the closing take place in a year or two?

Another immediate story update could be an interview with the person in charge of the depot-arsenal. Interviews with people who work at the arsenal would also be appropriate and provide interesting insights on the situation. Bankers, local government officials and real estate people would also be able to give some type of economic assessment of the closing and the possible impact on the community.

These are all stories that could be done immediately to provide your listeners with updated information relating to the depot closing. These story updates are pertinent to the original closing announcement and will give your listeners the type of information they want to know about the news event.

LONG TERM

The closing of a military ordinance depot and ammunition arsenal is an event that will take months or years to complete and it could be an ongoing story during that time. This type of story has many ramifications for a community, and the long term aspects should be a concern of the news department. Some long term stories, which could be undertaken, would be the impact on the local tax base which will affect schools, city or community services, housing, welfare rolls, churches, etc.

Some questions that should be answered are will the government transfer workers to other jobs or will employees be fired and have to find new jobs in the community? This leads to what jobs are available in the community and will community/government leaders try to get new industries to move into the area? An interesting story might be to find another community that experienced a military base closing and report how that community reacted. Did the community fold up and die or was new industry brought in and did the community prosper?

Another aspect of the story might be the community's fight to keep the arsenal and depot open. In most instances, local officials will try to fight a closing and enlist the aid of local senators and representatives. They will dig out information to support their argument and will be able to determine how the depot functioned and how it compared with other depots and ammunition arsenals.

The final aspect of the story would be the closing of the depot and monitoring the community to find out the actual consequences of the action.

The closing of a military depot and ammunition arsenal is an unusual type of story because it can have such a devastating impact on a community. More typical news stories to update and rewrite would be city commission, county commission or zoning hearings. These three governmental bodies are fairly common in most municipal or county governments, and these three governmental organizations generate a great deal of news on a regular basis. Most city and county commissions and zoning boards meet regularly and, by their very nature, deal occasionally with controversial events that arouse people in their respective communities. Knowledge of how each of these governmental units operate is quite important for news reporters/writers who must cover meetings and write stories about what transpired. Knowledge of how commissions and boards operate can help you know how to update stories. For example, the evening news report immediately following a zoning board hearing will stress what happened in the meeting. The first report will generally stress hard news and deal with what *IS* happening or has just happened.

TEMPERS FLARED AND ANGRY WORDS WERE HEARD AT THE LANSING ZONING BOARD MEETING THIS AFTERNOON. MORE THAN 50 REDWOOD AREA RESIDENTS ATTENDED THE MEETING IN AN EFFORT TO STOP A REZONING REQUEST BY THE L AND J STEEL COMPANY. L AND J WANTS COMMISSIONERS TO REZONE PART OF THE REDWOOD AREA FOR A PROPOSED TWO MILLION DOLLAR PLANT EXPANSION. L AND J ATTORNEYS SAY THE PLANT EXPANSION WOULD MEAN 200 NEW JOBS AND A SUBSTANTIAL BOOST TO THE ECONOMY.

SEVERAL REDWOOD RESIDENTS SHOUTED DOWN THE L AND J ATTORNEYS, DEMANDING TO KNOW WHAT THE PLANT EXPANSION WOULD DO TO EXISTING PROPERTY VALUES.

COMMISSION CHAIRMAN PAUL CLAYTON SAYS THE COMMISSION WILL STUDY THE MATTER AND MAKE A DECISION AT NEXT WEEK'S ZONING MEETING.

This story would be sufficient for the evening newscast immediately following the zoning commission meeting. The problem that news writers face is how to update this story for early morning newscasts before the city and county government offices open. Once people are up and about, several different aspects of this zoning story could be pursued. However, without access to Redwood residents or city/county officials, writers must produce early morning stories that are not identical to the story that was run the night before. Morning news writers can rewrite this story by looking at what is to come. This really involves nothing more than logical projections of what will happen. For example:

LANSING ZONING COMMISSIONERS HAVE A TOUGH DECISION TO MAKE THIS WEEK. AT LAST NIGHT'S ZONING MEETING...

Or:

LANSING ZONING COMMISSIONERS WILL BE STUDYING THE IMPACT OF A PROPOSED EXPANSION OF L AND J STEEL COMPANY ON PROPERTY VALUES IN THE REDWOOD AREA...

Nothing in the story has changed overnight. Newswriters have merely projected what will be happening to update the story lead and revise the story.

ORGANIZATION

Outside of being able to write a simple declarative sentence, most news editors would probably say the ability to organize is the next most important accomplishment for newswriters. News reporters/writers must be able to gather a lot of information in a limited amount of time; organize that information; distill the important facts and quotes; and organize it into a complete, clear news story.

This may seem like a simple request but it is not. It takes experience and an ability to work under pressure in a noisy newsroom. Some people do not have the type of personality which easily fits into this work environment. Some people cannot focus their attention when others are talking, public service monitors are blaring, there are only minutes before airtime, and the producer is pacing behind your chair. The pressure of the moment is too much to handle and some people cannot function in this type of pressurized work situation. Good news writers must be able to work under pressure and consistently make right decisions about what information should be in news stories and how stories should be organized.

Until you are in a newsroom facing critical deadlines you may not really know how you will react to pressure and deadlines. There are, however, some things that you can do, or practice doing, that will help you function in a noisy newsroom. The first thing you must learn is how to focus your attention on the story you are working on and block out everything else. This takes intense concentration.

The second thing that you must be aware of in pressure situations is that you will never have enough time to do everything you want. This means that you must learn how to compromise and what you can compromise. For example, when a quickly moving news event occurs shortly before your airtime, you probably will not have sufficient time to call everyone you would like or to get all of the information you would like to get. But there are certain crucial facts that you must have in your stories and these are the items that you pursue. Other items or interesting aspects of stories will have to wait for other newscasts or updates.

The third thing that you must know is when to stop gathering information and start writing. You must always allow writing time unless you are ad-libbing live reports. You must know your own abilities and how long it will take you to distill the information you gathered and write clear well-organized news stories.

Once you have gathered all of the information that you can possibly gather in the time available to you, carefully go through your notes, wire copy, and other information and underline the facts that are crucial for your listeners to know. Leave out all interesting events or unusual things that would be nice to include but are not crucial for your listeners. Organize the crucial facts in chronological order or time sequence. Remember, you will probably gather your information in bits and pieces and out of sequence, so you want to organize your information to explain chronologically how the news event happened. From the chronological order, you can start at the beginning and tell your news stories in a clear manner that most people will easily understand. This chronological structure is the way you would normally tell someone about something you had seen. For example, if you witness an accident and later see a friend, you would probably tell the story in time sequence. You might say, "did you see the car accident at the intersection of Central and Broad Streets? One of the cars ran through a picture glass window of the Pizza Shop. No one was injured but both cars were badly damaged. Traffic is tied up on both Central and Main."

The story has come out in chronological order. The accident happened; no one was hurt; cars were damaged and traffic is tied up. You started with the original act and the rest of the story flowed out naturally--in a conversational manner. Broadcast writers stress the conversational writing style and narrative organization, but we really demand something more structured than normal conversation. In normal conversation, we repeat ourselves, forget items and sometimes get out of sequence.

In Example 3-4 you will see how information flows into a newsroom and how it eventually gets organized into a news story.

In a news event, such as a bank robbery, the writer/reporter will often get the same information from several different sources. Sometimes the information will conflict. However, almost from the beginning at 3:23, the writer is aware that this will probably be a bank robbery story. At 3:25 the second major element is known. The writer can start mentally organizing the story based around the bank robbery and the guard getting shot. Other information is important and can be added to the story, but the basic outline of the story is known after the police officer reports from the scene at 3:28 p.m. At 3:50 the writer stops overtly gathering information for the 4:00 p.m. newscast and starts writing. Based on the information gathered, Example 3-5 is what the first radio news story might look like.

The news story in Example 3-5 is a straightforward story written in chronological order. The lead summarizes the event and talks about what IS going on at that moment. The body of the story then summarizes the bank robbery in chronological order. Each time the story is rewritten and updated, the lead changes and the body of the story will also be revised to include new information. See Example 3-6.

In updated news stories, leads are the key to story organization. Updated leads will contain the freshest information and writers should try to relate each succeeding sentence to the ones preceding. If, for example, the lead deals with injuries then the following sentences should concentrate on injuries. Compartmental-

EXAMPLE 3-4

TIME	SOURCE	INFORMATION
3:23 pm	Police monitor	Silent burglar alarm sounded at First National Bank of Fullerton. Two squad cars sent to scene using flashing lights but not siren.
3:25 pm	Police monitor	Bank robbery in progress. Shots fired. Two additional squad cars sent to bank along with ambulance unit.
3:28 pm	Police monitor	Police at scene report two male Caucasians robbed bank, shot guard and escaped on foot. Following description.
3:30 pm	Wire Service	BULLETIN (FULLERTON, CALIFORNIA) A BANK GUARD HAS BEEN SHOT AND AN UNDETERMINED AMOUNT OF MONEY TAKEN FROM THE FIRST NATIONAL BANK OF FULLERTON. TWO SUSPECTS ARE BEING SOUGHT.
3:30 pm		<u>You send reporter nearby to bank location with orders to call you before air time</u>.
3:40 pm	Police monitor and telephone	From police monitor, you know to which hospital wounded guard was taken for treatment. You call emergency room and talk with supervisor going into surgery--bullet wound in chest. No condition report, no ID on guard, was conscious.
3:50 pm	Reporter at scene	Calls with following information. FBI at scene. No amount given - although more than $20,000. Calm - very calm - announced "hold up." Jumped counter - cleaned out drawers. Main safe already locked - time lock. Asst. bank mgr. ordered to open small safe. Walked out around corner. Police think had car around corner. Everyone forced to lie on floor. Bank guard shot when he got up as they were leaving.

EXAMPLE 3-5

Bank Robbery
3:50 pm - 4-4
Staehle-Rhodes

FULLERTON POLICE ARE SEARCHING FOR TWO MEN WHO SHOT A BANK GUARD AND ROBBED THE FIRST NATIONAL BANK OF FULLERTON OF MORE THAN 20-THOUSAND DOLLARS.

WITNESSES SAY THE TWO ROBBERS WALKED INTO THE BANK SHORTLY BEFORE 3:30 THIS AFTERNOON AND CALMLY ANNOUNCED A HOLD-UP. WHILE ONE MAN HELD THE CUSTOMERS AT GUNPOINT...THE OTHER MAN JUMPED OVER THE BANK COUNTER AND CLEANED OUT ALL THE OPEN CASH DRAWERS. THE ASSISTANT BANK MANAGER WAS FORCED TO OPEN A SMALL SAFE BUT THE MAIN SAFE WAS ALREADY CLOSED AND ON A TIME LOCK.

THE TWO ROBBERS FORCED EVERYONE TO LIE FACE DOWN ON THE FLOOR WHILE THEY MADE THEIR ESCAPE. ONE MAN GOT UP...HE WAS THE BANK GUARD AND HE WAS SHOT IN THE CHEST. THE WOUNDED GUARD IS NOW UNDERGOING SURGERY AT THE FULLERTON MEMORIAL HOSPITAL. THERE IS NO REPORT ON THE GUARD'S CONDITION.

THE ROBBERS SIMPLY WALKED OUT OF THE BANK AND DISAPPEARED. POLICE THINK THEY HAD A CAR WAITING FOR THEM AROUND THE CORNER.

THE F-B-I CRIME LAB IS AT THE SCENE AND BANK OFFICIALS ARE CONDUCTING AN AUDIT TO DETERMINE PRECISELY HOW MUCH WAS STOLEN.

EXAMPLE 3-6

Bank Robbery update
1:00 pm - 4-5
Staehle-wire-police

POLICE IN ARIZONA ARE SEARCHING FOR THE TWO MEN WHO SHOT A BANK GUARD AND HELD UP THE FULLERTON NATIONAL BANK YESTERDAY, ESCAPING WITH MORE THAN 36-THOUSAND DOLLARS. A SERVICE STATION ATTENDANT NEAR THE CALIFORNIA-ARIZONA BORDER NOTIFIED POLICE THAT TWO MEN... ANSWERING THE BANK ROBBERS' DESCRIPTION...STOPPED AT HIS ALL NIGHT GAS STATION EARLY THIS MORNING.

YESTERDAY...THE TWO MEN WALKED INTO THE DOWNTOWN FIRST NATIONAL BANK OFFICES...HELD 14 CUSTOMERS AND BANK EMPLOYEES AT GUNPOINT...AND LOOTED CASH DRAWERS AND ONE SAFE. AS THEY MADE THEIR ESCAPE THEY SHOT THE BANK GUARD WHO IS NOW LISTED IN GOOD CONDITION WITH A CHEST WOUND.

FULLERTON POLICE SAY IT WAS A PROFESSIONAL JOB BECAUSE THE MAN WAS SO CALM DURING THE ROBBERY AND THE ESCAPE WAS SO WELL PLANNED.

ize stories as best you can. In Example 3-6, the lead stresses that the search for the bank robbers has now focused in Arizona. The second sentence supports the lead explaining why the search has moved to Arizona. Once the new aspects of the story have been covered then the bank robbery is summarized and new information added.

Each succeeding update will change the story organization and new aspects of the story will be stressed. However, each time the story is run there will generally be a summary of the original bank robbery to remind people or to inform those who may not have heard the original story. There may come a point in the news process when nothing new might be the lead. For example, if we take our bank robbery story a step further:

POLICE AND FEDERAL OFFICIALS SAY THEY HAVE RUN OUT OF LEADS IN LAST MONTH'S ROBBERY OF THE FIRST NATIONAL BANK OF FULLERTON. TWO ROBBERS SHOT A GUARD AND ESCAPED WITH MORE THAN 36-THOUSAND DOLLARS IN WHAT POLICE DESCRIBE AS A PROFESSIONAL JOB...

The point is that news events will often generate a number of follow-up stories or updates. As long as stories are pertinent and interest your listeners, you should follow events, rewriting and updating stories. Stories may, after a few days, no longer be of interest unless some new aspect is uncovered or revealed. The only way to effectively assess how much effort you should continue to devote to stories, and how stories should be covered must be based on news judgments, strong feelings for your community, and knowledge of how police, government and other official agencies do their jobs.

QUIZ

1. What purpose does a broadcast lead serve?______________________________

2. Briefly define the difference between a newspaper lead and a broadcast lead.

3. What are the four basic types of broadcast leads? Explain when or under what circumstances you would use each lead.

   a.

   b.

   c.

   d.

4. What is the Paul White formula?

5. Explain what the "IS factor" helps you determine.

6. What is meant by the term "localizing?"

7. What is a "chronological" order?

EXERCISES

1. Assume that you have just collected the following information and now must write a 30-second story for the next regularly scheduled radio newscast at 11:00 a.m.

10.09 AM	Police monitor conversation indicates two car traffic accident at NW 14th and Main Streets.
	You call police and determine that one person was taken to the hospital.
	A hospital spokesman you talk with says the person has been injured. The victim's injuries have not been fully evaluated, but the person will be admitted for treatment.
10:35 AM	Another call to police department dispatcher says that it appears one car failed to stop for a red light and hit the other car broadside.
	Car #1, 1982 white sedan. Driven by William Sweet, 22, 2341 NW 44th Street. Car badly damaged.
	Car #2, 1979 blue economy import. Driven by Maggie Powell, 41, 735 Westwood Drive. Powell was taken to Riverside Hospital for treatment.
	Police still at scene. That's all the information he has.

2. Rewrite the facts in Exercise #1 for the 12:00 noon newscast. Remember to update your lead.

ASSIGNMENTS

1. Monitor a national radio network and record newscasts throughout a day. Compare and analyze how various stories are developed over a period of time by rewriting and updating.

2. Select two local stations--one noted for having a good news department and the other for not having a strong news department. Alternate listening to the stations' newscasts and compare the way each news department handles its news. Look specifically for how often the stories are rewritten and updated; how leads are changed, even if nothing substantial has changed, and how the body of the story will change with a new lead.

3. Select five hard news stories from your local newspaper. Rewrite each of the stories in broadcast style, using only the newspaper facts, not the newspaper language. Update each story with the purpose of using them in the next hourly newscast and consider each story as happening right now. When you are done, staple the newspaper stories to the back of your copy and hand in to your instructor.

ENDNOTES

1. Copyright 1981. National Broadcasting Company. All rights reserved. NBC Nightly News. October 6, 1981.

2. *The Associated Press Broadcast News Style Book* (New York: Associated Press, 1976) p. 11.

3. Courtesy of Mutual Broadcasting System. Mutual News. October 25, 1981.

4. Copyright 1981. Columbia Broadcasting System. All rights reserved. CBS News-On-The-Hour. October 5, 1981.

5. Copyright 1981. National Broadcasting Company. All rights reserved. NBC Radio News. October 25, 1981.

6. Reprinted Courtesy of ABC News. ABC Radio News. October 19, 1981.

7. Courtesy of Mutual Broadcasting System. Mutual News. October 25, 1981.

8. Reprinted Courtesy of ABC News. ABC Radio News. October 19, 1981.

9. Copyright 1981. National Broadcasting Company. All rights reserved. NBC Radio News. October 25, 1981.

10. Courtesy of Mutual Broadcasting System. Mutual News. October 25, 1981.

11. Reprinted Courtesy of ABC News. ABC Radio News. October 19, 1981.

12. Copyright 1981. Columbia Broadcasting System. All rights reserved. CBS News-On-The-Hour. October 5, 1981.

13. Courtesy of Mutual Broadcasting System. Mutual News. October 25, 1981.

14. Reprinted Courtesy of ABC News. ABC Radio News. October 19, 1981.

15. Copyright 1975. Columbia Broadcasting System. September, 1975. CBS Evening News with Walter Cronkite.

4

INTERVIEWS, LEAD-INS, TAG LINES

News editors, journalism teachers and reporters all agree that the central skill of any journalist is the ability to write well. There is another skill, however, that is extremely important but generally overlooked. This is the ability to gather information through interviewing. The reason this skill is often overlooked is because most people think interviewing is something that you learn on the job through trial and error. Many older journalists have learned interviewing just this way: through trial and error. There are, however, certain interviewing skills and procedures that can be taught and practiced before you face your first real news interview.

Just how important is the ability to interview? It is extremely important because through interviewing we gather information for news stories we are working on. Try to write news stories or update leads without talking to someone or gathering new information. Without the ability to clarify information or get more information, news becomes a stagnant process. The ability to interview people is quite important for newspeople because without information your news writing skills are not terribly important.

The point is that broadcast journalists must be good writers, but to gather information and quotes for news stories, they must also be good interviewers. Journalists are conduits between the public that wants to know what happened and the people who create news or get involved in news events. Journalists are surrogates for news listeners or viewers, and the questions journalists ask must reflect what listeners or viewers want to know or what interests them.

Interviews take place in all types of situations and places. Reporters sent to accidents or fires try to get information from busy police or fire officials while they are trying to direct traffic or the activities of people working to put out the fire or clean up the accident. Some interviews have been done in planes, buses, trains, or cars as busy politicians move from one campaign stop to another. In all types of interviewing situations, whether interviews are electronically recorded or not, certain basic interviewing principles and procedures are the same because the goals are the same. The interviewing goals of broadcast journalists are to elicit new information about topics and obtain quotes from people which can be used in news stories. Quotes from newsmakers are electronically recorded and later edited for use in newscasts. The terms *sound bites*, *interview cuts*, or *cuts* refer to the small portions of film or electronically recorded interviews which are edited and inserted into news stories.

Interviewing is nothing more than an information gathering technique used by journalists when they talk with police, politicians, judges, elected officials, or other people who are involved in newsworthy events. Broadcast journalists talk with, or interview, people throughout the day as an important part of their job. One aspect of interviewing is the standard information gathering interview that is not usually recorded for inclusion in news stories. Newswriters who hear an accident report on the police monitor only get a few facts about the accident, such as where it happened and if someone was injured. The extent of damage, injuries, names of people involved, causes, or where the injured were taken are seldom mentioned on the police monitor. Writers must telephone police departments and talk with the police records officers or dispatchers to get further information for the news story. More telephone calls will probably be made to hospitals or accident investigators before enough information is available for a complete story. These types of informational interviews concentrate on the five Ws: who, what, when, where and why. The answers to these questions, gained from police and hospital sources, will flesh out that accident report and become a story in the newscast.

Broadcast journalists also spend a great deal of time and resources getting recorded interviews that provide information and quotes which are used in news stories. Listening to, or viewing, a few local or network newscasts will quickly show you the importance broadcast journalists place on recording the sounds and voices of newsmakers or seeing those caught up in news events. Nothing matches the impact of hearing or seeing a president talk about inflation or the survivors of a plane crash describe the experience. Hearing and seeing people who make the news or witnessed dramatic news events brings an excitement and reality to broadcast news that newspapers cannot match. With the use of sound and video, broadcast journalists allow people to become part of world and local events by watching over the reporter's shoulder. Even if newswriters could better summarize interviews or more clearly describe situations, and in many instances they can, the actual voices or sounds of newsmakers provide viewers or listeners with vicarious feelings of witnessing history.

Recorded interviews demand a greater degree of concentration and intensity than non-recorded interviews. Newspaper reporters may go through all of the same interview steps or use the same techniques used by broadcast reporters, but when the audio or video recorder is turned on, the tension increases and the stakes go up. Broadcast interviewers and interviewees are more careful of what they say and how they say it. The fear of making mistakes or revealing too much during recorded interviews is a constant worry for interviewees.

Another aspect is that non-recorded interviews can take place in several sessions and interviews can be disjointed and rambling. Reporters can then shape news stories back in the newsroom, reconstructing the best portion of the interviews from notes. Broadcast interviewers are expected to shape stories in the field and, in the case of television and cable, record narration tracks or stand up opens and closes to fit with interviews in nice concise news stories. Even though film, video and audio tape can be edited and rearranged in editing rooms, broadcast reporters are expected to obtain recorded interviews which have a good flow and need minimal editing. Editing takes time, and video tape or film edits are visually obvious to viewers and require editing techniques to avoid jump cuts. Not only do broadcast reporters have to ask the right questions, but the questions have to be succinct, clear and in the right order to provide organized interviews with a natural flow.

INTERVIEW PROCEDURES

Unlike newspaper reporters, broadcast and cable journalists face a series of deadlines throughout the day. News is an ongoing process and electronic journalists have the ability to cover important news events and report them immediately in scheduled newscasts or by breaking into regularly scheduled programs with news bulletins.

There has been a dramatic increase of news programming in the past ten years. In many major markets there is at least one all-news radio station that carries news 24 hours a day. In a few major cities, television stations are experimenting with all-news formats, and with the advent of *C*able *N*ews *N*etwork (CNN), many people who have cable hookups can watch cable news 24 hours a day. Even in more traditional radio and television stations there are many hours of news programming daily. Most radio stations program news every hour throughout the day, and most television stations program major newscasts in the morning, noon, in the early evening and at night.

This increase in news programming has placed greater pressure on electronic journalists to be more efficient and do more stories throughout the day. One way of being more efficient is for newspeople to cover a news event and create two or more news stories about the same event. An example would be if a reporter was sent to cover a city commission meeting where a city-county coordinating committee was approved. For the evening newscast, the reporter might interview the mayor about the commission's action and what it means. During the same interview, the reporter might ask questions about another aspect of the newly created committee which could be run in later newscasts. The one interview, with minor re-editing and script changes would produce two different stories. For example:

QUESTION: Mayor, what is the significance of the council's action today?

MAYOR: Well, Bob, as you know, the Commission has been trying to find a solution to the uncontrolled growth that has been taking place in the city and county.

What we did today will bring the city and county administrations closer together on matters of mutual concern because it sets up a procedure where certain issues will not be voted on until members of a city-county co-ordinating committee...that we created today...discuss the issue and make recommendations.

QUESTION: How will the committee work?

MAYOR: Actually it's quite easy. We appoint two members to the committee and the county appoints two members. The four member committee will then discuss any issue set before it by either the city or county. It merely takes a majority vote to send an issue to the committee.

QUESTION: Who will be appointed to the committee by the city?

MAYOR: That is a good question. Right now the commissioners will be looking for qualified people to represent the city on this committee. Whoever is appointed to this committee will have their work cut out for them because this is going to be a lot of work. This is going to be a tough job and whoever is on the committee is going to help make some tough decisions.

QUESTION: What type of tough decisions are you talking about?

MAYOR: Well, just take a look at the major issues facing our city-county area right now. We have a bankrupt bus service that really should be expanded to provide service to county residents if we want to cut energy use and reduce traffic. But how do we keep it going and what type of service do we provide? Another matter is growth. We have forces on one hand pushing to develop everything in the city and county. On the other extreme we have forces that want to stop all growth and preserve our quality of living. No matter what the committee decides on development there are going to be some angry people.

EXAMPLE 4-1

EARLY EVENING NEWS STORY

MAYOR ON CITY-COUNTY COMMITTEE
SOPER-WILLSON
7-4, 6 PM

REDIVILLE CITY COMMISSIONERS ARE TAKING THE FIRST STEP TOWARD COORDINATING CITY ACTIVITIES WITH THE COUNTY. COMMISSIONERS CREATED A FOUR MEMBER CITY-COUNTY COORDINATING COMMITTEE WHICH WILL DISCUSS ANY MATTER SENT BEFORE IT BY EITHER THE CITY OR COUNTY GOVERNMENTS AND THEN MAKE RECOMMENDATIONS. MAYOR CHARLOTTE SCOTT SAYS COMMITTEE MEMBERS WILL HAVE A TOUGH JOB AHEAD OF THEM.

CART :29 "going to be some angry people."

TEXT OF SOUND BITE:

"Well, just take a look at the major issues facing our city-county area right now. We have a bankrupt bus service that really should be expanded to provide service to county residents if we want to cut energy use and reduce traffic. But how do we keep it going and what type of service do we provide?
Another matter is growth. We have forces on one hand pushing to develop everything in the city and county. On the other extreme, we have forces that want to stop all growth to preserve our quality of living. No matter what the committee decides on development there are going to be some angry people."

MAYOR SCOTT SAYS THIS WILL BE AN ACTIVE COMMITTEE WITH A LOT OF WORK FACING COMMITTEE MEMBERS.

EXAMPLE 4-2

LATE NIGHT NEWS STORY

MAYOR ON COMMITTEE
SOPER-WILLSON
7-4, 11 P.M.

REDIVILLE CITY COMMISSIONERS FINALLY PASSED THAT CONTROVERSIAL CITY-COUNTY COORDINATING COMMITTEE PROPOSAL. TWO TOUGH ISSUES FACING THE NEW COMMITTEE ARE THE BANKRUPT BUS SYSTEM AND THE RATE OF CITY-COUNTY DEVELOPMENT. AT TODAY'S COMMISSION MEETING MAYOR CHARLOTTE SCOTT SAYS CREATING THE COMMITTEE IS JUST THE FIRST STEP.

<u>CART</u> :15 "make some tough decisions."

TEXT OF SOUND BITE:

"Right now the commission will be looking for qualified people to represent the city on this committee. Whoever is appointed to this committee will have their work cut out for them because this is going to be a lot of work. This is going to be a tough job and whoever is on the committee is going to have to help make some tough decisions."

MAYOR SCOTT SAYS THE CITY COMMISSION IS LOOKING FOR THE RIGHT PEOPLE TO APPOINT TO THE COMMITTEE. THE QUALIFICATIONS ARE A LIKING OF HARD WORK AND AN ABILITY TO MAKE TOUGH DECISIONS THAT MAY NOT PLEASE ANYONE.

Broadcast or cable news interviewers cannot be content with getting one good audio cut or sound bite in an interview. You must be thinking about what questions you can ask that will get interviewees to talk about the news event in future terms on what will happen later. In effect, you are trying to update the news stories by getting someone to talk about what will be happening in the future. Not all news events or news stories can be updated in this manner, but a surprising number of interviews can gain information about the future.

Most good broadcast interviewers go through a series of steps in obtaining and conducting interviews. They may not mentally realize that they are going through the steps, and they may even deny it, saying "if you want to interview someone you just do it." However, there do appear to be some common procedures or steps that many good broadcast and cable interviewers go through to obtain and conduct good interviews. These six steps are:

1. *Defining* the interview purpose

2. *Obtaining* the interview

3. *Researching* the topic or person

4. *Determining* questioning strategies and questions

5. *Establishing* rapport and conducting the interview

6. *Concluding* the interview

Defining the interview purpose sounds like something so obvious that it need not be discussed. That is not true because you would be surprised at the number of harried and hurried news reporters who race out to interview someone without really knowing the story background or thinking about what they want to talk about. Defining the purpose is simply sitting down for a few minutes, or discussing the interview with other people in the newsroom, and determining what area or areas you are going to concentrate on in the interview. Interviewing your local mayor, for example, could result in a smorgasboard of unrelated questions and answers. There are probably so many issues that could be discussed that you might end up with a series of shallow questions and answers about many topics. However, if you choose a few areas of major interest and then question the mayor in depth about those issues you will produce a much better interview. Defining the interview purpose is really just deciding about which important or interesting areas you are going to question someone.

Obtaining the interview is probably going to be as simple as calling up a person and asking for an interview. Most public people who get involved in newsworthy events expect to be interviewed for broadcast, newspapers, and magazines. Some people even seek out newsworthy or controversial events which will generate news media interest and gain notoriety and publicity for themselves. There are people, however, who do not particularly want to be interviewed or gain notoriety and this is where obtaining an interview can become a problem.

The key to interviewing reluctant people is to find out what might motivate them to talk with you in front of a camera or with a tape recorder running. Most people, even reluctant people, have some psychological, motivating force that, if correctly tapped, will lead them to say yes to interview requests. Your job is to figure out what that motivating force is and to phrase your request in a manner that stimulates that motivation. Some common motivating forces are:

to get revenge

to tell your side of a story

to clear up misconceptions

to help the reporter

to get notoriety

All of these motivating forces can be used to get you inside doors and talking with people who initially said no to your request for interviews. Many reporters have called reluctant people and told them they had a news story that they were going to run. The story, however, would be incomplete without someone telling the other side of the story or defending a particular point of view. The fear of having news stories aired which are biased against deeply held convictions or beliefs will motivate many people into granting interviews.

A request for an interview should always be clear. It should contain your name, your news organization, and the request for the interview. For example:

Interviewee: Hello.

Reporter: Hello, is Mr. Simpkins available?

Interviewee: This is Mr. Simpkins, what can I do for you?

Reporter: Mr. Simpkins, my name is Sheila O'Conner and I'm with WWWW television news. I am doing a story on the downtown merchants association and I would like to talk with you about your opposition to the suburban mall for the story.

Interviewee: Oh. Well,...I don't think so. That is something I really don't want to talk about at this time.

Reporter: Mr. Simpkins, I'm doing a story on the controversy and you are the most knowledgeable person in the merchants association who can talk about this issue. Now, I already have an interview with the mall developer George Builder and he really outlined his side of the issue. I am going to run the story tonight, but it would be incomplete without you clearly representing your side.

Interviewee: Look, why don't we just talk on the telephone and you can get your information this way.

Reporter: Mr. Simpkins, I am going to use part of Mr. Builder's interview on the air. I do not think my trying to represent your side, even though I will do it to the best of my ability, will be nearly as effective as you outlining your opposition to the mall.

Interviewee: Yes...I see what you mean. Well, when do you want to do this?

Clearly state your purpose, name and the news organization you represent and be prepared to sell your interview. Do not take no for an answer initially, and try to convince people that it is to their benefit to grant an interview. Do not lie or set up interviews under false pretenses. Lying could result in your being thrown out of an office or being denied admittance, and it will certainly ruin your credibility. Falsely representing yourself and talking to people without them realizing they are being interviewed also opens up the possibility of invasion of privacy. You should be explicit about your intentions to record interviews and the probable line of questioning. Knowing the general line of questioning in advance allows people to prepare mentally for interviews and formulate possible answers. People may examine files or scan pertinent information prior to the interview, which will make their answers much better. If possible, avoid giving people specific questions before interviews. Knowing specific questions beforehand is bad from two points of view. First, interviewees start rehearsing specific answers to your specific questions, and answers will sound rehearsed and spontaneity will be lost. Secondly, if there are potentially sensitive areas reporters wish to cover, interviewees can rehearse answers which will avoid sensitive topics or put them in the best possible light.

In some instances, where people refuse to talk with you about your main areas of interest, you may be able to obtain interviews by promising not to discuss certain topics. For example, if you wish to interview a city official who has been charged with a crime the person might refuse to talk about the charges or the court case. However, if approached correctly, the city official might agree to talk with you about other matters not pertinent to the court case, such as how his life has changed since the charges were filed and he was suspended from his job. Even though the primary topic will not be discussed, the interview can be quite revealing and interesting to your listeners. Also, once the person is on camera or in front of the tape recorder, he might bring up certain things he initially said he would not discuss.

Researching the topic or person to be interviewed is an important part of interviewing. The more that you know about the topic or the person you are interviewing, the better your questions will be and the better answers you will receive. It just makes sense that perceptive, well-informed questions come from solid research and knowledge of the topic.

Research can take on many forms. Simply talking with other reporters in the newsroom can provide you with excellent information about a topic or some pertinent questions to ask. Most newspeople keep fairly good files about many topics and asking around the newsroom might produce a file of clippings or notes. Good newsrooms also contain reference books, such as encyclopedias, almanacs, and statistical yearbooks. Some news departments also put old news stories on computer for quick reference. Other good research sources are local reference librarians, who can assist you with current information on a person or topic. A few telephone calls to local colleges or universities can also reveal great quantities of information. Call the recreation, physical education, or physiology departments if you need information about fad diets or controversial exercise programs. An interview with an African ambassador might prompt calls to the history, political science or African studies departments for background information on the nation, political systems, economic factors or personalities.

Most newspeople are generalists and do not have detailed information about a lot of topics. However, good newspeople know where to find information about a wide range of topics and quickly assimilate that information for use in interviews and news stories. This ability to quickly get information, analyze it, and use it is extremely important if you wish to conduct good interviews. Only through information can you determine if the person you are interviewing is telling the truth, shading answers, or lying outright. Unless you know what the person is talking about you will not be able to ask good follow up questions or challenge answers that are not correct. Whenever a news interviewer on CNN, NBC, ABC, NPR or CBS challenges the statement of a person they are interviewing, you can be assured that the newsperson has done a good deal of research on the topic and knows what the answer should have been.

Determining questions, interview strategies and the *role* of the interviewer are personal types of decisions based on what you found out researching the topic or person to be interviewed. Based on research and the interview purpose, you should develop an outline of topics to be covered during the interview and a series of interview questions. As a novice interviewer, it is a good idea to take this outline and list of questions into the interview situation. This will provide you with a guide to make sure that you cover the important areas and ask the important questions. Do not use the outline or list of questions as a rigid format, because interviews take on a life of their own, and you must be able to follow unexpected lines of questioning that open up. If you have to ask a particularly tough or sensitive question, a good policy is to write out the question and then memorize it so that you will not have to refer to your notes. This way you will ask the question precisely without stumbling or hesitating.

Particularly sensitive questions that might lead to hard feelings or strong language directed at the reporters should be saved for the end of interviews. Starting out with particularly hard or sensitive questions could result in the interviewees getting up and walking out without saying a word. This might result in dramatic video but your questions would still remain unanswered. You should first build up a pattern of question and response with interviewees before asking tough or sensitive questions. Once people have started talking and responding it is harder for them to break off interviews. Even if interviewees do get up and walk out, you have information gained during the first part of their interviews and some dramatic video of their responses to your final questions.

Avoid asking questions that lead to "yes" and "no" answers. You should ask questions that lead to narrative responses, questions that seek to find out why. Why has something happened and why has it happened this particular way? How do you feel about it now? The key to good answers are good questions that elicit personalized responses from interviewees. You should ask people you interview questions that require their opinions.

Novice interviewers have a hard time determining how they should act during interviews. Until you become an experienced interviewer, the safest role is for you to be moderate and act neutral. In other words, do not act tough or take sides by trying to play the devil's advocate. Remain moderate in your demeanor and ask questions in a firm businesslike manner. Asking tough questions does not mean you have to act tough. You can ask hard questions in a businesslike manner and this will generally produce good answers. Tough language or an accusing tone in your questions may sound like biased reporting, while the same questions asked in a moderate tone of voice and a businesslike manner will get an open response. The question, "Mr. Wylie, are you a crook?" asked in an accusing manner may result in the interview being terminated. Virtually the same question asked in a moderate voice with some softening language may result in a good answer. For example, "Mr. Wylie, you've been accused of taking bribes; of being a crook. How do you respond to these charges?"

Tough questions or questioning should never be avoided. It is your responsibility as a newsperson to ask hard questions and expect answers to your questions; not evasions or blanket statements. Some people evade answering tough questions by going off on tangents or giving lengthy answers without really answering the questions. You should not fall for this ploy and you should continue to pursue the line of questioning firmly but politely. For example:

REPORTER: Congressman, you were voted into office because of your stand on ecology. You just voted against a major ecological bill that will affect this district. Why?

CONGRESSMAN: I'm really glad that you asked that question because it's an issue that has been on my mind for months. It touches the economy. And you know what poor shape our economy is in. As a matter of fact, the recent economic indicators say the economy is getting worse while interest rates are going up. And when interest rates go up...no one can buy homes and businesses can't borrow money to expand their businesses.

REPORTER: Congressman, you must have misunderstood my question. I wanted to know why you voted against the ecological bill.

CONGRESSMAN: I just answered that question.

REPORTER: No sir, you did not. Now why did you vote against the ecological bill when most of the voters in your district favored the bill?

CONGRESSMAN: Not going to give up, are you?

REPORTER: No sir. The people who put you in office have a right to know why you voted the way you did.

You do not need to raise your voice or yell. You just need to politely but firmly pursue the line of questioning until either your questions are answered or you get a flat refusal to discuss the issue. Sometimes a refusal to answer a question or a "no comment" is the story. However, never accept a "no comment" answer. Always ask that person why they are refusing to comment and you might get a good answer.

REPORTER: What about these charges of bribery levelled against you?

INTERVIEWEE: No comment.

REPORTER: No comment! Why can't you comment?

INTERVIEWEE: Well, my attorney has told me not to talk about the charges until we file our million dollar libel suit. He says we'll do our talking in court.

That is not a bad story to run. It is certainly better than a "no comment."

Establishing rapport with the people you are going to interview and *conducting the interview* is, in most respects, the culmination of the interview process. Establishing rapport with people you are going to interview is rather important because rapport is nothing more than building a relationship of trust between people. If the interviewee distrusts you and is wary of your motives then your interview will be stilted, formal, and not very revealing or productive. Your attitude when you first meet the person to be interviewed is important. You should be friendly but not overly familiar with the interviewee. You should try to be friendly and open, but you should let the person you are going to interview set the pace of the relationship. Someone busy and on a tight schedule may not want to engage in a little informal conversation prior to the interview. Trying to force informal conversation will just make the person tense and uncooperative. If, on the other hand, someone seems willing to chat for a few minutes about world events, golf, or the weather, don't rush the person into the interview. Let this informal conversation prior to the interview build into two people enjoying each other's company, because this feeling of friendship will carry over into the interview.

When you arrive for the interview and start to build rapport, this is a good time to again casually outline areas for questioning. This might correct any misunderstanding, and the person being interviewed might open up new areas for questioning. Many times, people being interviewed can be helpful by providing you with background information that makes your questions and their answers better and more pertinent. If the interviewee is an expert in an area, rely on that person's judgment to a degree. During this informal conversation prior to the interview, you can become aware of possible strong responses or new areas to probe when the camera or tape recorder is turned on.

Informal conversation prior to interviews serves purposes other than building rapport and opening up new lines of questioning. Equipment can be set up and voice levels taken while you talk with the interviewee. You can also size up the interviewee and watch for patterns of speech or possible problem areas. For example, a busy telephone could interrupt the interview, and the problem can easily be solved by taking the telephone off the hook or having the secretary hold calls during the interview. Some individuals, not used to being interviewed, may be unusually tense and need to be reassured. A simple explanation of equipment and assurances that editing can take care of coughs, stumbles or answers that do not make sense will help put people at ease. A word of warning, though, never let a person being interviewed gain editorial control over which questions and answers will be used in the news story. Some interviewees may request hearing or viewing the interview before it is run. A simple way of avoiding that problem is to say that your station has a policy that forbids you from playing or showing interviews to anyone outside the news organization prior to the news story being aired.

Once an interview starts and the recording equipment is turned on, a good policy is to get the person's name and job title on the front of the tape or film for identification. Nothing is more frustrating in a newsroom than to have a film or taped interview and not know who was interviewed. Having the person pronounce his or her own name also provides a pronunciation guide for the newscaster and makes sure that you have the correct name for the news story. It is also wise for the newsperson to get the correct spelling of the interviewee's name for an identification "super" or "chromakey" over film or video tape.

During an interview, you should not fiddle with the tape recorder, cords or other equipment. The person being interviewed needs someone to respond to and communicate with. Set your audio levels and then look the interviewee in the eye and start the interview. An important aspect of face-to-face communication is eye contact and body language. By looking the interviewee in the eye and physically responding to the person you can build a communication bond. The interviewee may forget about the equipment and carry on a candid, animated conversation with you. The process of interviewing really comes down to human communication with a recording device present to record what happened.

During an interview don't feel that you have to encourage a person to keep talking by nodding your head or giving encouraging verbal responses by saying "Yes, yes," or "Un huh, un huh," "I see" or "I understand." There is no need for you to continually respond to the interviewee. A reporter's verbal responses, while the interviewee is talking, ruins the tape or film because these comments cannot be edited out. Once you ask a question you should remain quiet until the interviewee is done talking or you need to ask another question. Another thing to be careful of is "overstepping" the words of the interviewee. In normal conversation, it is natural for people to interrupt or overstep others' remarks by not allowing them to finish a statement. In broadcast news, overstepping creates editing problems. Only one person should be talking at any one time during an interview, so let pauses develop between the end of an answer and your next question.

Concluding the interview is a procedure that, it is hoped, will predispose the interviewee to let you come back on relatively good terms. Even when you ask tough or sensitive questions that upset an interviewee, you can try to reestablish rapport before you leave. Once the tough or sensitive questions are asked, you should continue the interview and move on to safer subjects that will allow you and the interviewee to reestablish a friendly atmosphere. Once the interview is over, remain for a few minutes to talk unless the interviewee is busy and gives off signals that he or she must do other things. A good idea is to ask people if they would mind a telephone call if you need further information. Try to get them to verbally commit to answer your telephone calls if you need to clarify a point or ask another question.

There are a number of *interview hazards* that electronic journalists face. One of the major problem areas is the "off the record" interview. The reason this is a problem is because people have different ideas as to what "off the record" means. It is important to make sure that you and the interviewee understand what each other is thinking when you talk about information given to you "off the record." For example, does "off the record" mean that you can use the information but not reveal the person's name? Or does "off the record" mean that you can use the information if you can get someone else to confirm or act as an attributing source? These are questions that should be clarified between reporters and interviewees before the interviews are given or the information used in news stories.

Another common interview hazard that journalists frequently face are people who will not grant an interview until they know what questions will be asked. A good way to avoid giving all of your questions to people is to tell them a few of the questions but caution that their answers will prompt other questions. Explain that an interview is a give and take discussion and one answer will raise other unforeseen questions.

EDITING PROCEDURES

Despite the best efforts of news interviewers, most interviews run in peaks and valleys with a few good statements separated by other parts of the interview that are not especially newsworthy. The following interview is a good example:

Q: Commissioner, would you summarize the issue that the city commissioners discussed at today's meeting?

A: Okay, the city wants to spend 18 million dollars to buy a percentage of the power eventually generated by a nuclear power plant. That 18 million dollars just goes for building the plant. We will still have to pay for any power that we want in the future at the going rate. So the 18 million we are talking about now is merely option money and we'll have to pay more later.

Q: Commissioner, you voted against the proposal for the city purchasing part ownership in the proposed Port St. Lucie Nuclear Power Plant. Why?

A: Well, there are a number of reasons why I voted against it. The main reason is that I am basically opposed to more nuclear power plants. They are not safe and this has been proven by the Three Mile Island disaster and recent problems with nuclear reactors in Japan.

Q: You said there were a number of reasons. What are your other reasons?

A: Well, one big reason is that I think we could spend the same amount of money on energy saving devices and get greater financial gains through savings over the years.

Q: Explain what you mean.

A: My solution is simple. Don't buy into the Port Saint Lucie plant. Use that money for energy savings devices here in the community. Instead of having to continue to pay for electricity and be dependent on electricity, we should invest in energy saving devices and what we save now will continue to save in the future.

Q: Given me an example of what you mean.

A: Well, we take this 18 million dollars and spend it on solar water heaters or other devices like that. That solar device reduces our energy needs and pays for itself over a period of time. The investment actually reduces our energy needs. So the 18 million we invest cuts down the amount we spend in the future. The nuclear plant, however, calls for us to spend 18 million now and more in the future.

Q: What other types of energy saving devices would you recommend?

A: Well, that's really up to energy specialists. But we could invest money in better windows--double glazed or storm windows. We would also buy more insulation for older homes and city buildings or buy energy efficient mass transportation vehicles.

Q: What do you think your chances are of convincing other commissioners to go along with you on the final vote?

A: Not good at all. I don't think my plan has much of a chance at all.

The interview contains a number of potentially interesting sound bites that could be used in a news story for radio, television or cable. Depending on what type of coverage this story has already received, what is new or different in the interview, and the amount of time available in the newscast are factors which will help you determine which sound bite or sound bites will eventually be used. If, for example, you only have 45 seconds for a news story you might go with only one sound bite and try to summarize other important aspects of the interview in your news copy. If you have the time, however, you might edit the best sound bites and appropriate questions together into a long interview. For example:

A: The city wants to spend 18 million dollars to buy a percentage of the power eventually generated by the nuclear power plant. That 18 million just goes for building the plant. We will still have to pay for any power that we want in the future at the going rate.

Q: What's your solution?

A: We take this 18 million dollars and spend it on solar water heaters or other devices like that. That solar device reduces our energy needs and pays for itself over a period of time. The investment actually reduces our energy needs. So the 18 million we invest cuts down the amount of money we spend in the future. The nuclear plant, however, calls for us to spend 18 million now and more in the future.

Q: What do you think your chances are of convincing other commissioners to go along with you on the final vote?

A: Not very good at all. I don't think my plan has much of a chance at all.

To make the interview flow and sound logical, we edited together three answers and two questions which provided a 52-second sound bite. Questions were left in or inserted into the interview to provide logical transitions between answers. Although there has been some slight manipulation in editing the interview, the content has not been changed. The purpose of editing is to help convey the meaning of the story, not change what was said to fit pre-existing feelings on the part of news-people or editors.

In most news stories utilizing sound bites or interview cuts, the script actually tells the story and the interview is used primarily to support the script. Most good news writers can organize the five Ws into tight news scripts that tell the story better than someone in an interview. However, sound bites are used to add source credibility; epitomize what is happening; tell an anecdote; convey an emotion; or elaborate on one important element of the story. Since the script will tell the story the sound bite can be rather short. Most radio interview cuts are less than thirty seconds long and sound bites for a television news story seldom run longer than forty-five seconds.

If you go through the time and trouble to edit an interview, it is a good idea to take a few extra minutes and try to clean up some of the rough spots. The first question was edited out because the news writer will summarize the question in the script leading into the interview. A few other minor editing changes were made. "Okay" and "So the 18 million we are talking about now is merely option money and we'll have to pay more later," were edited out of the first sound bite. The deletion does not change the content, but it does streamline or tighten up the statement. In the second sound bite, only "Well" was edited out. Many people will start answers to questions by either repeating the question or using hesitation words, like "well" to give themselves a moment to think or organize their answer. These hesitation words or redundant statements can be edited out quite easily and this will keep the sound bite short.

Sophisticated editing requires time, and, in many instances, newspeople may only have time to edit the desired sound bite. Many radio news operations do not edit audio tape unless it is absolutely necessary. If a reporter has not overstepped the sound bite chosen for the news cut or actuality, the news cut may simply be dubbed or transferred onto a tape cart without the original tape physically being cut or edited.

LEAD-INS

Writing lead-ins to video tape, audio tape, or sound film stories requires the same basic style, organization, grammar, and lead used in other broadcast news copy. Lead-ins, though, must do three and, in some instances, four things. They must:

1. Justify your use of tape or film

2. Focus attention

3. Identify people speaking on the tape or film

The fourth item depends on the people interviewed and how widely known they are. Sometimes merely identifying people in sound bites is not sufficient. You may have to build people's credibility so that news viewers or listeners understand the impact of what they are saying or can evaluate their credentials for speaking on the topic. So, the fourth item, if needed, is:

4. Establish source credibility

Most lead-ins range in length from about ten to twenty seconds. Under ten seconds and you face the possibility of not saying enough in the lead-in to justify the story, focus attention or identify the person speaking. If the lead-in runs longer than twenty seconds, the whole story may run too long or the lead-in could overshadow the sound bite and reduce its impact. Occasionally, in a feature story or national news story that has been localized with an interview, you may have to give more background or justification in the lead-in than you would prefer. An ability to summarize complex situations and concentrate on important aspects of the news stories are very important in keeping your news copy to a reasonable length. You must be able to justify the interview and the news story without giving away what the interviewee says in the sound bite.

INTERVIEW SUMMARY

SOUND BITE Commissioner Bowles against nuclear plant purchase

TAPE #16

Bowles says he would rather see the 18 million dollars that will go for buying into the nuclear plant used for energy saving devices. He says that if we spent 18 million dollars on solar water heaters and other energy saving devices...our electricity costs will be cut immediately and the energy saving devices will continue to save residents money on future utility bills.

In the nuclear power story examples, leads and lead-ins to the tape summarize sufficient information to prepare news listeners for the interview with Commissioner Bowles. Listeners understand the story background and know that Bowles is the one vote against buying into the nuclear plant. The lead-ins also clearly identify the voice on the tape as that of Commissioner Bowles.

In Example 4-3 the writer avoided using a sentence fragment or *dead end lead* to the sound bite. Dead end leads demand very tight production or the stories and newscasters come off looking and sounding amateurish. A few examples of dead end leads are:

THE MAYOR RESPONDED...

HE REPLIED...

SENATOR SMITH HAD THIS TO SAY...

THE MAYOR DECLARED...

If, for whatever reason, tape or film is not aired on time,dead end leads set up an awkward situation for the newscaster. Dead end leads clearly indicate that tape or film should immediately follow the news copy. Newscasters can only apologize and mumble through some type of excuse as to why film or tape was not aired.

With the type of lead-ins used in the nuclear power plant examples, if tape or film is not aired newscasters can go on with the story with only a slight pause. Some news organizations require that for every sound bite prepared for a newscast the writer must also type out a short summary of what the bite contains. Newscasters carry the summaries into the studio for emergency use.

News writers and editors should avoid writing scripts or editing tapes which *echo* or *parrot* each other. There should obviously be a strong connection between the lead-in and the first words on tape or film, but they should not be identical. Echoing or parroting is when the first words in the sound bite are virtually identical to the lead-in. See Example 4-4.

If newsroom policy is to write news script content in all upper case or capital letters, then it is a good idea to write production directions in lower case, to set them off visually from content. If the policy is to write in upper and lower case, then, conversely, use upper case or capitals for all production directions. This helps to avoid mistakes, as newscasters have been known to accidentally read out cues or production directions.

As part of production directions, you should always include the length of sound bites and give five or six word out cues as was done in Examples 4-3 and 4-4. This production information is vital because announcers and technicians can gauge the time of the sound bite and be prepared for the out cue signifying the end of the tape or film. In television, these production directions are also vital because directors must co-ordinate the activities of many people to make sure video tape is rolled on time and the right cameras and microphones are used exactly at the end of the sound bite.

Each news organization has its own style of writing production directions on radio, television, or cable news scripts. Obviously, you should follow whatever policies are used where you work to be consistent with what others are doing and to avoid confusion.

EXAMPLE 4-3

Nuc Power Plant-Bowles
Staeyle-Novell
7-22, 5pm

CITY COMMISSIONERS HAVE TENTATIVELY VOTED TO BUY PART OF THE PORT SAINT LUCIE NUCLEAR POWER PLANT. AT A PRELIMINARY MEETING TODAY, COMMISSIONERS VOTED FOUR-TO-ONE TO START RAISING 18-MILLION DOLLARS THROUGH THE SALE OF BONDS TO BUY EIGHT PERCENT OF THE PLANT. ONE COMMISSIONER...RALPH BOWLES...IS AGAINST THE IDEA AND SAYS THE MONEY COULD BE BETTER SPENT...

tape cart #16 (Bowles) :52 "...has much of a chance at all."

COMMISSIONER BOWLES SAYS PART OF HIS RELUCTANCE TO SUPPORT THE ISSUE IS BECAUSE OF RECENT NUCLEAR PLANT ACCIDENTS IN THE UNITED STATES AND JAPAN.

EXAMPLE 4-4

NUC Power Plant-Bowles
Staeyle-Novell
7-22, 5 pm

CITY COMMISSIONERS VOTED TENTATIVELY TO BUY PART OF PORT SAINT LUCIE NUCLEAR POWER PLANT. AT A PRELIMINARY MEETING TODAY, COMMISSIONERS VOTED FOUR-TO-ONE TO START RAISING 18-MILLION DOLLARS THROUGH THE SALE OF BONDS TO BUY EIGHT PERCENT OF THE PLANT. COMMISSIONER...RALPH BOWLES TOLD REPORTER CAROL NOVELL THERE ARE A NUMBER OF REASONS WHY HE VOTED AGAINST THE PROPOSAL...

TAPE CART

"Well, there are a number of reasons why I voted against it. The main reason is that I am basically opposed to more nuclear power plants. They are not safe and this has been proven by the Three Mile Island disaster and recent problems with nuclear reactors in Japan."

COMMISSIONER BOWLES THINKS THE MONEY USED TO BUY PART OF THE POWER PLANT SHOULD BE USED TO BUY ENERGY SAVING DEVICES FOR CITY RESIDENTS.

-30-

BRIDGES

Bridges are exactly what you think they are. They are devices used to get from one point to another. In geography they are man-made structures used to get from one side of a gorge to another without getting your feet wet. In broadcast news, bridges are script devices used to get from one sound bite to another. Bridges are really script transitions that reporters and newscasters read in between two sound bites.

If tape or film sound bites are not edited together as we did in Example 4-3, then news writers must provide newscasters with bridges in their scripts. See Example 4-5.

Many times bridges will contain questions that lead to the next sound bite. If this is done, then the questions are edited out of the tape or film to avoid echoing or parroting.

Using bridges between three short sound bites changes the pacing of a news story. Using longer sound bites tends to build a slower paced newscast. Short sound bites with quick transitions between bridges and sound bites builds a quicker newscast pace that might be more appropriate for a younger listening or viewing audience. Even though the same information is carried in both stories, the three short punchy statements build a quick pace and add a certain excitement to the story. Many news editors prefer using shorter sound bites because they have greater impact and use less air time.

TAG LINES

Tag lines, lead-outs or out lines are important parts of all radio, television or cable stories that contain sound bites. They are important but they are often neglected by newswriters. Ideally, tag lines should reestablish identities of people being interviewed and add new bits of information to news stories. Re-establishing the identities of people in sound bites is appreciated by listeners who were not devoting their full attention to news stories and missed identifications in lead-ins. Some tag lines merely mention names and positions of interviewees, but this is not a good or creative writing technique. This reestablishes identities, but it adds nothing new to stories. In most broadcast news stories there is information that cannot be included in lead-ins or interviews for lack of time or because including it would create organization problems. The tag line is the ideal place to include that interesting bit of information that did not fit anywhere else.

EXAMPLE 4-5

Nuc Power Plant-Bowles
Staeyle-Novell
7-22, 5 pm

CITY COMMISSIONERS HAVE TENTATIVELY VOTED TO BUY PART OF THE PROPOSED PORT SAINT LUCIE NUCLEAR POWER PLANT. AT A PRELIMINARY MEETING TODAY, COMMISSIONERS VOTED FOUR TO ONE TO START RAISING 18-MILLION DOLLARS THROUGH THE SALE OF BONDS TO BUY EIGHT PERCENT OF THE PLANT. ONE COMMISSIONER...RALPH BOWLES...IS AGAINST THE IDEA BECAUSE BUYING THE PLANT IS JUST THE FIRST PAYMENT...

tape cut #16 (Bowles) :15 "...future at the going rate."

BOWLES SAYS HE HAS AN ALTERNATIVE ENERGY PLAN THAT WILL PAY OFF DOUBLE FOR CITY TAXPAYERS...

tape cut #17 (Bowles) :21 "...more in the future."

REPORTER CAROL NOVELL ASKED BOWLES WHAT HE THOUGHT HIS CHANCES WERE OF CONVERTING OTHER COMMISSIONERS TO HIS ENERGY SAVINGS PLAN...

tape cut #18 (Bowles) :04 "...has much of a chance at all."

CITY COMMISSIONER BOWLES SAYS HE IS AGAINST NUCLEAR POWER PLANTS BECAUSE OF RECENT NUCLEAR ACCIDENTS IN THE UNITED STATES AND JAPAN.

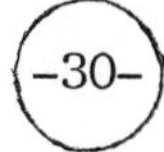

QUIZ

1. What is the purpose of interviewing?
2. What are the six steps you should go through to obtain and conduct a good interview?
3. What are two psychological motivations you might use to obtain an interview with someone reluctant to be interviewed?
4. When should sensitive or hard questions be asked in the interview?
5. What should the novice interviewer's role be in the interview?
6. The correct procedure for you as an interviewer when someone avoids answering a question is to do what?
7. Explain what "establishing rapport" is intended to do?
8. What is "overstepping"?
9. What should a lead-in accomplish?
10. What is a "dead end lead"?
11. Define "echoing"?
12. What is the purpose of a narration or script "bridge"?
13. What should a "tag line" accomplish?

EXERCISES

1. Define the interview purpose; research the topic or person and determine questioning strategies and interviewer's role for interviews with:

    a. The mayor of your town

    b. The president/chancellor of your university

    c. Yasir Arafat

    d. Robert Vesco

    Also, consider the possibility that these people may not want to be interviewed. What psychological motivations might be used to get him or her to grant an interview?

2. Audio tape record an interview with a campus leader about a current issue. Determine which sound bites are the best and write a news story for class utilizing those sound bites.

ASSIGNMENTS

1. Spend a day with a radio, television or cable news reporter observing how that person obtains and conducts interviews. Write a report outlining that person's interview style and critique the interview procedures.

2. Watch ABC's "NIGHTLINE" and critique the interview style of the newsperson doing a live interview.

3. Visit a local radio or television station that conducts live news or public affairs interviews. Observe the interviewer as he or she prepares for the interview and conducts the interview on the air. Write a critique of the interview procedures.

5

WRITING NEWS FOR CABLE AND TELEVISION

When media critic Marshall McLuhan said "the medium is the message" he started a debate that has continued to this day. Whether or not "the medium is the message" is still debatable but the fact is the medium does shape the message. This is quite obvious in any analysis of news written for radio or cable and television. A number of factors, some quite obvious, differentiate the roles of radio, television, and cable news operations. The economic influences, listenership-viewership patterns and the role each medium plays in our daily lives will be discussed in Chapter 8. However, one major difference that will be discussed in detail in this chapter is that unlike radio, cable and televison news are visual; they have pictures.

There is very little difference, if any, between writing for cable or television news. The real difference between cable and television news is in the delivery system each medium uses to reach its audience. Other minor differences are in the length of newscasts and formats. Cable systems also have a much smaller and more geographically defined audience than most television stations.

The visual element of television and cable is, in itself, a major aspect with which newswriters have to contend. Visuals also complicate the television and cable news production process because it requires significantly more people who specialize in a greater number of jobs. In addition to announcers and writer/reporters, television and cable news require photographers, editors, field producers, studio producers, television directors, and a whole studio production staff. Television news is a team effort of highly specialized people. Radio news, except in the larger markets, is primarily an individual effort of the newsperson on duty who monitors wire services; rewrites news stories; makes telephone calls to gather news; conducts and records interviews; and delivers the news during regularly scheduled newscasts.

Except in the largest broadcast markets, television and cable newswriters are also reporters who cover stories and conduct recorded interviews. Some very small television and cable markets have news writer/reporters also doing photography and video/film editing. Most television and cable news operations want versatile people who can do a variety of different jobs inside the news operation. This is especially true for small and medium sized markets which use people directly out of college with limited news experience. The tight budgets of these smaller operations call for people who can do many different news jobs.

There are three distinct production processes involved in television and cable news with which newswriters must be familiar. They are: (1) studio news production, (2) field news production, and (3) live field news production.

STUDIO NEWS PRODUCTION

Studio news production is the regular, formal presentation of television and cable newscasts on the local or network levels. Examples of studio news production process are regularly scheduled nightly news programs on local television or cable outlets. Examples of network studio news productions would be the evening ABC, NBC, CBS or CNN newscasts. (See Exhibit 5-1.) Newscasts are produced live in studios and involve production people operating equipment which is not considered portable. Locally, studio news productions involve segments of news, sports, and weather. Announcers read news and sports scripts and introduce field production packages, live field reports and other video or film shot in the field.

FIELD NEWS PRODUCTION

Field news production of television and cable news segments involves small crews, usually consisting of reporters and photographers (a field producer and lighting technician are used at the network level) who go to news events; gather information; record interviews and shoot video tape or film (See Exhibit 5-2.) Examples of the field production process would be when news teams are sent to cover fires, plane crashes or meetings at City Hall. The culmination of field productions take place at the television or cable station when news scripts are written, narration tracks recorded, and video or film edited to match the script. These packages, voice over video, and interview sound bite stories are inserted into studio-produced newscasts.

LIVE FIELD NEWS PRODUCTION

Live field news production is a mixture of studio and field production. (See Exhibit 5-3.) Utilizing highly portable electronic equipment and microwave transmitters, reporters and photographers in the field transmit live reports or visuals back to stations for inclusion in newscasts or as bulletins inserted into other programs. An example would be a reporter conducting a live interview from the scene of an ongoing event such as a night meeting of City Council or a natural disaster.

Helicopters with microwave capabilities have quickened the newsroom pace and provided another tool for instantaneous news coverage. (See Exhibit 5-4.) Helicopters hover over events, providing platforms for photographers and, at the same time, providing the necessary height to bounce TV signals back to stations off stationary microwave reflectors. Helicopters have proven to be quick transportation for newscrews who must travel over miles of crowded highways to get to a breaking news story.

Television and cable news writers, working in this highly visual and complex medium must be familiar with the demands of these three different production processes and know how to write and adapt news scripts for each. Through news scripts, writers become video editors and television directors. Finished news scripts dictate to video or film editors which shots will be used and in what order. When announcers read scripts during in-studio productions, the work of newscasters and television directors are coordinated by news scripts. Television directors direct newscasts according to directions written in the video column of news scripts, rolling video tapes, opening studio microphones, and inserting video at appropriate times dictated by the scripts. Newswriters are central to the production process because their news scripts coordinate the efforts of large news and production teams.

There is irony in the fact that in these electronic media of broadcasting and cable we rely on old technology to help us do our job electronically. For example, television/cable news crews go into the field and electronically record stories on video tape. Back in newsrooms, video tape is electronically edited on sophisticated editing equipment, while reporters sit down at typewriters and type out hard copy. Then hard copy or news scripts are taken into studios and read before electronic

EXHIBIT 5-1. STUDIO NEWS PRODUCTION

Photograph: Courtesy of WUFT Television, Gainesville, Florida

EXHIBIT 5-2. FIELD NEWS PRODUCTION. RCA's Hawkeye color field camera incorporates a video recorder on the camera providing greater field maneuverability.

Photograph: Courtesy of RCA Broadcast Video Systems

EXHIBIT 5-3. LIVE FIELD PRODUCTION. All necessary equipment for live field production can be carried in a small van with a microwave transmitter and retractable microwave antenna.

Photograph: Courtesy of Wolf Coach and WFLA Television, Tampa, Florida

EXHIBIT 5-4. LIVE FIELD NEWS PRODUCTION. JetRanger III helicopter provides quick transportation and an excellent platform for news photography and field-station microwave transmission.

Photograph: Courtesy of Bell Helicopter Textron

television cameras and electronically broadcast to electronic home receivers (television sets).

Some newspeople liken the use of typewriters to create hard copy to highly skilled surgeons using pocket knives in open heart surgery. They say typewriters are out of place in our electronic news gathering process because the job can be done better and cheaper with electronic equipment which some stations are already using.

The electronic medium is finally becoming electronic in the newsrooms. Two major changes for broadcast and cable newsrooms have been the invention of television character generators and newsroom computers. Both of these devices are similar and resemble small micro-computers like those sold by Radio Shack and IBM.

Character generators and newsroom computers are similar to each other in looks and technology (See Exhibits 5-5 and 5-8.) Both have key boards, visual display screens (similar to television sets), and memory storage capacities. In general, the more expensive character generators and computers deliver more sophisticated graphics and memory storage systems. Character generators produce high resolution graphics, numbers, and letters that are used to visually present information seen by viewers on home television receivers. Newsroom computers are used for writing news, information recall, and information storage. Newsroom computers are low resolution devices used internally, and viewers do not normally see computer information on home television receivers.

Newsroom micro-computers or visual display terminals (VDT) are basically electronic typewriters that use television screens instead of paper and have electronic disc memory storage units. Depending on the memory storage capacity, a VDT can perform many newsroom functions which reduce costs and time needed to produce radio, cable, and television news. VDTs are used by newswriters to type out draft news stories; store completed stories until needed; or search through files of audio and video which can be used in story preparations.

Most newsrooms converting to micro-computers find that efficiency increases after a week or two of transition. Some newspeople resist converting to computers but most people find that micro-computers save them time and energy. For example, when newspeople are typing out stories, corrections, changes, additions, and deletions are electronically made without using erasers, correcting fluids, strikeovers or new sheets of paper. When newswriters are satisfied with stories, the stories are electronically stored until they are recalled. Stories can be recalled onto hard copy and/or electronically transmitted to studio teleprompters or monitors where the announcers read them directly on the air.

Both character generators and micro-computers are nothing more than electronic tools for the news and production processes. The information collected, organized, and stored in these electronic units is the important element. These electronic tools help news and production people do better, more efficient jobs.

While most television news operations are basically the same, there are several factors that affect the people who work in newsrooms. Market size and unions affect the way that newsrooms operate. In small, non-union markets, newspeople must be able to do a variety of jobs. For example, in some small markets, newspeople may have to perform as writers, reporters, photographers, editors and announcers. Newspeople in small markets may pair up as they go out in the morning, and while one person reports, the other person films or video tapes interviews and cover video. On the next story, the newspeople switch jobs, and the morning reporter now becomes the photographer and vice versa. With two stories completed, they go back to the station to write and edit their individual news stories. Two newspeople, able to do a variety of news jobs well, help small markets stretch their tight news budgets.

In large television markets there is a tendency for specialization in newsrooms. This is encouraged by unions, which try to define and limit what union members do.

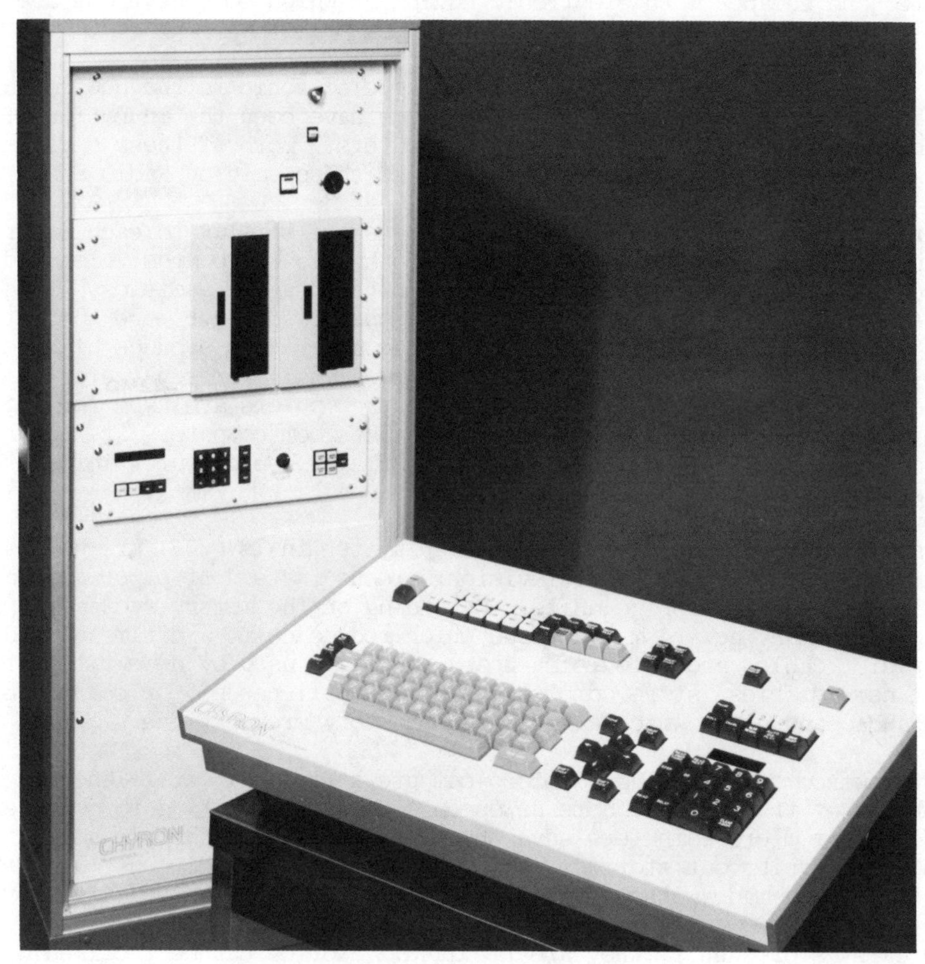

EXHIBIT 5-5. CHYRON CHARACTER GENERATOR. Chyron character generator with electronic keyboard and disc storage unit in equipment rack.

Photograph: Courtesy of Chyron Corporation. Chyron is a registered trademark of Chyron Corporation.

EXHIBIT 5-6. DESERT CLASSIC

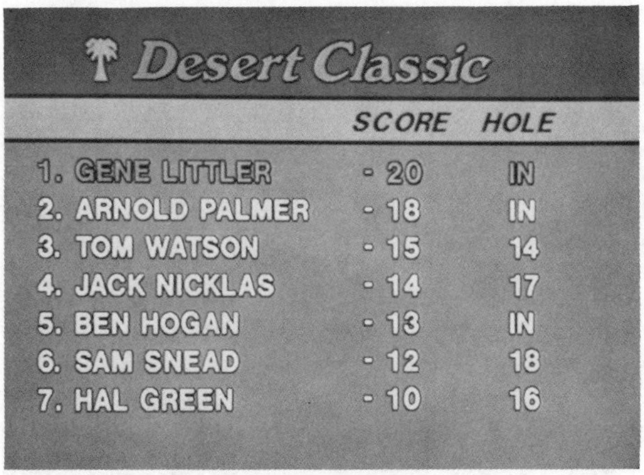

Desert Classic
SCORE HOLE
1. GENE LITTLER - 20 IN
2. ARNOLD PALMER - 18 IN
3. TOM WATSON - 15 14
4. JACK NICKLAS - 14 17
5. BEN HOGAN - 13 IN
6. SAM SNEAD - 12 18
7. HAL GREEN - 10 16

EXHIBIT 5-7. AFGHANISTAN USSR DEPLOYMENT

Afghanistan
USSR DEPLOYMENT
80,000 IN KABUL
895 WITH IN RANGE

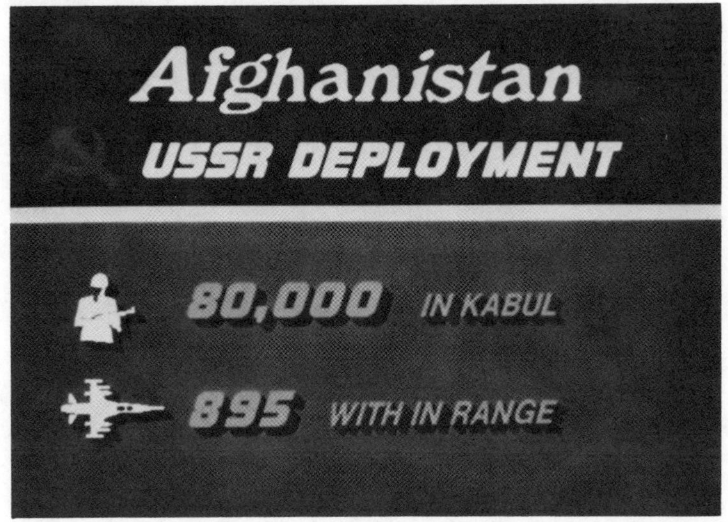

CHARACTER GENERATOR INFORMATION. Character generator material can be highlighted by type size, color, edging or computerized graphics.

Photographs: Courtesy of Chyron Corporation. Chyron is a registered trademark of Chyron Corporation.

EXHIBIT 5 8. VDT IN OPERATION. News writer using a newsroom computer, or Visual Display Terminal (VDT), to compose a news story.

It is not unusual for writer-reporters to be forbidden, by union contracts, from video editing or photographing. Union issues aside, the philosophy behind specialization is that you can hire the best photographers, writers, reporters and editors and have an efficient news operation. The counter-argument is that specialized people become narrow and this hurts the news process.

SCRIPT FORMAT

Television news scripts reflect the complicated studio production process requiring close coordination of news and production people.

The simplest television or cable news stories have newscasters reading scripts on camera without supporting visuals. See Example 5-1. In this example, the news writer typed in ANNCR in the video column or left portion of the script indicating that no visuals will be used while the story is being read by the newscaster. The rest of the space in the video column is not wasted because the television director uses this space to write comments, reminders, or directions for camera shots or events coming up later in the newscast. In this particular example, Bill-1 is the director's shorthand symbol that he wants this story read by Bill on camera 1. At the end of the story, the director plans to go to Debra on camera 2 (Debra-2) for the next story and then "ready" the production staff (R) to roll a video tape on tape machine 2 (R-VTR #2).

In this example, the audio column is indented at nearly every sentence. Indentations make it easier for newscasters to keep their place in stories when reading off a teleprompter. Maintaining eye contact with the camera is very important in television and cable news, and newscasters must continually be looking up from scripts without losing their places.

In the upper left corner of Example 5-1 just below the slug, the newswriter penciled in the time of the story. Part of the newswriter's job is to time each story by reading it aloud, approximating the time and inflection of the newscaster. Story times are written near the slug or at the top of the page so that producers or news editors can quickly ascertain the length of stories when they start planning and timing out newscasts.

STILL VISUALS

Script formats for stories using still visuals are quite similar to stories without visuals. The most common still visuals are art cards, or 35 mm slides which are chromakeyed, or electronically matted, behind newscasters.

The development of chromakey has significantly altered studio television news production. Chromakey is an electronic process that allows studio directors to mat two color pictures together without losing picture quality. The newscaster on one television camera can be electronically superimposed, or matted, over a picture on another camera. Pictures or slides matted behind newscasters can come from art cards, 35 mm slides, photographs, film or video tapes. To avoid visual confusion and present visually balanced shots, newscasters are usually placed in one portion of the television screen and the chromakeyed picture in another portion. See Example 5-3 and Exhibit 5-8.

EXAMPLE 5-1

U.S. OUT OF MONEY
FRANCO-AP
Nov. 22

:20

VIDEO	AUDIO
ANNCR Bill-1	TECHNICALLY, THE UNITED STATES IS BROKE AND OUT OF MONEY. HOUSE AND SENATE LEADERS WERE UNABLE TO WORK OUT A COMPROMISE BUDGET BILL BEFORE THE MIDNIGHT DEADLINE LAST NIGHT. WITHOUT A BUDGET...FEDERAL AGENCIES DO NOT HAVE ANY MONEY FOR PAYROLLS OR PROGRAMS.
Debra-2 R-VTR#2	HOUSE AND SENATE LEADERS ARE STILL MEETING....TRYING TO WORK OUT A BUDGET BILL THAT PRESIDENT REAGAN WILL SIGN INTO LAW.

EXAMPLE 5-2

SLUG: MIAMI TOURISM OFF	PAGE# 1
ANCHOR: BILL	SLIDE: 1026-1761
DATE: 11-15	WRITER: ROSENWASSER

BILL/ CK 1026 (Miami skyline)	MIAMI IS STILL CONSIDERED THE LAND OF SUN AND SAND... WHAT IT DOESN'T HAVE IS TOURISTS. FLORIDA TOURISM OFFICIALS SAY PUBLICITY ON THE CITY AND STATE'S HIGH CRIME RATE IS KEEPING TOURISTS AWAY FROM THEIR HOTEL AND BEACHES. SINCE MUCH OF FLORIDA'S ECONOMY IS TOURISM BASED, THE STATE'S ECONOMY HAS TAKEN A NOSE DIVE.
BILL/ CK 1761 (Gov. Graham)	FLORIDA'S GOVERNOR AND OTHER STATE OFFICIALS ARE TRYING TO CUT 56-MILLION DOLLARS FROM THIS YEAR'S BUDGET BECAUSE OF A REVENUE SHORTFALL. -30-

A typical television news script using chromakey visuals (CK) to illustrate the story.

Left side of page is used for production directions.

BILL/CK 1026, indicates Bill is the newscaster and CK 1026 is the first chromakey visual of the Miami skyline.

BILL/CK 1761. Bill continues to read and at this point a new slide showing Governor Graham is taken by the director.

:25 - in the upper right portion of script indicates length of the new story which was timed by the newswriter.

EXAMPLE 5-3

Camera 1

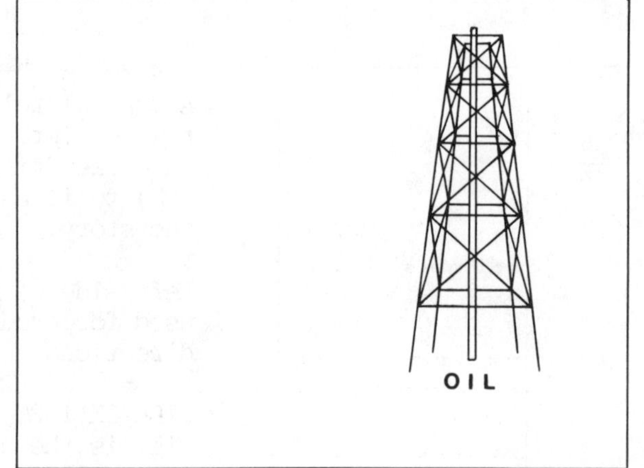

Studio Art card

or

35 MM slide

Camera 2

Newscaster

Composite picture seen on home television receiver

Art card or 35 MM slide chromakeyed behind newscaster.

EXHIBIT 5-9. TELEVISION NEWS ANCHOR TOM WILLS. Over Wills' left shoulder is a chromakeyed graphic. Electronically matted over Wills' chest is a station logo and newscaster identification.

Photograph: Courtesy WJXT, Jacksonville ©: Post-Newsweek Stations, Florida, Inc., 1981

MOVING VISUALS

Moving visuals for television news are created by film or video tape. In the United States, most television news operations are using video tape or electronic news gathering (ENG) equipment in field work. Some news departments, mostly for economic reasons, have not made a total transition to ENG and there are still many news departments which retain a film capacity as backup to ENG. For a number of reasons, primarily speed and ease of editing, portable video tape technology is dominating the visual reporting aspects of television news. Because video tape does not have to be processed like film, television has been able to move news reporting deadlines much closer to airtime. The only determining factors for deadlines are now the length of time needed for writing and video editing. The development of portable equipment for live coverage, which will be discussed in Chapter 6, has actually done away with television deadlines, allowing live inserts into news or other programs whenever the event's importance dictates live coverage.

Part of the reason that television news departments made such a quick transition to ENG technology was the realization that video tape, while creating some initial problems, solved most film editing problems that had haunted television newsrooms for more than twenty years. Film editing is complex and cumbersome because film editing technology is not as sophisticated as current editing technology for video tape. Film editing is a mechanical process that requires physically cutting and splicing film segments together. Sound visuals are separated on the film, which creates synchronizing problems. Film has only one audio channel which limits audio mixing. The electronic editing process of video tape technology revolutionized news production. Video tape editing and packaging has moved into editing rooms, whereas, complex film packaging, in many stations, had to be done live while newscasts were on the air.

Video editing is based on two important assumptions:

1. Dubs or duplicate video tape copies can be nearly as good as the original, especially after electronic processing. (See TBC, or time base corrector, in glossary.)

2. It is much easier and quicker to electronically edit video tapes than physically cut and splice together two or more pieces of film.

Another highly desirable trait of video tape over film is that video tape audio and video are synchronized. Video tape audio is in the same spot as corresponding visuals. See Example 5-4. In film, there were problems with sync because audio was 28 frames (slightly more than one second) ahead of the visuals. Editing sound film was always awkward and one-second gaps appeared between film segments.

Not only does video tape synchronize audio with video, but video tape has two audio tracks which can be used for different sound sources. For example, audio channel one can be used to record primary audio, such as an interview. Audio channel two can be used to record background or ambient sound. During editing or playback, the two different audio channels can be mixed or controlled, so that the background noise will be at the proper level under the interview.

Another reason that video tape technology was embraced so quickly by newspeople is that it allowed fast, sophisticated editing not available with film technology. With video tape, editors could electronically black out the video or one or more of the audio channels replacing them with different audio or video without affecting the other channels. In effect, electronic editing gave video editors the ability to completely combine a variety of audio and visual sources into one easily handled package. With news film, this complex process was not totally handled in editing rooms, and directors had to finish the packaging process during live studio news presentations where mistakes commonly occurred.

EXAMPLE 5-4

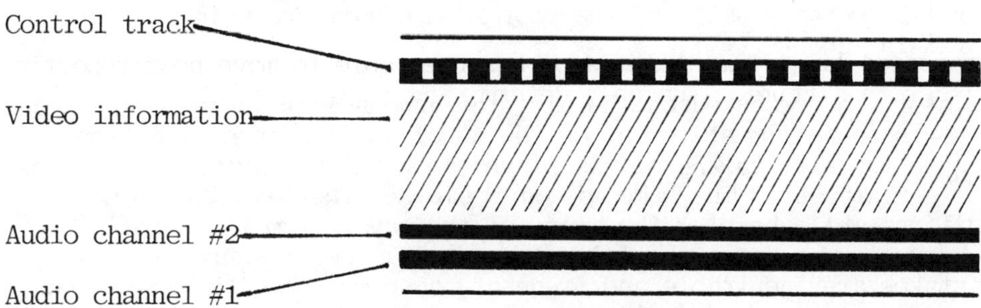

Control Track. The control track is composed of electronic pulses that indicate at what speed the tape was recorded. There is some variance in field tape recorders and the control track tells the playback unit, through a series of internal controls, at which speed the tape should be replayed for compatibility.

Video Track. Video information is recorded helically on the video track. The information on the video track is synched with the audio information.

Audio Tracks. Both audio channels are synchronized with the video channels. This means that during an interview, for example, the person's words would synchronize with the picture of the person talking.

NEWS FILM PRODUCTION

A film photographer obtains a soundfilm interview with the mayor, who talks about poor road conditions. Following the interview, film is obtained showing the poor road conditions; cars hitting potholes; large cracks in the streets; cars swerving to avoid hitting large holes or slowing down to save tires and suspension systems.

Back at the television station, a film editor prepares two rolls of film. The A-roll, or primary roll of film, contains the mayor's edited interview. The B-roll, or secondary film roll, contains shots of the poor road conditions which illustrate what the mayor is talking about.

When the news story is presented on the air, the announcer reads a script introducing the mayor's soundfilm statement on the A-roll. At a specified time, while the A-roll is on the air, the B-roll is played showing the pictures of the bad road over the mayor's statement. The home viewer would see the B-roll film shots of the poor road conditions while hearing the voice of the mayor from the A-roll. In effect, the studio director packages the film story during the pressure of a live newscast, where mistakes are inevitable and frequent, as compared with video tape production.

VIDEO TAPE NEWS PRODUCTION

With current ENG technology, the same video shots would be obtained in the field but the production process would take place entirely in the editing room. The video editor would, electronically, insert shots of poor road conditions over video of the mayor while retaining the interview audio. The end result is one video tape instead of two rolls of film, played back on the air showing poor road conditions with the mayor's audio discussing the road problem.

Video tape or film news stories are divided into three basic types: (1) cover video or voice over stories, (2) sound bite stories, and (3) the package stories.

Cover video or voice over (VO) stories are short news stories read live by the anchor, and cover video or film is chromakeyed behind the anchor person or taken full screen. When the video tape or film is taken full screen the news viewer hears the anchor person reading over video tape or film. (See script Example 5-5.) Sound bite stories contain interview sound bites inserted into the news story. (See script Example 5-7.) Package stories contain cover video and sound bites which are edited together with a field reporter narration and/or standup. Packages are played during the newscast after short live opener scripts read by the anchorperson. (See script Example 5-8.)

Cover video stories, as previously explained, utilize video to reinforce or illustrate scripts. Cover video stories develop in several ways. Most cover video stories are not good enough (because of news content or visuals) to be expanded into long package stories utilizing a reporter in the field. Cover video stories are normally fifteen to forty-five seconds in length.

Writing cover video stories is a team effort of news photographers, video editors, and newswriters. When members of the team understand each other's needs, producing cover video stories and scripts is easier. Photographers who understand that video editors need many cutaways and specific sequences of shots are better photographers, because their video will be easier to edit. Newswriters who understand the video formula will write better scripts that do not violate accepted film or video continuity and confuse news viewers.

Writing cover video stories may be the hardest job television newswriters face, if stories are done well. Cover video stories are usually a compromise between words and pictures. Writers organize, write, and time stories to make the best use

EXAMPLE 5-5

LINCOLN ST. BRIDGE
WEISS-GRANZOW
AUG 19, 1976

VIDEO	AUDIO
ANNCR	THE LINCOLN STREET BRIDGE IS A TROUBLED BRIDGE OVER TROUBLED WATERS.
VTR, 45-sec	STATE BRIDGE INSPECTORS SAY THE OLD BRIDGE IS UNSAFE...AND WILL HAVE TO BE CLOSED TO HEAVY TRUCK TRAFFIC.
	HIGHWAY PATROLMEN HAVE BEEN STATIONED AT EITHER END OF THE BRIDGE TO KEEP OFF HEAVY TRUCKS.
	THE CITY IS RUSHING TO GET WARNING SIGNS POSTED...BUT THAT WILL TAKE SEVERAL DAYS.
	THE PROBLEM IS THAT THE STRONG RIVER CURRENTS OF THE COLUMBIA RIVER ARE ERODING THE BANKS AND DIRT SURROUNDING BRIDGE SUPPORTS.
	THERE ARE SEVERAL THINGS THAT CAN BE DONE TO ALLEVIATE THE PROBLEM IN THE LONG HAUL.
	BUT...THE FIRST THING IS TO REDUCE HEAVY TRAFFIC ON THE BRIDGE AND GET ENGINEERS TO PUT UP TEMPORARY SUPPORTS.
	THE CLOSING OF THE LINCOLN STREET BRIDGE WILL CREATE SOME PROBLEMS...BUT THERE ARE SEVERAL DETOURS FOR HEAVY TRUCKS.

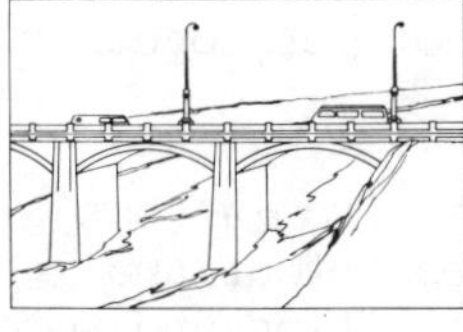

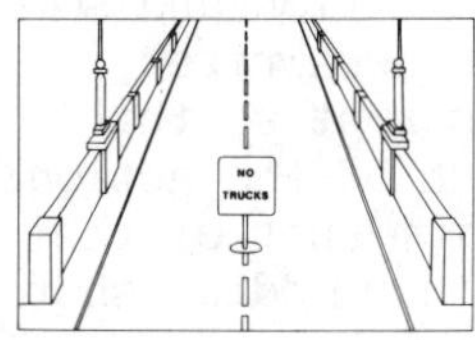

-30-

A cover video or voice over (VO) story.

As indicated in the AUDIO and VIDEO column, the announcer reads the entire script while the director inserts a 45-second video tape.

Live opener: The first paragraph read by the newscaster while on camera is called the live opener.

VTR, 45-sec: Indicates the point where the studio director should roll the video tape while the announcer continues to voice over the script.

Home viewers will continue to hear the newscaster reading the voice over while seeing the video of the Lincoln Street Bridge which has been edited to match, or sync with, the script.

of video and words. An aspect of a news story, deserving only a quick three- or four-second mention, might end up eight or ten seconds long because extra time is needed for editing or to make the best use of a particular video sequence. Writers must understand the problems of film and video tape editing, because scripts become editing guides for editors. Editors will cut film or edit video tape to match scripts, synchronizing video shots and sequences to words and sentences.

Novice news writers generally assume that words must dominate every news story. After all, they assume, words are those symbols that carry meaning and tell what has happened. This is not always true, because certain stories are dominated by visuals while other stories are dominated by words or content. Words should dominate stories that utilize general visuals because the visuals are not overpowering and they support the script. General or stock video, like that of city council meetings, requires that words dominate the story and explain what happened. Conversely, specific visuals, such as shots of the mayor jabbing his finger angrily at a person, can only be used in relation to a specific event. Words, or script, should support visuals of the mayor. When video is action oriented or highly specific, visuals will dominate and words should take a secondary position. When cover video dominates, video tape or film will be edited first to highlight the strong visuals and the script written to match the film or video tape.

Before writing cover video or voice over stories, writers should study shot sheets, if available, and view films or video tapes to get clear ideas of what shots were taken, shot length, and any film or video tape peculiarities which might affect writing. This information will dictate, to a degree, how stories are written and the length of stories. The amount of time left to air time may be the deciding factor in whether scripts are written to video or video edited to scripts. If time is critical, a producer or news editor may make all decisions based on a photographer's shot sheet, such as the shot sheet in Example 5-6. The producer will tell the writer how to write the story and the video editor to edit specific shots together in a specific order to match the script. The writer and editor may not get together or even see each other's work until the story is put on the air.

The Lincoln Street Bridge cover video story (Example 5-5) written from a shot sheet, did not use all of the cover video shot in the field. Shots one, four and six were not used. Remaining shots were edited to match script organization and some shots were shortened to synchronize video to specific sentences. The newswriter, aware of standard video continuity and the video formula, wrote the script so that the first video shot is a wide angle establishing shot showing as much of the action as possible. The script is written so that the next shots are a medium shot of the patrolman on the bridge; a long shot of the bridge and water and another medium shot of the "no trucks" sign.

Television news production demands that people follow certain common procedures or the system breaks down. It is expected that photographers will obtain certain standard video shots referred to as the *video news formula*. Writers and editors assume that photographers will follow the video news formula or have a good reason for breaking the rules. The video news formula follows film conventions developed by Hollywood and television photographers and is based on how people see things. For example, if you walked into a room full of people your eyes would probably first try to scan the whole room to get an overall perception of who was present and what was taking place. Then your eyes would focus in on small groups and finally your eyes would focus in on individuals. In video news formula terms, your eyes obtained a wide shot of the action, a medium shot of small groups, and close ups of individuals.

The video news formula follows the same shot sequence and is illustrated on the following page. Shots in the video news formula relate to preceding shots in a continuity that tells a visually pleasing story. If photographers do not follow the video news formula, video may be technically good but editing will be difficult and visuals will not relate well to other visuals and the script.

VIDEO NEWS FORMULA EXAMPLES

VIDEO NEWS FORMULA		FIRE SEQUENCE	ACCIDENT SEQUENCE
Long shot (LS) or Wide Shot (WS)	Establishing shot showing relationships	WS - showing fire scene, trucks, house and firefighters	WS - accident scene with two cars, person directing traffic and injured person on ground
Medium shot (MS)	Focusing in on small action scene	MS - firefighters holding hose, spraying house	MS - injured person on ground receiving first aid
Close up (action) (CU)	Specific action in above action scene	CU - firefighter's face showing tension, dirt and sweat	CU - face of injured person grimacing with pain
Close up (reaction) (CU)*	Specific reaction to previous action shot*	CU - spectators watching firefighters	CU - person administering first aid
MS	Focus in on another small action scene	MS - two medics working on injured firefighters	MS - person directing traffic with wrecked cars in background
CU (action)	Specific action in this small action scene	CU - injured fire-fighters	CU - person directing traffic
CU (reaction)	Specific reaction to previous action shot	CU - person giving first aid to firefighter	CU - traffic moving

Keep repeating the formula of WS - MS - CU (action) - CU (reaction) until all pertinent visual aspects of news story have been recorded.

*Remember your laws of physics. For every action there is a reaction. When you show a CU action shot you should always try to show the CU reaction shot.

EXAMPLE 5-6

EYEWITNESS NEWS SHOT SHEET

Story LINCOLN ST. Bridge

Date AUG. 19

Photographer GRANZOW

Shot No.	Length	Type	Content
1	10-15	LS	Bridge-No traffic
2	10-15	LS	3/4 ANGLE-Bridge-sign-Cars
3	10	MS	COP ON Bridge
4	8	LS	cars backed up-Shaky video
5	10	LS	sideview Bridge + supports
6	8-10	MS	Supports
7	10	MS	"No TRUCKS" Sign
8	15-18	LS	cop directing traffic +
			"DEtour" Sign

Normally newswriters will not list specific shots in the video column of scripts. About the only time specific shots are listed is when cover video is edited longer than the scripts and newscasters must synchronize their reading to specific shots.

There is a tendency for most novice newswriters to overwrite cover video or voice over scripts. Packing too many words into the script results in sync problems, or else video runs out before the newscaster finishes reading the script. If video is edited to the script, sync problems will be reduced because editors time out script segments and edit video tape to match the announcer's pace. In most instances, video editors add a second or two to each shot giving announcers and directors a few seconds of leeway or a pad. If there is more video tape than story, announcers can pause or slow their reading pace to let video catch up. Underwriting by a few seconds so there is more video tape than script is common practice, and it provides studio directors with a time cushion and helps avoid production problems.

Most sync problems occur when scripts are written to video tape or film that has already been edited. Trying to sync words to every shot results in choppy news stories that have an awkward flow or cadence. It does not hurt to have the copy a little ahead or behind a particular shot as long as the story retains a natural rhythm. Newswriters and video editors should only sync major points in stories, allowing portions of the script to run longer or shorter than video shots. Major sections of video should be synchronized to the script, not every shot. There are times, however, when shots need to be synchronized carefully to the script and, in these instances, it is easier to write the script first and edit video to the script.

Synchronizing identifications in voice over or cover video stories is risky business for novice newswriters. If, for example, a shot of the mayor starts twelve seconds into the video tape and the shot runs for eight seconds, identification should occur near the middle of the eight-second shot or about fifteen seconds into the cover video. Even if the announcer's pace is off or the studio director rolls the video tape early or late, there will be a four-second leeway and the right person will probably still be identified as the mayor.

When identifying someone in a crowd shot, avoid inadequate identifications such as:

THE MAYOR...SEEN SHAKING HANDS WITH POLITICAL SUPPORTERS...

Or:

THE MAYOR...TALKING WITH COUNCIL MEMBERS...

These identifications are not specific. When there are more than two people in a shot, identifications must be very specific, because viewers might not be able to distinguish one person from the other. In cover video or voice over stories, avoid phrases such as: seen here, shown here, or here we see. These phrases assume the film or video tape is synchronized with the script. While every effort is made to sync script and video, it is not always possible. A video tape machine may break down and the video tape may not be rolled; or the director may roll the film/video tape early or late, throwing off sync. It looks amateurish to see newscasters, unaware the film/video tape is not rolling, reading phrases such as "seen here" or "here we see."

Identify people with specific references. View the video tape or film and find identifying characteristics that will make it easier for news viewers to recognize someone instantly without visually searching through a crowd of people who look much the same. Use identifying phrases, such as:

THE ONLY ONE WITHOUT A COAT WAS MAYOR POWERS...

Or:

THE MAYOR WAS THE CENTER OF ATTENTION AS HE CUT THE RIBBON...

Scripts and video should not be overly redundant. Let film or video tape tell as much of the story as possible and use scripts to support or explain things the visuals cannot. Being redundant and having scripts explain every visual in detail creates a feeling that newscasters are talking down to viewers.

Script and video should never compete with or contradict each other. Studies show that when words and visuals conflict, viewers almost always believe the visuals. An example would be if the script says the mayor was highly distressed at the city council's vote and, at the same time, showing a visual of the mayor smiling. The script and visual contradict each other and most viewers will assume that the script was in error.

SOUND BITE STORIES

Television newswriters treat film or video sound bite stories in much the same way that radio newspeople treat audio bite stories, except for the split page television format. (See Example 5-7.)

In radio, cable, and television, sound bite stories come from interviews with newsmakers or people involved in news events. In small cable and television news departments, newswriters will probably exercise editorial judgments and select which sound bites to use in news stories. In larger news operations, news editors or producers may make these editorial judgments and inform writers and film/video editors which sound bites will be used in stories. No matter who makes editorial decisions, the process is usually the same. The person who makes the decision will review available information on the story; view and time film or video tape sound bites with a stop watch; and make notes on in cues and out cues of various sound statements. Once the decision is made on which sound bite will be used in a story, a film or video editor prepares the sound statement for insertion into the newscast. The film or video editor tells the newswriter the precise time of the sound bite and the out cue, or last four or five words of the sound bite. Newswriters include this information on script as a production aid for studio directors.

PACKAGE STORIES

Package stories are just what the name implies; everything is packaged, or edited, together in one neat package for playback in the newscast. There are actually two separate scripts written for package stories. The first script is written by the reporter who narrates the package. The second script is written for the newscaster who introduces the package in the newscast. (See Example 5-8 for the newscaster's script and Example 5-9 for the reporter's script.)

Package stories take much more time and effort to produce than cover video or sound bite stories. When reporters are assigned to package stories by news editors it is because some stories merit more air time or the sophisticated production of a package. Some news events, even if they are not terribly important, look better if they are packaged.

Package stories usually include at least one sound bite; a reporter's narration track; a reporter standup open or close; and cover video. (See the package script in Example 5-9.)

While each news package story tends to be different from other package stories, there are certain structural similarities. For example, in package stories without controversy or an opposing view, the following structure is quite common.

EXAMPLE 5-7

Mayor on roads
Novell
3-16/6 pm news

VIDEO	AUDIO
ANNCR:	THIS IS NOT REALLY NEWS TO MOST OF OUR AREA MOTORISTS...BUT OUR ROADS ARE IN TERRIBLE SHAPE.
	THE NEWS IS THAT THE FEDERAL GOVERNMENT SAYS IT WILL NOT HELP THE CITY TO REPAIR THE WINTER DAMAGED ROADS.
	MAYOR SYLVIA POWERS SAYS WITHOUT FEDERAL MONEY THE ROADS WILL GET A LOT WORSE....
VTR: :26 Sec.	
:08 /Mayor Powers	
"spring road repair crews."	
ANNCR:	MAYOR POWERS SAYS SHE WILL MEET WITH FEDERAL OFFICIALS IN WASHINGTON NEXT WEEK...AND TRY TO FIND SOME ROAD REPAIR MONEY.

-30-

As indicated in the AUDIO and VIDEO column, the announcer reads the live opener on camera.

VTR:26 Sec. At the end of the live opener, the director rolls and inserts a 26-second video tape full screen.

:08/Mayor Powers. At eight seconds into the video tape, the studio director will chromakey the words "Mayor Powers" over a shot of the mayor speaking on film or tape.

"spring road repair crews."
This is the outcue or final four words that are on the tape or film. At the end of the outcue, the studio director goes back to the announcer in the studio for a tag.

ANNCR. The last paragraph read by the announcer live in the studio is called a tag or tag line.

EXAMPLE 5-8

VIDEO	AUDIO
ANNCR	ATTORNEYS FOR CONVICTED MURDERER RAY SMITH WON A STAY OF EXECUTION FOR THEIR CLIENT WHO WAS TO DIE IN THE STATE'S ELECTRIC CHAIR THIS FRIDAY. EYEWITNESS REPORTER MARK NOVELL FILES THIS REPORT FROM THE STATE CAPITOL....
VTR: 1:44	
:08 / Mark Novell Reporting	(SOC)
:30 / Milt Truefoot Defense Attorney	
1:10 / Sally Whithead State Attorney	
1:30 / Mark Novell Reporting	
	-30-

Anncr: The announcer reads the live opener on camera to introduce the package story.

VTR: 1:44 Indicates to the director where to roll and take the video tape package and the story is 1:44 seconds long.

:08 / Mark Novell Reporting indicates to the studio director that eight seconds into the story the first chromakey identification should be inserted.

:30 / , 1:10 / and 1:30 / indicate other chromakey identifications and when they should be inserted.

SOC indicates Standard Out Cue. Which, in this story is, "Mark Novell, Eyewitness News at the State Capitol."

EXAMPLE 5-9

Package Script

Novell on Smith
1-22, 6:00 p.m.

VIDEO	AUDIO
LS, scale of justice pull back to WS of court building	THE LIFE OF CONVICTED MURDERER RAY SMITH IS AGAIN GOING BACK ONTO THE SCALES OF JUSTICE
LS, defense attorneys in room	DEFENSE ATTORNEYS FILED A MOTION TODAY REQUESTING A NEW TRIAL ON THE GROUNDS THE STATE ATTORNEY'S OFFICE WITHHELD CRUCIAL EVIDENCE. THEY CLAIM THE STATE SUPPRESSED EVIDENCE THAT WOULD HAVE PROVEN THEIR CLIENT INNOCENT OF MURDERING TWO PEOPLE DURING A HOLDUP IN MELBOURNE.
MS, state attorney's office	THE STATE ATTORNEY'S OFFICE SAYS ALL EVIDENCE THEY HAD WAS USED IN COURT AND AVAILABLE TO THE DEFENSE. SMITH WAS FOUND GUILTY OF ROBBERY-MURDER IN 1981 AND SENTENCED TO DIE IN THE ELECTRIC CHAIR THIS FRIDAY.
MS, Truefoot	DEFENSE ATTORNEYS SAY THEY SHOULD NOW GET A NEW TRIAL THAT WILL PROVE SMITH INNOCENT...
SOUNDBITE: Truefoot :16	(soundbite with Truefoot)
	SMITH WAS ARRESTED LESS THAN TWO BLOCKS FROM THE CRIME SCENE. ARRESTING OFFICERS TESTIFIED THEY HAD TO CHASE SMITH THROUGH BACK ALLEYS AND THAT HE FIRED A WEAPON AT THEM. THE WEAPON WAS NEVER FOUND BUT WITNESSES SWORE SMITH WAS IN THE MARKET WHEN THE SHOTS WERE FIRED.
	THE STATE ATTORNEY WHO PROSECUTED SMITH SAYS THE CASE WAS SOLID...
SOUNDBITE	
:22	(soundbite with Whithead)

VIDEO	AUDIO
Novell standup close in front of State Supreme Court Building	THE STAY OF EXECUTION FOR SMITH IS TEMPORARY... ONLY UNTIL STATE SUPREME COURT JUSTICES CAN REVIEW THE CASE AND SEE IF WHAT DEFENSE ATTORNEYS CLAIM IS TRUE...THAT THE STATE KEPT EVIDENCE THAT WOULD PROVE SMITH'S INNOCENCE OUT OF THE DEFENSE'S HANDS. THAT DECISION...COURT OBSERVERS SAY...WILL TAKE LESS THAN 10 DAYS. MARK NOVELL...EYEWITNESS NEWS AT THE STATE CAPITAL.

PACKAGE STORY STRUCTURE

VIDEO	AUDIO
Cover video supporting, synchronizing with reporter's narration	REPORTER'S NARRATION SETTING PARAMETERS OF STORY. INDICATING WHY STORY IS IMPORTANT TO VIEWERS AND RETAINING VIEWER ATTENTION.
Sound bite	SOUND BITE WITH PERSON INVOLVED IN STORY.
Reporter in field	REPORTER STAND UP CLOSE SUMMARIZING THE STORY, SHOWS WHAT IS WRONG, HOW TO CORRECT PROBLEM, ETC.

The package utilizes the following elements: cover video, which is edited to match the narration; sound bite with someone involved in the story; and the reporter's standup closing the package.

In package stories with controversy or an opposing point of view, the structur remains basically the same but, if possible, pro and con interviews are utilized.

PACKAGE STORY STRUCTURE--CONTROVERSY

VIDEO	AUDIO
Cover video supporting synchronizing with reporter's narration	REPORTER'S NARRATION SETTING PARAMETERS OF STORY. INDICATING WHY STORY IS IMPORTANT T VIEWERS AND RETAINING VIEWER'S ATTENTION. SETTING UP CONFLICT TO FOLLOW.
Sound bite (pro issue)	SOUND BITE WITH PERSON SUPPORTING ONE SIDE OF CONTROVERSY.
Cover video	REPORTER'S NARRATION SERVING AS BRIDGE FROM INTERVIEW TO CON INTERVIEW. (This is option and may be left out depending on circumstan
Sound bite (con issue)	SOUND BITE WITH PERSON AGAINST THE ISSUE OR ON THE OTHER SIDE OF THE CONTROVERSY.
Reporter in field	REPORTER STAND UP CLOSE SUMMARIZING THE STORY AND THE SIDES OF THE CONTROVERSY. SHOWS WHAT IS WRONG AND/OR POSSIBLE SOLUTIO TO CORRECT PROBLEM.

Two examples of how the networks handle package stories follow in Examples 5-1 and 5-11.

In Example 5-10, Dan Rather read the live opener leading to Ray Brady's packag The first part of Brady's script was read at a normal pace. The script has been expanded to indicate how the editor synchronized various visuals to the script. Th package contains controversy in the way that government figures are generated and there are two sound bites separated by Brady's narration bridge.

In Example 5-11, John Chancellor read the live opener, which is included. The

EXAMPLE 5-10

CBS NEWS
11-24-81
6:30 PM

VIDEO	AUDIO
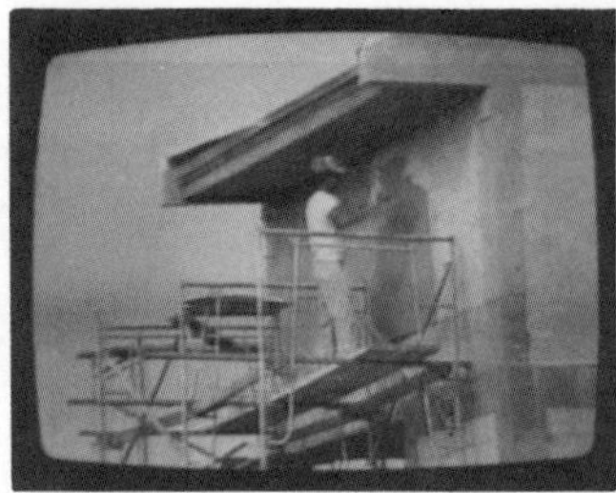	THE LABOR DEPARTMENT FIGURES SHOW AN EASING IN THE COST OF LIVING, LARGELY BECAUSE OF WHAT'S HAPPENING TO THE VALUE OF THE AMERICAN HOME.

	THE FIGURES SHOW ITS PRICE DOWN LAST MONTH SEVEN-TENTHS OF ONE PERCENT.
	AND THE FINANCING COSTS OF BUYING ONE DOWN ONE-TENTH OF ONE PERCENT.
	THAT DOUBLE DIP HELD THE ANNUAL RATE TO JUST FOUR-POINT-FOUR PERCENT.

VIDEO	AUDIO
	THE REAGAN INDEX, THE CBS NEWS MEASURE OF INFLATION SHOWS THAT WHAT COST ONE DOLLAR WHEN MR. REAGAN TOOK OFFICE NOW COST ONE DOLLAR AND SEVEN CENTS. CRITICS ARE AGAIN SAYING THAT HOUSING IS DISTORTING THE CONSUMER PRICE INDEX. ONLY COMPARATIVELY LOW PRICED HOMES ARE USED IN THE COMPUTATION AND EVEN SMALL CHANGES IN PRICE FOR MORTGAGE RATES CAN SEND THE FIGURES UP OR DOWN SHARPLY AND THAT HAS A MAJOR AFFECT ON THE OVERALL C-P-I.
	EARLIER THIS YEAR, HOUSING MADE THE INFLATION FIGURES LOOK WORSE. NOW, SAY CRITICS, THEY'RE MAKING THE FIGURES LOOK BETTER THAN THEY ARE.

VIDEO	AUDIO
	NEUBERGER SOUNDBITE: In the month of October, both home purchase prices and the ceiling rate on mortgages declined. These two factors have combined to pull the CPI down below what it would have been had home ownership been measured...let's say...on rental equivalence basis. THE LABOR DEPARTMENT ADMITS THE CRITICISM IS VALID AND WILL CHANGE ITS MEASURE, BUT NOT UNTIL 1983.
	NORWOOD SOUNDBITE: I agree that the home ownership component would be better measured with a cost of shelter concept rather than the total purchase of an asset, which is what we now have in the index.

VIDEO	AUDIO
	THE LABOR DEPARTMENT'S NEW FIGURES WILL USE WHAT IT CONSIDERS A MORE REPRESENTATIVE MEASURE, WHAT PEOPLE ARE PAYING FOR RENT. IF THAT MEASURE WERE IN USE NOW, THE OCTOBER INFLATION RATE WOULD NOT BE FOUR-POINT-FOUR PERCENT BUT NEARLY DOUBLE THAT, EIGHT-POINT-FOUR PERCENT. A FIGURE MOST ECONOMISTS FEEL IS CLOSER TO THE REAL INFLATION RATE.
	EVEN A NEW FORMULA MAY BRING A LOT OF CONTROVERSY WITH IT BECAUSE IF IT WERE IN USE NOW IT WOULD HELP PUSH UP THE COST OF SOCIAL SECURITY, SOME UNION WAGES, THE PAY OF MANY STATE AND LOCAL GOVERNMENT WORKERS, EVEN SOME ALIMONY PAYMENTS. ALL OF WHICH ARE TIED TO THE CONSUMER PRICE INDEX, RISE WITH IT AND, SOME SAY, FURTHER FUEL INFLATION. RAY BRADY, CBS NEWS, NEW YORK.

EXAMPLE 5-11

NBC NIGHTLY NEWS

11-24-81

6:30 PM

CHANCELLOR

THE LAST BIG EXERCISE OF THE EGYPTIAN-AMERICAN MILITARY MANEUVERS KNOWN AS OPERATION BRIGHT STAR ENDED TODAY WITH SOME VERY BIG BANGS.

A GROUP OF AMERICAN PLANES, WHICH HAD FLOWN NON-STOP FROM THE UNITED STATES DROPPED LIVE BOMBS ON A DESERT TARGET.

AN AIR FORCE COLONEL CALLED THEM DEAD ON TIME AND DEAD ON TARGET.

PAUL MILLER REPORTS.

VTR 1:25

THIS WAS A MAJOR SHOW OF AMERICAN AIR POWER.

B-52S DROPPED FIVE-HUNDRED POUND BOMBS FROM SIX-HUNDRED FEET ABOVE THE EGYPTIAN DESERT.

(pause)

A-10 THUNDERBOLTS AND F-16S BOMBED DESERT TARGETS,

AND, ABOVE IT ALL AN AWACS KEPT TRACK OF THE WAR GAMES.

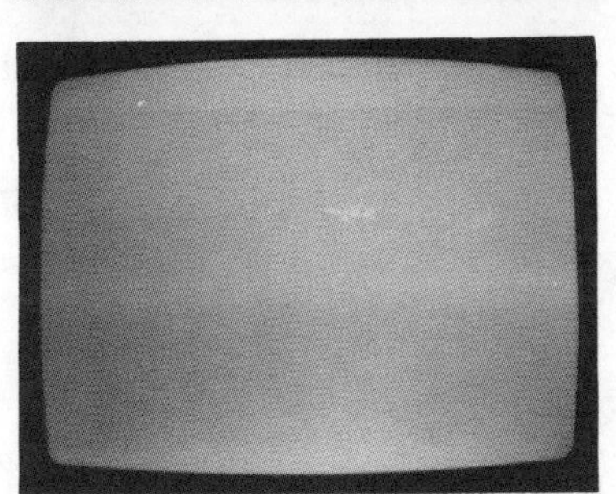

THE SIX B-52S FLEW SEVEN-THOUSAND MILES NONSTOP FROM NORTH DAKOTA TO HIT THE TARGETS 70-MILES FROM CAIRO.

THEIR FLIGHT WAS ANOTHER SHOW OF AMERICAN MUSCLE AND DETERMINATION TO RESPOND QUICKLY IN THE EVENT OF TROUBLE IN THE MIDDLE EAST.

OTHERWISE, THE B-52S HAD LITTLE TO DO WITH THE REST OF BRIGHT STAR 82 IN EGYPT.

MOST OF THE JOINT EXERCISES WITH EGYPTIAN TROOPS TESTED AMERICAN INFANTRY, TANKS HELICOPTERS AND FIGHTER PLANES IN DESERT CONDITIONS.

THE EXERCISES ENDED WITH TODAY'S LIVE AMMUNITION DISPLAYS. GENERAL ROBERT KINGSTON SAID THE PERFORMANCE OF THE RAPID DEPLOYMENT FORCE WAS GOOD, BUT NOT GOOD ENOUGH.

KINGSTON SOUNDBITE: I don't like to use the word perfect because I like the carrot and the stick--and when you get up to a certain professional standard, you raise that standard. And I intend to raise the standards.

Miller THE RDF WANTS TO COME BACK TO EGYPT FOR MORE TRAINING.

THE EGYPTIANS ARE INTERESTED TOO. THEY SEE THE RDF AS A DETERRENT TO AGGRESSION IN THE MIDDLE EAST AND THE BRIGHT STAR MANEUVERS AS A WAY OF IMPROVING THEIR OWN MILITARY CAPABILITIES.

PAUL MILLER, NBC NEWS, CAIRO.

structure of Paul Miller's report on Operation Bright Star is rather straightforward and the package contains only one soundbite.

STORIES WITHOUT SCRIPTS

Stories without scripts are somewhat of a misnomer. In broadcasting and cable, there are always scripts or else the report is being adlibbed. The phrase "stories without scripts" really refers to stories so visually exciting or interesting that scripts are not needed except to introduce film or video tape. The video tape or film, usually with natural (wild) sound, is so self-explanatory that a script is not necessary.

During the Nigerian Civil War, CBS television news showed a sound film of the execution of two Nigerians. The newscaster, Walter Cronkite, introduced the film by warning people that the film might offend some people. But, he said, the story had to be told. During the long film story the only sounds heard were background noises of the crowd, the officer giving commands to the execution squad and the shots being fired. The story was powerful and words would have detracted from its terrible impact. Nothing needed to be said.

Stories without scripts or narrations do not have to be as grim as the CBS story of the Nigerian executions. The news event can be exciting or happy, such as a 30 or 40 second video tape showing the locker room of the team that won the World Series. The sounds, commotion and excitement carry the story meaning better than words. Another example of a story without words occurred during the Ohio State Fair when a television station showed the start of hot air balloon races and under the film played an audio tape of a choir singing "Up, Up and Away."

QUIZ

1. Differentiate between the purposes of a character generator and a newsroom computer.

2. What does VDT stand for?

3. What are the two main reasons that video tape technology, or electronic news-gathering equipment, have made film mostly obsolete in the daily operation of most television newsrooms?

4. What purpose does the control track on a video tape perform?

5. If you have a photographer go out into the field to obtain video tape, you expect that person to come back with certain types of shots, sometimes referred to as the video news formula. What shots would you expect?

6. The left portion of a television news script contains what?

7. Whose job is it to time out scripts and write those times on the scripts?

8. What should be the deciding factor in whether or not a cover video story is dominated by words or visuals?

EXERCISES

1. Consider yourself as a newswriter for the local television station. Your editor tells you to take a look at the CBS news story (Example 5-10) on the cost of living and recut the story for the 11 p.m. news. You can take whatever you like from the CBS story except the CBS reporter's narration. Write a 45-second television story for your late news.

2. The same situation exists in this exercise as in exercise #1 except you should use the NBC news story (Example 5-11). For this exercise write two television news stories--one using only cover video and the other General Robert Kingston's soundbite.

ASSIGNMENTS

1. View the 10:00 p.m. or 11:00 p.m. news in your community. Carefully analyze package, voice over and soundbite stories. Try to determine why stories ended up as packages, soundbites or voice over stories.

2. Arrange to spend a day with a local television or cable news crew. Follow the crew throughout the day through field reporting, editing, writing and the newscast production. Write a report on how the stories developed and were finally shaped for use inside the newscast.

3. Discuss with a local television producer what the person takes into consideration when deciding whether or not stories should be packages, soundbites or cover video stories.

ENDNOTES

1. Copyright 1981. Columbia Broadcasting System. All rights reserved. CBS Evening News with Dan Rather. November 24, 1981.

2. Copyright 1981. National Broadcasting Company. All rights reserved. NBC Nightly News. November 24, 1981.

6

NEWS JUDGMENT

News judgment! That phrase has come to mean different things to many people. News judgment, in broad terms, has come to mean human judgments because news involves people. The phrase also implies a certain savvy, sophistication, or understanding of the news process. News judgment, to many people, embodies a mind set synonymous with good judgments. "That person has good news judgment" can mean many different things and the phrase must be judged in terms of the situation in which it is used.

Good news judgment has been used to ascribe to newspeople the ability to accurately judge news source credibility or facts; to spot a newsworthy story when other reporters may walk by it; to ask the right question in the right manner at the right time; to handle a news story objectively, accurately and clearly; to understand or have a good feel for the people in your market; to handle touchy issues or potentially dangerous legal, social, or ethical situations; and to judge accurately the importance of one story over another and determine how much time and effort a story deserves.

WHAT IS NEWS

Certainly this is an important issue to address in this chapter dealing with news judgments. John Masterman, former NBC newsperson, says news is easy to spot. It flies by you and it is "tough, chewy, and has a certain texture." He's right. News is "tough, chewy, and has a certain texture," but it's hard to spot because so many things get between newspeople and news events. Sometimes news is obscured by our own failure to see or hidden by a barrage of propaganda. News is sometimes right in front of us but we are blind to the importance of a situation until someone else, without preconceived notions, sees through our eyes. For example, a Pennsylvania reporter complained to another reporter about the poor quality of interstate highways between Pennsylvania and Ohio. The complaining reporter spouted off a litany of complaints about crumbling roads, narrow and poor quality berms, and the steeply angled on/off ramps that were short and forced drivers to accelerate quickly as they entered the highway or slam on their brakes as they exited. The other reporter, not blinded by daily contact with the situation, did some investigation and several months later developed a major story on a highway construction scandal.

News can sometimes be hidden by propaganda. The term propaganda is used here in its connotative meaning which might be applied to one-sided or purposefully slanted information from sources which try to shape news for ideological purposes. News, to be considered news, must reach certain standards. It must be *accurate, clear* and *objective.*

How accurate is accurate? That debate goes on continually in newsrooms all over the world. It used to be said that the only absolutes in life were death and pregnancy. They were clear issues; black and white. You could not be partly dead or halfway pregnant. Now, physicians, philosophers, theologians, attorneys, and legislators argue violently over the issues of abortion and death. These two former absolutes have fallen into the broad gray area with most other worldly things. Accuracy is a relative term that also falls into the broad gray area and must be judged with one eye on the conditions present at the time of the event.

What type of conditions might affect how we view accuracy? Accuracy standards will vary with the type of event and the deadline pressure newspeople face. For example, during fast breaking hard news events, such as riots or disasters, news reports may contain inaccuracies. Newspeople and public officials may overestimate casualties, damage, number of people involved, or even the significance of the event. Sometimes these inaccuracies are recognized and corrected before stories are used, but fact errors are bound to slip by the most careful writers or editors. News will contain mistakes, but you should strive for complete accuracy even though you will fail to meet your goal. The test for accuracy would be much tougher on stories that take time to develop and on which the reporters have time to check and recheck facts before the stories are utilized. Even the courts have recognized two standards of accuracy and are more lenient with mistakes made during breaking news situations with tight deadlines.

Clarity is an obvious criterion of news. Communication, the transmission of information, occurs only when the message is understood and received. A garbled message is not communication. A poorly written news script, poor audio tape quality or bad video can hinder communication and affect clarity. Sometimes in radio the pressure to include audio tape is so great that muffled or poor quality audio is used and the stories suffer. In these types of situations, the particular demands of the medium affects our news judgments and we garble the news story because of poor audio or video. Some good advice is not to allow the pressures of the medium to affect your editorial responsibility of clarity in communication.

Total objectivity, like total accuracy, is impossible to achieve. Your perception of the world is colored by your past. You are shaped by your parents, friends, enemies, schools, books, teachers, and so on. We develop certain philosophies or perceptions about the world we live in and the way we think it should be shaped. We are biased. Biases occur all through the news selection process. Deciding which stories will be covered, time allocated to each story, and serial order or placement in the newscast shows individual biases or news judgments. A news editor with Republican leanings makes a decision on how to cover a Democratic party story. A Democratic news producer takes the story and makes a decision on where the story will run in the newscast and how long the story will run. All of these decisions in the news process can and will affect what is seen or heard on television, cable or radio.

Newspeople must try to overcome biases, report events fairly and balance news coverage of events. You are not expected to report every minor detail in chronological order without making news judgments. You must make editorial judgments, summarize events, and present news in a balanced, fair manner. Deliberately leaving out important facts or bending perceptions of the news event to fit personal prejudice is the trick of the propagandist, not the newsperson exercising good news judgment.

News must be clear, objective, and accurate, but this definition still does not divide events into news and non-news categories. What is news? What makes one event newsworthy and another event not worth air time or newspaper space? One experienced news editor said news was whatever he decided it was. This simplistic answer contains a strong degree of truth. What that experienced editor decided was news got into the newspaper and was read by newspaper subscribers. What he felt was not newsworthy was left out of the newspaper and few people heard of the event.

Comparing newspaper front pages, radio, cable, and television newscasts shows that few newpeople, even experienced news editors, agree precisely on news or the relative merits of news stories. Successful and highly paid news editors will have their newspeople covering events that other editors, just as well paid and successful, do not consider worth coverage. Even if there is agreement on covering the same story, editors will disagree on placement in the newscast, amount of time allocated to the story or whether or not the story rated a report from the field, sound bite or package. For example, see the ABC, NBC, and CBS news stories on the same event in Examples 6-1, 6-2, and 6-3. Each editor, combining past experience, research, intuition, and a little crystal ball gazing, tried to decide what would be interesting and significant for the news consumer. These editors are exercising their news judgments and they may all be right in their particular decisions.

Willard G. Bleyer, a prominent journalism educator, said "news is anything timely that interests a number of persons, and the best news is that which has the greatest interest for the greatest number." It is easy to split hairs and expand on Bleyer's definition but it is flexible enough to encompass all news. Bleyer's key words are *anything*, *timely* and *interest*.

News must be timely to have great meaning. Timely generally means reporting news events within a short time after the events occurred. It would not be timely to report a car accident in your community a week after the accident took place, especially if other media had already reported the accident. It would be timely, however, to report a week-old car accident if the accident had just been discovered. This situation happens frequently in rural or sparsely populated areas. It also happened in Columbus, Ohio, when a car carrying two adult women and five children ran off a road into a city reservoir. For more than a week, the news media did not cover the story because police treated the event as a simple missing person story. Eventually, a city worker hearing of the missing people remembered seeing a bent over guardrail near the reservoir the morning after the people were reported missing. A massive dragging operation near the bent guardrail eventually found the car and the victims. Another story not reported immediately was the My Lai massacre, which took place during the Vietnam War. Even though the first news reports of My Lai came nearly a year after the event, the news reports had great impact and the story was timely in relation to when information on the massacre became available. The Columbus accident and the My Lai massacre were old events, but the first news reports told news listeners something important or interesting that they had not known before.

Another aspect of timeliness is the seasonal feature story. Thanksgiving, Christmas, July 4th, and other holidays provide ideas for news stories. Summer always brings on water, boating,swimming, lawnmower and car safety stories. Christmas results in toy safety stories and human interest stories about families facing a bleak holiday. Feature stories do not have the same timely quality as hard news stories but there must be some type of peg on which to hang the story. The change of seasons and events related to various times of year are good story pegs.

Another element in Bleyer's definition of news is interest. Whatever interests a large number of people could be considered news. Recently, there has been much debate over this concept. Some news purists are outraged over this concept, saying that it calls for presenting soft feature stories that interest people and avoiding hard, gritty news stories that might upset people but contain information they should know. Others argue that newspeople have always been sensitive to what interests their particular audiences and news operations, to be successful, must have a large audience to pay for equipment, personnel, and operating expenses. It appears, as with most things in life, that this concept depends on the degree to which either position is carried and a balanced approach appears to work for most news organizations.

EXAMPLE 6-1

THE SOVIET UNION GAVE ITS PERMISSION TODAY TO SWEDEN TO QUESTION THE SKIPPER OF A RUSSIAN SUB THAT RAN AGROUND NEAR A RESTRICTED SWEDISH NAVY BASE LAST WEEK. SWEDISH TUGS PULLED THE SUB FREE AS THE DIPLOMATIC INCIDENT APPEARED TO BE MOVING TOWARD A PEACEFUL CLIMAX.[1]

This news story was aired by ABC radio on November 2, 1981 at 4:00 pm.

EXAMPLE 6-2

THE SWEDISH GOVERNMENT HAS SAID THE SOVIET SUBMARINE WILL NOT BE RELEASED UNTIL THE CAPTAIN TELLS THE WHOLE STORY OF HOW THE SUBMARINE GOT STRANDED LAST TUESDAY IN A RESTRICTED MILITARY AREA. CBS NEWS CORRESPONDENT DOUG TUNNEL SAYS THE SWEDISH OFFICIALS APPARENTLY HAVE A LOT OF QUESTIONS.

> Audio tape of Doug Tunnel:
>
> The Soviet captain left the submarine about six hours ago and has ever since been under questioning by Swedish military officers and intelligence officials. Along with the Russian captain are his navigational commander and also two Soviet diplomats who travelled to Karlskrona about three days ago from Stockholm. It is, according to officials here, one of the Soviet requests that if they are going to interrogate the captain, which they are now doing, that those two diplomats be present throughout. That is taking place on board a torpedo boat well outside the military zone that leads into the Karlskrona naval base where the submarine is now anchored. The submarine is in an archipelago of islands. It was moved today in a mission of mercy during the storm.

CORRESPONDENT DOUG TUNNEL IN KARLSKRONA, SWEDEN. WHEN HEAVY WEATHER AND HIGH SEAS STARTED POUNDING THE RUSSIAN SUB TODAY IT GROUNDED ON THE ROCKS OFF THE SWEDISH COAST. THE CREW SENT UP DISTRESS FLARES AND THE SWEDISH NAVY TOWED THE SUB TO CALMER WATERS. THE SWEDES SAY THE SUB WILL BE KEPT THERE UNTIL THEY ARE SATISFIED WITH WHAT THE SUBMARINE CAPTAIN HAS TO TELL THEM.[2]

This news story was aired by CBS radio on November 2, 1981 at 3:00 pm.

EXAMPLE 6-3

SWEDISH OFFICIALS SAY THAT THE SOVIET UNION HAS AGREED TO GO ALONG WITH FOUR SWEDISH DEMANDS FOR THE RELEASE OF A SOVIET SUBMARINE AND ITS 56 CREW MEMBERS INCLUDING PAYMENT FOR SALVAGE OPERATIONS. ALAN SIMON HAS A REPORT FROM STOCKHOLM.

Audio tape of Alan Simon

Swedish interrogators completed the first round of questioning of the Soviet submarine commander and his navigator aboard a Swedish torpedo boat. The questioning may continue tomorrow along with the agreed on inspection of the Soviet submarine. Sweden's commander-in-chief believes the U-boat was on a spy mission to either practice putting people ashore or marking channels through Swedish waters for use by Soviet forces in the event of war.
Alan Simon for NBC News, Stockholm.

This news story was aired on NBC radio on November 2, 1981 at 5:00 pm.

Bleyer's definition is not only limited to important events. He said news is anything timely that interests a number of people. Certainly world events interest news consumers, but Bleyer's definition is audience-centered rather than news event-centered. Whatever the audience perceives as worthy of interest becomes news. "Anything" is rather broad, but news is a broad subject because people have wide-ranging, diverse interests. In this open definition, though, there are some common elements of news that tend to interest large numbers of people. These common elements are stories that contain conflict, human interest values, prominent or familiar people, and the unique or unusual event.

ELEMENTS OF NEWS

CONFLICT

More than 2,000 years ago, Greek dramatists knew that conflict, rivalry, combat, fighting, and duels interested and excited their audiences. News audiences also respond to these elements. Conflict, as the Greeks found out, though, does not always have an element of violence. The Greeks perceived the three great conflicts as man against man, man against nature, and man against himself.

Man against man obviously involves some rivalries, which may or may not contain violence. Fighting in Poland, Ireland, or the Mideast interests news listeners. Reports from the scenes of fighting or rioting have great emotional impact and some historians feel that television and radio reporting of the Vietnam War helped polarize the American people. Other types of man against man conflicts would be political races, crime stories and labor strife. One of the major labor conflict stories of the 1980s was the air traffic controllers' illegal strike against the U. S. government.

Man against nature also creates great interest. People caught in severe weather or fighting against hostile climates are interesting news stories. The space program is also a story of man against nature--man trying to tame a universe.

Man against himself may be the most emotional and moving type of news story. For example, Terry Fox, a young Canadian dying of cancer, attempted to run across North America to raise money for cancer research, despite having only one leg. His determination to reach his goal despite his own weakening body said a great deal about the human spirit. Fox failed to complete his run across North America, but his fight, seen nightly on cable and television newscasts, so aroused people that contributions poured in for cancer research.

HUMAN INTEREST

The difference between human interest stories and hard news stories is that human interest stories stress emotion while hard news stories stress information. Sometimes it is hard to separate human interest from hard news because the news event contains both aspects. An example of a hard news story with human interest possibilities would be a fire leaving a widow with three children homeless.

Human interest stories do not have to be tragic stories, such as widows losing everything in fires. Human interests can be comical or deal with unusual events. Where, for example, does a nine-feet-tall basketball player buy clothes and how much does he pay for size sixteen shoes? Who are the lonely people who join computer dating services and do they really find someone compatible? Human interest stories which look at human beings in humorous or unusual situations are stories that interest us all because we can identify with people caught in funny or embarrassing circumstances. The response we touch is "but for the grace of God there go I."

Many human interest stories are overlooked because writer-reporters are looking for hard news stories and fail to see human elements. Human interest stories can generate tremendous audience involvement and interest. The Terry Fox story is one such example. Various charities, causes, and fund raising ventures know the value of human interest. A crippled child is chosen yearly as the symbol of a national charity because the child creates human interest and an emotional response. In Kansas, a television station ran a package story about the last wish of a child dying of leukemia. The child wanted to see Disney World before dying, but the parents, already financially drained by medical costs, could not afford the trip. Within days following the newscast, enough money was raised to send the child to Disney World only weeks before he died of cancer.

Human interest is that emotional quality of a story that cuts through our exterior shield and gets us involved with other people.

PROMINENCE

News consumers are generally interested in hearing about prominent people or places. A crime wave created by drugs and illegal immigrants turns a famous Florida city into a place where people are afraid to go out alone day or night. That story was the cover story on *Time* magazine and ABC, NBC and CBS carried long packages investigating crime in Miami.

Most people are interested in the doings of nationally or locally prominent people. Divorce is a common occurrence that seldom rates a mention in the news unless, of course, the person getting divorced is your mayor, governor, or senator. Common occurrences may take on great significance or interest if prominent people or places are involved.

UNIQUE

The unusual, bizarre, or unique is always interesting. Some of the major news stories of this century involved the unusual or unique. The birth of quintuplets or sextuplets is an unusual event which generates a lot of news coverage. A child, born with a rare aging disease which will lead to an early death, is unique and when three of these children meet it is a very interesting story.

Setting unusual records, such as pie eating, parachute jumping or hot air ballooning are good visual stories. The first time an event is done or attempted may also be a good story with unusual ramifications.

There are also some specific factors that affect your listeners' interest in news. These factors are personal impact, proximity to the news event, market size and time of day.

PROXIMITY

As was discussed in another chapter, proximity or closeness to news events increases viewer/listener interest. News events close to us may have a direct impact on our lives. A fast moving forest fire in the Pacific Northwest may have moderate interest for someone living in North Central Florida. However, a forest fire twenty miles away from your home will have much greater interest, especially if the wind is blowing your way.

PERSONAL IMPACT

Personal impact obviously increases interest in particular news stories. A person working in a tire plant will be quite interested in declining auto sales. A news story about decreasing personal income taxes will rank much higher on an interest scale than a news story about an earthquake in Tibet. Anything that affects the quality of life or the lifestyle of large audience segments will have great viewer/listener interest. American farmers and consumers followed the news of the 1975 Mid-western drought in Kansas, Iowa, Nebraska, and Missouri. Farmers in other regions were interested in the story because what was happening to the Midwest could also happen to them. Another aspect to the story was that crop destruction in one region makes the crops in another region more valuable. Another example would be the medfly infestation in California that spread to other states. The destruction of citrus fruit in California and Florida eventually drove up the price of orange juice in the supermarkets.

Government, labor or business actions that affect prices, products or lives will also have great impact on nearly everyone who listens to news. A five percent increase on the price of new cars will add hundreds of dollars to the sticker price on the average car sold in the United States. Most safety or pollution devices for autos will also drive up the price of new cars and further hurt an ailing auto industry.

Other news stories that have audience interest are stories that help people cope with their daily lives. These stories may be called features or consumer news but they tackle problems common to large numbers of people and they generate interest. These consumer stories may include advice on when and how to start work on your yard in the fall; save money; increase your leisure time; make your home safer; or increase your satisfaction with living. People want to better themselves; make more money; save on major purchases; avoid getting cheated; and have better health.

The Associated Press has commissioned several research studies to find out what news interests people. Their studies confirmed the old saying that people want to hear news that deals with *health, heart* and *pocketbook*. These are three strong personal interest factors that we all have.

MARKET SIZE

The size of your community also determines what is considered to be newsworthy. In Miami, Detroit, Chicago or New York, the evening news may not even mention fatal accidents or homicides unless something about the story makes it unusual or unique. Newscasters may not even give the names of people killed--only the total number of victims that day. In some major metropolitan areas, crime and accidents are so common that they cease to become news unless some unusual angle makes them newsworthy. Quite the opposite may be true; a day without drug related homicides in New York or Miami might be worthy of a news story.

In medium or smaller sized markets, news becomes more personalized and detailed. An accident story that might be ignored in New York City might be the lead story in El Paso, Texas; Boise, Idaho; or Lima, Ohio. In small markets, it is not uncommon to mention funeral arrangements or visiting hours at funeral homes in fatality stories. Some small market radio stations also have sponsored programs where all of the fire or emergency runs during the preceding twenty-four hours, no matter how trivial, are recounted in detail. Birth and death report programs are common and these program chores may fall to news departments. If you think that they are a waste of time and have little interest, just get a name wrong and you will see how much interest is generated.

News takes on a gossip function in small and medium sized communities. People in smaller markets tend to be more interested in news events or activities in their communities and this is reflected in their news demands. People in smaller communities also tend to identify more with their local radio stations, and they use the medium in a more personal manner. Listeners in small markets truly consider the local radio station as part of their community. Radio announcers and newspeople are local celebrities and they are almost considered community property. In small and medium sized markets, it is not uncommon for people to stop newspeople on the street and comment on the news or a particular news story.

TIME OF DAY

The time of day may also have a direct bearing on news selection, placement and time allocated to news stories and even the scheduling of newscasts. For radio, the heaviest listening occurs during the morning and afternoon drive times, when people are going to and from work. During the morning hours, radio news listeners want to be brought up to date on world and local events and assured that basically everything in the world is all right. The morning radio listeners also want to know about weather conditions and traffic reports. Newscasts may be scheduled more frequently during the morning hours. Instead of every hour, news may be scheduled every half hour with headlines and weather every fifteen minutes. Newscasts may also be lengthened to accommodate heavier news and commercial loads. Many news departments also give frequent road reports and will mention road construction, hazards, or other traffic problems that may call for an alternative route to work.

The Associated Press studies indicate that for some morning and afternoon drive time radio listeners, the quality and number of news, weather, and traffic reports may be more important than the type of music the station plays. In other words, some people may listen to a top 40 radio station for the weather, news and traffic reports and to some other station for their musical entertainment.

During the day, when most men are not listening to radio, news departments may shift their emphasis from hard news to features, human interest, or consumer news that might appeal to homemakers. The major audience group available to listen to radio during the day is homemakers, who may use radio as background while they work in the home, run errands, shop, or do yardwork. News departments may try to target their news to the homemaker by appealing to the self-interest of these listeners.

REAL TIME COVERAGE

One of the big advantages of electronic journalism over the print medium is radio, television, and cable's ability to respond quickly to breaking news events. News stories of disasters, riots, or major accidents can be on the air within minutes of the events. Audio tape, film, or video tape can be back to the station, processed or edited, and on the air within an hour. For some events, cable, television, and radio stations will provide live or real time news coverage. In the past, live or real time news coverage was limited to events over which broadcasters could exercise some control. Weeks, sometimes months, of planning went into real time coverage of news events like political conventions, elections, space shots, or sporting events. The equipment to provide this live coverage was bulky and not portable by today's standards. Problems associated with real time coverage have only recently become acute for television and cable news reporters because of technological advances in portable television equipment. News vans carrying lightweight portable cameras, video tape recorders and low cost microwave units can be at the scene of breaking news events quickly, (see Exhibits 6-1 and 6-2) equipment can be set up in minutes, and signals carrying the drama of live news events can be beamed back to the stations. It is not unusual to see live coverage of major news events on a regular basis on local, network or cable newscasts. Satellites and helicopters, specially modified for news operations, have further expanded the live coverage capabilities of cable and television news.

The problem with live coverage is that it is live. There is no time between the event and when newspeople report on the event. Newspeople do not have the luxury of standing back from the emotion of news events to gather thoughts or put things in perspective. Live is live, and decisions must be made instantaneously. In the heat of the moment, newspeople may get caught up in news events, lose perspective, and pass along false or exaggerated information that may aggravate a situation. Real time coverage of a disturbance, some people say, could increase the seriousness of the situation and turn a controllable disturbance into a riot. Real time

EXHIBIT 6-1. PORTABLE MICROWAVE BEING SET UP AND VAN. Live field news production unit utilizing microwave transmission

Photograph: Courtesy of Wolf Coach and WFLA Television, Tampa, Florida

EXHIBIT 6-2. HELICOPTER WITH PHOTOGRAPHER HANGING OUT DOOR. Live field news production unit utilizing JetRanger III microwave equipped helicopter.

Photograph: Courtesy of Bell Helicopter Textron

coverage places heavy editorial responsibilities on reporters in the field and the station producer. Live coverage has done away with television deadlines and, in some instances, it does away with a reporter's ability to make one last check with authorities or obtain better and more reliable information.

Live or real time news coverage also opens up the possibility of accidentally airing libelous or obscene remarks and gestures. Obscene gestures or libelous remarks can be edited out of film, audio, and video tape interviews before the interviews are aired. Such editing cannot be done with real time coverage. Real time coverage can be risky for the station licensee who is legally responsible for anything broadcast by the station. In semi-controlled live coverage events, such as political conventions, reporters have field producers who screen prospective interviewees and weed out possible problems.

ETHICAL JUDGMENTS

Dealing with ethical judgments is bound to raise many more questions than there are answers. Ethics, like many things in life, have to be judged at the moment and in light of the circumstances or the situation. This discussion on ethics is not designed to answer your questions because it cannot do that. This discussion is designed to ask you questions and make you think about your own values and about what you would or would not do.

How far would you go to get a news story? This is a common problem or question that nearly all newspeople face at one time or another in their careers. Each person answers the question in a different manner because each situation is different. Some reporters say they would do almost anything to get a story. They'd break into someone's home, read through private papers or open someone's mail. They respond that anything is permissible as long as the cause is just and they are trying to keep the public informed. Other newspeople disagree with this attitude, saying it sets up a double standard. The newspeople expect one standard from officials, legislators and business leaders, and yet they live by another standard that tolerates unethical activities. There is no universal answer to this question.

Treatment and protection of sources is another ethical problem that newspeople constantly must deal with. One aspect is what is "on" or "off the record," and do you honor requests from sources that information is only for your background and cannot be used? One group of newspeople says that if you receive "off the record" information you should honor the conditions by which you got the information. Other newspeople say that depends on the circumstances and they are not in the business of receiving and not using information. This latter group feels that any information gained during investigation could be used in the story.

Another ethical problem of dealing with sources is how close should you get to people who have information you want. This is a problem that develops when reporters cover beats and socially get to know people they cover. Reporters who say it is not good to know sources socially say it becomes very hard to write critical stories about people you know. However, reporters who disagree with this philosophy say that only when you get to know people well do they open up and tell you sensitive things. These reporters say that social contact with sources is important because it builds a bond of trust between source and reporter.

Another question to consider when dealing with sources is whether to agree not to use someone's name if they give you information. This becomes a legal problem as well as an ethical problem, because the courts do not recognize a reporter's right to keep sources confidential. The legal problem arises when reporters face jail if they do not reveal the sources of their information. Some reporters have gone to jail and paid fines rather than reveal their sources of information. However, other reporters have revealed the identities of sources under court order.

Should you withhold information at the request of officials? This ethical problem will spur a vigorous debate among reporters who argue persuasively on both sides of this question. There have been numerous situations where officials have requested that information be kept out of newspapers or off radio, television or cable. For example, during the urban unrest in the 1960s, a police official called television and radio news editors asking that news of minor disturbances and some firebombings of vacant buildings in an area of the city be withheld until the next day. The rationale was that police and firefighters could handle that level of violence, but they were afraid that if information of the disturbances was broadcast it would advertise the situation and lead to a full scale riot. Some stations ran the news story that evening while some news editors complied with the police request and held the story until the next day.

Another example of official requests to withhold information occurred when three police officers chased a suspect into a dark area of a city. One police officer was killed during a shootout, and the suspect was eventually arrested and charged with murder. However, an autopsy proved that the bullet that killed the officer did not come from the suspect's pistol but from another police officer's weapon. Police officials and prosecuting attorneys requested that the identity of the officer who mistakenly shot his partner be withheld. Some radio and television stations withheld the name while other stations and the newspaper revealed the officer's identity.

Economic temptations can pose legal as well as ethical problems for newspeople. It is against the law for broadcasters to receive money, goods, or services to give free commercial mentions or plug someone's goods or services. However, what about presents, lunches, or dinners? Should reporters accept a free lunch from someone in business or government? What about a Christmas gift or a bottle of wine? Should reporters get free travel or lodging to cover certain events, such as the unveiling of new car models in Detroit? It used to be common practice for the car manufacturers to pick up the cost of travel and accommodations for business reporters who normally covered the new car product lines. The problem of presents, junkets, free travel, and accommodations is handled by newspeople in different ways. Some newspeople do not think it ethical to take presents or receive free travel. Other newspeople say there is nothing wrong with taking a free lunch or a junket unless it affects what you report. They feel that a present or free trip will not affect what they report and they can separate business from pleasure.

QUIZ

1. What three standards should newspeople try to attain with news stories?

   a. ______________________________

   b. ______________________________

   c. ______________________________

2. How might market size affect your news judgment?

   ____
   ____
   ____
   ____

3. The Associated Press has a little formula developed from their research into news. What are the three elements of that formula?

   ____
   ____
   ____
   ____

4. Should Willard Bleyer's definition of news be expanded or changed? How?

   ____
   ____
   ____
   ____
   ____

5. List three types of stories that you might utilize during the 10:00 AM to 3:00 p.m. period on radio targeted to the homemakers.

   ____
   ____
   ____
   ____

EXERCISES

Read and discuss the following situations:

1. Over a period of time you have become friendly with a few police officers in your community. You stop by the police department daily to check the booking slips as part of your daily news rounds. One morning you overhear one of the police officers talking about an incident that happened in the jail several weeks ago. It seems that a young officer on probation struck a person being booked for shoplifting. You start questioning your friends about the incident and get no information. As a matter of fact, one of your acquaintances in the police department tells you "off the record" that the police department has already taken care of the situation. The probationary officer is being let go. He warns you that if you persist in probing this minor incident you risk alienating the people who have fed you some major stories in the past. The threat is obviously that if you pursue this minor incident that the police have taken care of you will lose a good source of information. What do you do?

2. A police officer is killed and a suspect is arrested by other officers. The police department and prosecuting attorney meet with members of the press and answer questions about the arrest and events leading up to the killing. It appears that two officers chased the suspect into a dark area of the city. The officers split up and searched for the suspect. The officer who made the arrest told a story of coming down an alley and being shot at. He shot back and eventually chased the suspect out of the alley where an arrest took place. Later the police officer's partner was found in the alley dead of gunshot wounds. Several days later, an autopsy shows that the bullet which killed the police officer did not come from the suspect's gun, but from the gun of the other police officer. The prosecuting attorney asks members of the press not to run the story until after the funeral of the dead officer. He told reporters that the police officer and the family of the dead officer did not yet know of the autopsy results, which he wanted to hold until after the funeral. Should you hold the story until after the funeral or not?

ASSIGNMENTS

1. Interview a member of the news media about ethics. Try to determine how far the reporter would go in gathering information about a story.

   Also try to determine the reporter's policy about accepting gifts or lunches from sources. Is there a station policy regarding this practice or does the reporter follow a personal policy in this matter?

2. Evaluate a local television newscast and analyze the stories in regard to news judgments. How many of the stories deal with matters of health, heart, and pocketbook?

   Categorize the stories by proximity, prominence, conflict, human interest, and unusual aspects.

ENDNOTES

1. Reprinted courtesy of ABC News. ABC Radio News. November 2, 1981.

2. Copyright 1981. Columbia Broadcasting System. All rights reserved. CBS News-On-The-Hour. November 2, 1981.

3. Copyright 1981. National Broadcasting Company. All rights reserved. NBC Radio News. November 2, 1981.

7

NEWS SOURCES

A radio journalist once confided that his worst nightmare was arriving at work early in the morning to get ready for the 6:00 A.M. news and finding the wire service broken, jammed, or out of paper. Suddenly, a trusted major source of news is not available and he is forced to generate four minutes of news and weather in forty-five minutes without access to a wire service. Certainly this is not an impossible job for an experienced newsperson but it can strain the best journalist. Wire services are major sources of news, weather, sports, and stock information. Even if news organizations generally do not rely on wire services for local news, the wire services open up windows to national, international, and state news events.

Aside from news wire services, the most valuable sources of news and ideas in newsrooms are broadcast journalists. If your newspeople cannot recognize news possibilities, it really doesn't matter how many news sources your station has access to. Covering obvious news events, such as routine fires, accidents, or crimes, is the easy part of journalism and, after a while, the mundane and boring part. The difference between a mediocre and a good journalist is the ability to develop strong local news from a variety of news sources. We are talking about news judgment and the ability to exercise critical thinking and creativity in the way newspeople see events in their communities.

One prominent television news director says "you'll pay to be a broadcast journalist." He is really saying that good newspeople are seldom paid what they're worth for the dedication and amount of time they put into their jobs. Although it sounds "Boy or Girl Scoutish," good newspeople love their work. They immerse themselves in their communities and news becomes an obsession during waking hours. Good newspeople do not work 9 to 5; they are constantly watching, reading, talking to people, and analyzing events and situations in light of what would be a good news story. Driving home at night after a movie or date, a good newsperson will be observing and looking for things out of the ordinary or even the ordinary things that are overlooked but would make a good news story. Good newspeople are constantly reading newspapers and magazines looking for news they can localize. They listen to competitors and at night wear out channel selector knobs trying to watch all of the television newscasts at the same time. Few other professions demand so much dedication and thought outside normal working hours.

Broadcast journalists come from a variety of backgrounds, but the most common college majors are journalism and broadcasting. Most broadcast journalists are generalists and a liberal arts background is important because good newspeople have broad knowledge in many areas, such as history, government, archeology, political science, sociology, psychology, and economics. Broadcast journalists are like pack rats with information because they build files and create specialized areas of knowledge waiting for the time when they can be used to build good stories. Journalism training is important because it stresses a thought process that is research oriented. Journalists are basically researchers who gather information from a wide variety of sources. Abilities to research, synthesize information, and analyze critically are more important than broadcast mechanics or technology; although knowledge of the medium is necessary.

Good newspeople are constantly trying to develop their own *enterprise* stories which are not assigned through the assignment desk and do not come from other standard news sources. Enterprise or *initiative* stories are prized in news organizations because they are exclusive and indicate quality craftmanship.

NEWS WIRE SERVICES

News wire services are necessary expenses for broadcast and cable news operations. Local broadcast or cable news operations cannot afford the money or staff time necessary to compete with wire services on a regional basis, let alone on a national or international level. The news wire services really provide a pooling arrangement for subscribers who cannot individually afford to send reporters to Washington, Moscow, Peking, or Warsaw. However, the wire services, selling their services to many subscribers, can afford to send people all over the world.

The major news wire services operate twenty-four hours a day, seven days a week, 365 days a year. The Associated Press (AP) and United Press International (UPI), with their large staffs, thousands of part-time "stringers," and well organized distribution systems, are the largest merchants of news in the United States. Even the broadcasting networks, with their large domestic and international staffs, rely on wire services to keep them informed of national or international news events.

For a price, both AP and UPI will provide radio, television and cable operations with a variety of services. Prices are somewhat negotiable depending on a number of factors, such as paper costs, size of markets, and number of specialized services. In general, the more services contracted, the lower the cost of the basic news service and other specialized wires.

ASSOCIATED PRESS (AP)

The Associated Press is a cooperative news service owned and managed by its members, who vote and set company policies. Some 3,300 radio, television and cable operations in the United States subscribe to AP's broadcast news wires and are members of the cooperative.

The "A" wire is the major news service offered by AP. This service is written in newspaper style and most newspapers and magazines subscribe to this service. A few television stations and all-news radio stations subscribe to the "A" wire because news stories are written in great detail. Before "A" wire material is used on the air it must be rewritten in broadcast style. The content of the "A" wire is national, international, and regional news. This service carries some weather, sports, and market reports.

The "B" wire is AP's secondary service which carries the "A" wire overload. Stories on the "B" wire are usually of lesser importance or go into more detail. For example, the "A" wire might carry a story of a presidential speech on sanctions against the Soviet Union with reactions to the speech from heads of European governments. The full text of the speech, which would take too long to send over the "A"

EXHIBIT 7-1. AP Xtel PRINTER. Associated Press broadcast news wire printer.

wire, would be transmitted over the "B" wire. The "B" wire is also written in newspaper style and has to be rewritten for broadcast use. More broadcast stations probably subscribe to the "B" wire, as opposed to the "A" service, because the "B" wire has strong emphasis on regional and interpretative reporting.

The wire service used by most radio, television, and cable operations is AP's or UPI's radio wire. Radio wire stories are short and written in broadcast style so they can be inserted into radio newscasts without being rewritten or edited. Most radio wire stories are twenty to forty seconds long. Some stations do not even bother to rewrite radio wire news copy. Radio wires carry national, international, regional, state, and local news, as well as business and market features, women's news, sports, weather, and farm reports.

AP's radio wire, during a twenty-four hour period, transmits twenty-two national and international summaries at twenty-five minutes past the hour. Summaries are five minutes long, although they can be shortened to two-and-a-half minutes by using only the first paragraph of each story. Three times during the day, AP transmits ten-minute summaries. During the day, AP sets aside twenty-two time periods, or splits, for regional and state bureaus to insert local and regional news. This way each regional or state AP bureau can transmit news that interests its subscribers and will be useful.

The Associated Press Television Wire (APTV) is the first wire service attempt to meet the specific needs of television, all-news radio and all-news television stations. APTV is a high speed (1,200 words per minute) news wire service delivered by satellite that is compatible with newsroom computers. APTV could be fed directly into newsroom computers, annually saving thousands of dollars in paper costs.

APTV delivers three services to subscribers. These services are: (1) high speed news transmission, (2) geographically targeted news, sports, and weather information, and (3) story research and development.

AP's high speed news transmission takes place 24 hours a day and provides stations with a full range of international and domestic news, sports, and weather. National, international, and sports news is summarized in short form for breaking stories and then transmitted in longer form. Seven times a day AP sends in-depth block feeds containing national and international news. Many stories refer to specific photographs transmitted on AP's Laserphoto service or to AP's Photocolor slides which are purchased separately. The references alert news editors to still visual story possibilities.

APTV's high speed capabilities provide state and regional bureaus with greater opportunities to insert targeted news, sports, weather, and market information into scheduled splits. News is targeted geographically to have the greatest appeal to subscribers.

APTV also provides research and development services for subscribers. APTV personnel research and write stories which stations can localize. Individual stations get taped interviews and develop local angles. Many stories developed by APTV writer-researchers revolve around the health, heart, and pocketbook formula.

UNITED PRESS INTERNATIONAL (UPI)

United Press International is a commercial news operation, privately owned and operated. UPI subscribers are not involved in management decisions or setting company policy. The more than 2,500 UPI subscribers pay monthly service fees which are based partially on market size and number of services.

United Press International offers more variety in its radio wire than does AP. UPI transmits eighteen "World in Briefs" (WIB) which are five minute national-international news summaries. Regular WIBs contain ten to twelve stories, each about fifty to sixty words long. Six times daily, UPI transmits "World News Roundups" for stations scheduling longer newscasts. "Roundups" run ten to fifteen minutes long and go into greater depth and detail than "World in Briefs." Like the AP, UPI has regularly scheduled splits during the day in which regional and state bureaus insert targeted local and regional news, sports and weather.

AUDIO SERVICES

Both AP and UPI offer audio services to subscribers for a fee. Stations receive audio services by satellite or an open telephone line. Voice activated tape recorders at stations are turned on and off automatically when news feeds are transmitted. Both AP and UPI send hourly feeds containing an average of five to eight stories, which can be inserted intact into five minute radio newscasts or edited down for shorter newscasts. Depending on news flow, about half the stories will be voicers and have correspondents reporting from the scene of news events. The other stories are actualities containing interviews or sounds of news events. During a day, AP or UPI audio transmits sixty to eighty different stories over satellite or telephone lines. To assist audio users, several times a day the wire services transmit lists of stories in each feed, length of stories, whether each story is an actuality or voicer, and out cues.

Both wire services also offer network styled newscasts to local subscribers. *AP Radio* and *UPI Audio* hourly transmit five minute newscasts with commercial positions which can be sold locally and inserted into newscasts. Both *AP Radio* and *UPI Audio* focus on national and international news developments as the services must appeal to national audiences.

WIRE SERVICE LANGUAGE

The wire services have audio systems and specialized languages to communicate with station subscribers. When a story of importance is transmitted, a special circuit inside the teleprinter is activated and bells are rung to warn newspeople that a major story is clearing the wire. The number of bells rung indicates the importance of the news story being transmitted. A *flash* is for a story of "transcendental importance" such as a presidential assassination, war, person landing on the moon, or presidential resignation. This is a story of highest priority and twelve bells are rung to warn newspeople to standby for a major story which will probably result in program interruption. A flash is only two, three or four words long. For example:

POPE SHOT

AGNEW RESIGNS

SADAT IS ASSASSINATED

PRESIDENT SHOT

Immediately following a flash, the wire services will transmit other high priority information related to the flash in bulletin form. A *bulletin* is not so important as a flash; it is signaled by five bells and is written in paragraph form. For example:

(SUB WARSAW)

(WARSAW, POLAND)---POLISH PREMIER JARUZEKSKI HAS DECLARED MARTIAL LAW. SPECIALLY TRAINED RIOT TROOPS ARE TAKING OVER MINES AND INDUSTRIES BEING STRUCK BY THE POLISH UNION SOLIDARITY. UNION

LEADERS AND GOVERNMENT OFFICIALS HAVE BEEN ARRESTED IN THE CRACKDOWN.

SOLIDARITY LEADER LECH WALESA REPORTED TO BE UNDER ARREST.

Bulletins are major news stories which will affect, or interest, most listeners. A nationwide strike, major presidential proclamation, or death of a prominent person may rate a bulletin.

The third priority of the Associated Press is a *95* and for UPI it is an *urgent*. Urgents and 95s denote good stories which deserve to be transmitted outside normal splits, but they do not have the impact or importance of flashes or bulletins. Urgents or 95s are used to carry further developments on stories previously moved over the wires as bulletins or flashes.

PHOTOGRAPHIC SERVICES

Although wire services do not compete with networks in film or video tape distribution, they have a virtual monopoly on still news photographs. Many newspapers, television and cable operations subscribe to AP's *Laserphoto* or UPS's *Unifax* photograph services. Black and white photographs, which can be colored, are transmitted daily to stations by satellite or telephone lines. Photographs carry captions which can, if necessary, provide sufficient information for brief news stories, although, the photographs are tied to news stories transmitted over the "A," "B," "radio" or APTV wires. In some instances, photographs are so unusual that they find a place in newspapers or newscasts because of visual impact. The types of photographs transmitted range from hard news to sports, features, and weather maps.

SPECIALIZED WIRE SERVICES

AP, UPI, the New York Times, U. S. Weather Service, Reuters and other organizations offer specialized wire services, but few radio, television or cable operations have the desire or money to subscribe. In some major cities, private wire services have many circuits for business and market information. Because of operational costs, city wires can only be successful in major communities where enough subscribers are available to make services profitable. There are city wires in Washington, D.C., New York, and Chicago. Other specialized wires carry police and public safety information, weather bureau information and business news.

One major company offering specialized information to private individuals, radio, television, and cable operators is Reuters. Reuters is an international news service organized and operated much like the Associated Press. Reuters has bureaus, correspondents, and stringers in more countries and cities than any other agency. Reuter fulfills business information needs in the United States, Canada, Europe, and the rest of the world.

In the United States, Reuters' main service is REUTER MONITOR, which concentrates news services and supplies news items on business development; national and international news that affects business; and up-to-the-second commodity, money market, and stock quotations. Part of REUTER MONITOR is "NEWS-VIEW," which is not interactive, as the viewer can only sit, watch, and wait for the pages of information to change every 20 seconds. Information includes news of the day, sports, TV listings, theatre listings, weather, traffic reports, stock tickers (with a 15-minute delay), shopping tips, real estate listings, and horoscopes.

The commodity service receives information from domestic and international exchanges and money markets. The service condenses and organizes this information into various business categories, such as commodities, money markets, business news, or instant stock quotations. Other aspects of REUTER MONITOR are interactive. Users can use a keyboard to call up specific information listed on the menu in each category.

EXHIBIT 7-2. REUTERS MONITOR interactive equipment which allows subscribers to select desired data from a menu of business information listed by data group and page numbers.

Reuters services are fed to user stations by satellite or cable. Information is sent at high speeds of 70,000 words per second and it is presented in groups and pages. Subscribers use keyboards to call up a menu listing system contents numerically by groups and pages. Reuters has 127 information groups and a flexible number of pages in each group, depending on the amount of current information available. For example, group 24 is REUTERS' NEWS VIEW service:

Group	Page	Description
24 REUTERS NEWS VIEW	0	REUTERS GENERAL NEWS
	1	REUTERS FINANCIAL NEWS
	2	REUTERS FEATURES

Users would type into the system "group 24" page "2" to call up the feature section. Information would be visually displayed on the VDT.

Reuters ultimately wants to offer services to cable subscribers. However, this type of service would be essential for radio, television or cable operations concentrating on business news. This service, installed in newsrooms, would instantaneously provide business reporters with access to all types of national business news.

Wire services provide an invaluable product but, as Chapter 3 points out, wire copy is written for regional or national audiences and is not localized. Wire service writers cannot localize stories, because wire services cater to national or international audiences. Another problem with using straight wire copy, without rewriting, is that some wire services start out novice writers on the radio wire. The most skilled writers and editors work on newspaper oriented services, although this is changing and greater emphasis is being placed on wires used by broadcast and cable organizations. Less skilled writers obviously make more style and fact errors and some stories are quite hard to read. Another problem with wire services is that, with only two major radio wire services in the United States, several stations in the same market will obviously use the same service and be getting the same news stories. If news copy is not localized and updated, newscasts may sound nearly identical.

The only way to avoid some of these wire service problems is to always rewrite, localize, and update wire stories. The best news organizations seldom use straight wire copy on the air unless it is an emergency. These news organizations use wire stories as guides and as supplements to their own local news coverage. Writers always check out wire story facts as they try taking stories one step further by updating. For example, newswriters may get wire stories about local government actions. A few telephone calls to the mayor, council members or some local government official will verify factual information and may provide new quotes or further information for the story, telephone actualities, or appointments for interviews. These news gathering procedures insure your station will not sound like all other stations in town. Your news operation will be different and the difference will attract prospective advertisers. Whenever there are advertisers waiting for commercial openings in newscasts, news directors are in stronger positions to ask management for more personnel, larger budgets, new equipment and greater autonomy. Managers and program directors are usually wary of interfering in news operations that make money without requiring great sales efforts.

NETWORK SERVICES

The costs of networking have previously precluded narrow network services that did not have mass appeal. For many years, networking was limited to the big three television networks and the ABC, NBC, CBS and Mutual Broadcasting System (MBS) radio networks. The demand for specialized or narrow network services was growing, however, and it took the speed and economy of satellite transmission to make specialized networks possible.

The major television and radio networks are still the primary source of national and international news for local radio and television stations. ABC, CBS, and NBC television transmit major newscasts in the early evening. Shorter, five-minute newscasts are presented at other times during the day, and all three television networks transmit one-minute news updates during prime time hours. CBS programs an hour newscast in the morning while ABC and NBC present magazine programs with news and weather inserts. One major innovation in network news has been ABC's NIGHTLINE created during the Iranian hostage crisis. ABC was surprised at the acceptance of a late night newscast and NIGHTLINE remained on the air following release of the American hostages.

Throughout the day, network television news staffs gather video and package stories which are sent to New York for use in early evening newscasts. Because the networks' early evening newscasts are only thirty minutes long, some news stories sent to New York are dropped from the network news line-ups. The stories which have been cut may be sent to affiliates in *Daily Electronic Feeds* (DEF) for use in local newscasts. DEFs are generally fifteen minutes long and contain national and international stories. DEF feeds take place in the afternoon when local affiliates are presenting local programs and the network telephone, satellite, and microwave links are not being used to transmit on-air network programs. Prior to DEF feeds, networks send to affiliates, by Telex, scripts and run-downs of stories, video, and soundbites scheduled for DEF transmission.

Networks also allow affiliates to video tape network evening newscasts and take video and packages for use in local late evening newscasts. Affiliates cannot use the voices or faces of primary anchors such as Dan Rather, Max Robinson, or Peter Jennings. Since most network stories are rather long, affiliates usually edit stories considerably and rewrite scripts updating and, in some cases, localizing certain elements.

ABC, CBS, NBC, RKO, and MBS radio networks provide affiliates with hourly five-minute newscasts; sports, commentary, and business news are fed to affiliates at other times during the day. ABC, RKO, and NBC have created specialized networks, which are targeted to specific audience groups. ABC has four radio networks which are programmed to reach certain demographically distinct audiences. News, features, and commentaries are carefully programmed to fit with various radio music formats, which appeal to different age groups. ABC, RKO, and NBC are capitalizing on the fact that certain age groups have common music and news preferences, and the specialized radio networks program to meet the needs and interests of these groups.

National Public Radio (NPR) feeds two major news and public affairs programs to some 260 affiliated public radio stations each weekday. *Morning Edition* is a two-hour news block that is fed at different times during the morning to accommodate public radio stations in different time zones. *Morning Edition* is formatted in such a way that local stations can take the entire two-hour news block or they can insert local news headlines or newscasts into predetermined windows. A window is a time segment in a network program that is made available to local stations to insert local material. *All Things Considered* is a ninety-minute, early evening news and public affairs program that is also fed at different times to accommodate stations in other time zones. *All Things Considered* is a tightly structured program and there is only one window available for local affiliates.

CABLE NEWS NETWORK (CNN)

A major news networking innovation has been the development of CNN1, CNN2 and CNNRADIO by Atlanta, Georgia, entrepreneur Ted Turner. Both CNN1 and CNN2 operate television news services twenty-four hours a day providing news, sports, features, and weather information. CNN services are delivered to cable and radio stations by satellite, and television services are available only to people who are cable subscribers. CNN relies on people wanting information and news programming at various times throughout the day rather than at regularly scheduled times. There is constant audience turnover as people tune in briefly to CNN1 and CNN2 and then go on to other activities.

CNN offers two television services and one all-news radio service. CNN1 is the traditional long form network style news with long package, interviews and even extensive live coverage if news events warrant. CNN2 is a short form news service similar to all-news radio. CNN2 audio, called CNNRADIO, is being offered to local radio stations who want to join an all-news network.

CNN offers national and international news and there are CNN news bureaus in key U. S. cities and in several foreign countries. CNN offers specialized reports on health, finance, sports, science, medicine, and consumer affairs.

SPECIALIZED NETWORKS

Because of CNN's successful effort to build an alternative news network, other communication groups have created specialized programs which are fed to stations by satellite. Westinghouse Broadcasting and ABC television plan to start their own all-news service for cable operators which will compete with CNN2's short form news format.

There are many other specialized services offered by satellite to radio, television, and cable operators. John Coleman's all-weather cable channel based in Atlanta is fed to cable operators in North America. Financial News Network (FNN) offers, by satellite, seven hours of business programming to television and cable operators. FNN reaches an estimated 25 million cable and television households with hard financial news, market information, and business features.

Independent television station news operations have always been at a disadvantage competing with network affiliates which get national and international news from network DEFs and network nightly newscasts. To fill this need for national and international news, a number of news film or video news companies have started servicing independent television stations. VISNEWS, UPITN, Independent Television News Association, Independent Network News (INN), Associated Broadcast News Service, and other companies have news services which offer specialized news and features or regular national and international news services to subscribers. INN provides the same basic service for independent television stations as do the major television networks for their affiliates. INN delivers, by satellite, a nightly, thirty-minute newscast at 10 p.m. which, at that time period, competes with network entertainment programs carried by network affiliates.

STATE AND REGIONAL NEWS NETWORKS

A number of states have state radio networks which serve the state news needs of local stations. Missouri, Ohio, Kansas, Florida and Maine have state networks which regularly transmit five-minute radio newscasts to affiliates via microwave, telephone line, or satellite. State networks make money by attracting regional advertisers. Affiliates are compensated for carrying state networks in several methods. The most common method of compensation is for the network to let local stations sell and insert local commercials in specified newscasts.

In many states, there are independent newspeople who act as state capital news correspondents for radio, television, and cable stations. Most capital correspondents send out daily audio or video reports to subscribers. If subscribers want special interviews or news stories, the capital correspondent can usually handle special requests for a fee.

FUTURE FILE

Future files or day books are the appointment calendars for news departments. All types of information which might lead to news stories are stored in future files and organized by day and month. Future files or day books are generally inexpensive and simple. Most work approximately the same way. Folders or dividers are numbered *one* through *thirty-one* corresponding to the days of the month. A thirty-second folder is marked *next month*. News conferences or possible news events taking place on the twenty-fourth day of the current month are put in the file marked "twenty-four." Stories scheduled for any day in the coming months are put in the file folder marked "next month." At the end of the current month, the news editor sorts through the next month folder; organizes and files all items by date in folders one through thirty-one. This continuing process insures that news or assignment editors keep track of newsworthy events in their communities.

Before leaving the station at night, assignment editors always check the next day's future folder to make sure reporting teams are scheduled to come early enough to cover possible news stories. While news or assignment editors are constantly working with future files, these files are not their exclusive property or responsibility. A future file belongs to the entire news department and everyone should feel responsible for clipping news stories or wire copy, saving news releases, jotting down future events, and filing them in the correct folder. The future file, and ultimately the quality of local news, is the responsibility of the whole staff. Those days when future files are empty can be agonizing for news editors and news staffs if spot news is scarce. On those days when the news flow is low, stories that might normally not be covered will end up in newscasts and reporters who have initiative or enterprise ideas are turned loose to work on their own stories. When future files contain eight or ten solid news possibilities, news or assignment editors can be more selective in what is given local news coverage.

INVESTIGATIVE REPORTING

To this point, the news sources which have been discussed are standard sources of information for most news departments and do not require active efforts by newspeople. Wire services transmit thousands of words of news copy; news releases flood assignment desks and network news feeds arrive precisely on time via satellite, telephone line or microwave. These sources would continue to be available even if the entire news staff took a vacation. None of these news sources requires any active investigatory efforts by newspeople. The information that arrives in your newsroom, however, also arrives in almost every other newsroom in your market. If you passively rely on this easily available information, your news will look and sound like all other mediocre news operations.

There are many potential stories in communities that no one covers because newspeople do not know these stories exist. Someone has the information or knows about the potential stories, but the person is not volunteering information or knocking on newsroom doors begging reporters to write stories.

The term investigative reporter has come to mean a special breed of reporter who is turned loose to do major investigative stories. However, any reporter who digs for information is an investigative reporter and capable of doing investigative work.

It is impossible in one chapter to cover adequately all sources of information available to investigative reporters. However, there are certain basic sources of information with which you should be familiar.

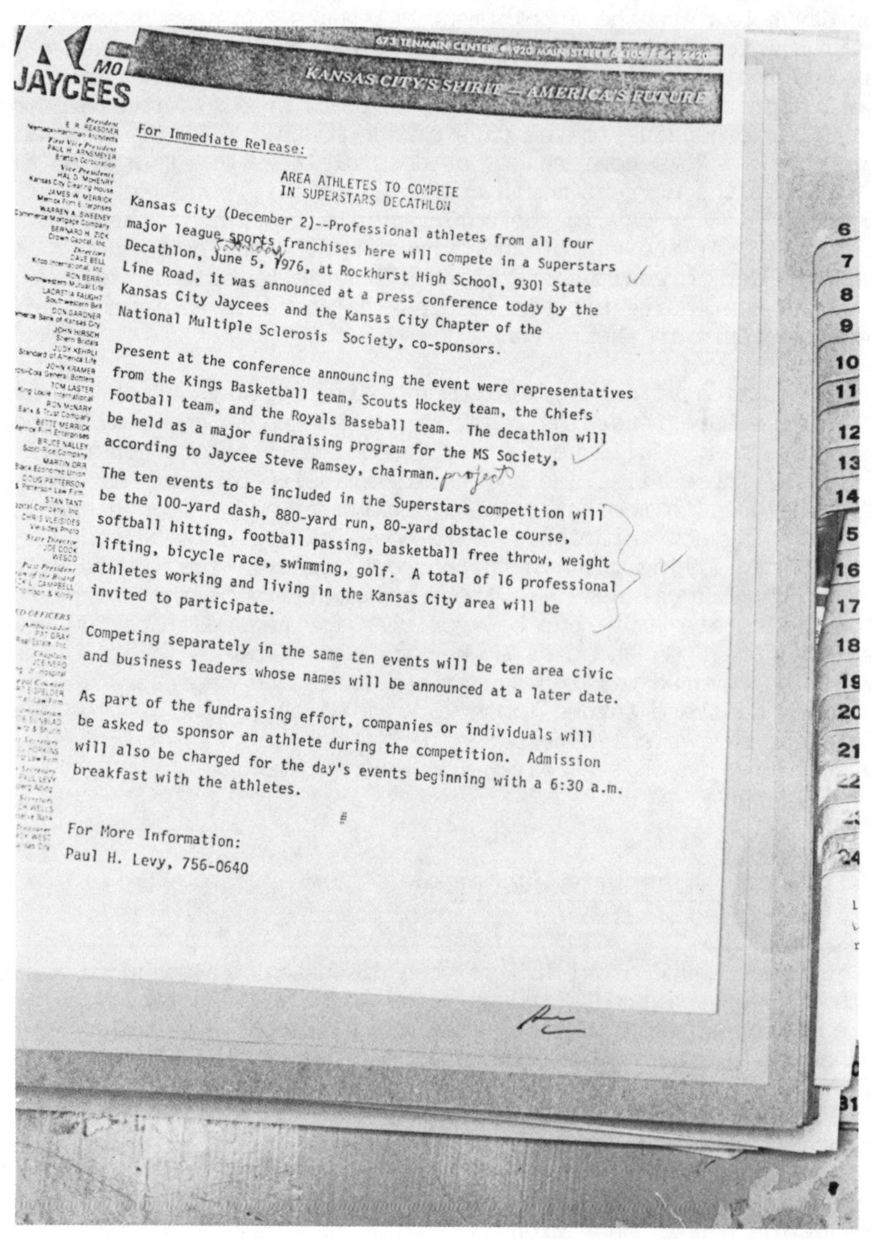

MO JAYCEES

673 TENMAIN CENTER • 920 MAIN STREET • [illegible]

KANSAS CITY'S SPIRIT — AMERICA'S FUTURE

For Immediate Release:

AREA ATHLETES TO COMPETE
IN SUPERSTARS DECATHLON

Kansas City (December 2)--Professional athletes from all four major league sports franchises here will compete in a Superstars Decathlon, June 5, 1976, at Rockhurst High School, 9301 State Line Road, it was announced at a press conference today by the Kansas City Jaycees and the Kansas City Chapter of the National Multiple Sclerosis Society, co-sponsors.

Present at the conference announcing the event were representatives from the Kings Basketball team, Scouts Hockey team, the Chiefs Football team, and the Royals Baseball team. The decathlon will be held as a major fundraising program for the MS Society, according to Jaycee Steve Ramsey, chairman.

The ten events to be included in the Superstars competition will be the 100-yard dash, 880-yard run, 80-yard obstacle course, softball hitting, football passing, basketball free throw, weight lifting, bicycle race, swimming, golf. A total of 16 professional athletes working and living in the Kansas City area will be invited to participate.

Competing separately in the same ten events will be ten area civic and business leaders whose names will be announced at a later date.

As part of the fundraising effort, companies or individuals will be asked to sponsor an athlete during the competition. Admission will also be charged for the day's events beginning with a 6:30 a.m. breakfast with the athletes.

#

For More Information:
Paul H. Levy, 756-0640

EXHIBIT 7-3. KMBC TELEVISION'S FUTURE FILE.

Source: Courtesy of KMBC TV Metromedia Television, Kansas city, Missouri. Photograph by Gary Mason.

REFERENCE BOOKS

Most news departments have some basic reference books available. These reference sources will probably be encyclopedias, statistical yearbooks, almanacs, and federal, state, and regional telephone directories. These standard newsroom sources are not designed to provide all of the information necessary for story research. They are designed to provide quick information so that you have a working knowledge of subjects when you go to more specialized reference works and experts. Each state government publishes annual reports and statistical studies of state and governmental functions. These specialized reference works can be found in library reference sections. At the federal level some important sources are: the *Congressional Directory* (lists Congressional offices, Senators, U. S. Representatives, and Congressional staff members); *U. S. Government Manual* (describes the purpose and function of government programs and lists top administrators); and *Federal Information Sources and Systems* (describes where to get information from each government office).

EXPERTS

Every community has people in various professions who qualify as experts in some particular area. Part of your job in using expert sources is to develop relationships with them so they will respond favorably when help is needed. Librarians are experts at collecting, organizing, and retrieving published information. Most librarians will answer questions over the telephone, but it is a good idea to make personal visits to libraries and establish personal contacts. Find out what reference librarians do, explain to them the needs you have, and ask for their help on those occasions when you do not have time to personally visit the library.

Other experts at filing and collecting information are government secretaries and file clerks. They may not know specifically what is in each file, but they know the basic file or record categories and can help newspeople locate information. Clarence Jones, WPLG Television investigative reporter says, "find the records clerk with moss between the toes and thick glasses from reading records for the past thirty years. They know everything and will save you hours." Jones advises telling clerks specifically what you are doing and asking for their help. In many instances this will be the most exciting thing that has ever happened to them and they will spend hours trying to assist you in your investigation. Jones tells an anecdote of asking a records clerk for help in checking the travel forms of a city council member. Jones explained to a clerk that he was looking for travel irregularities. Later when he came back to pick up the city council member's file, the clerk had two files and innocently asked, "You did want the mayor's file too, didn't you?" It took a moment to sink in but Jones realized what was happening and responded "Sure did, thanks."

Another local source of experts, often overlooked, is the faculty of nearby colleges or universities. Every college teacher has devoted his or her career to a particular topic and some professors qualify as experts in their respective fields. Professors can be interviewed for stories or provide reporters with leads or questions to ask someone else who is an expert. Colleges or universities can provide experts in business, economics, religion, law, medicine, veterinary medicine, zoology, weather, and so on.

There are many other experts in communities. Some can be located through telephone books, which are great sources of information. For example, do you need to know about rabies? Call local hospitals or veterinarians. Do you want to know about zoning or building? Call the local board of realtors or the city/county zoning commissions. Other experts in communities may not be categorized in telephone books and it is necessary to build your own list of experts. For example, one Ohio reporter kept a personal list of experts in a Rolodex. Every time he met someone he considered interesting, an expert, or a possible information source he jotted his or her name down in the Rolodex. One of those names was that of a retired psychiatrist and former head of the state hospital for the criminally insane. During a series of murders in the community, the reporter interviewed the psychiatrist, who gave a physical and mental profile of the type of person who would commit such a crime. The profile was amazingly accurate when it was later compared with the person charged with and convicted of committing the murders.

Depending on state public record laws, many, if not all, of the sources listed below can provide you with valuable information. Some state public records laws restrict access to certain types of information while other state public records laws are so broad that virtually anything on paper in government offices is open to inspection.

COURT RECORDS

Most court records are a matter of public record. Civil suit records and suit deposition files can provide valuable information about someone's private and public business activities. Many civil suits are filed by business associates who feel wronged or cheated. By using civil suit records, the plaintiff's attorneys do a great deal of investigatory work for you. It is not unusual to find all types of allegations, names and dates in civil suit files. You can find leads to other business associations and property ownership records.

Probate or family court records contain financial information and the property dispositions listed in wills or divorce settlements. Most people, to avoid long costly probate court battles, list all property and its disposition in their will. Divorce actions can also reveal financial information because who knows more about someone's activities than the person's angry husband or wife.

Bankruptcy records are kept in federal court buildings and are public record. Bankruptcy records contain lists of property, property dispositions, and assets and liabilities of people or businesses. The records will also contain lists of creditors.

LAND-MORTGAGE RECORDS

Land and mortgage records are public records and are scrupulously recorded in court houses. Land and mortgage records list what is owned by a person; how much was borrowed on the land; and who holds the mortgage. There are indexes which list sellers (direct index) and buyers (reverse index) of property.

Another investigative reporter says land-mortgage records are extremely important in finding money connections between people. You can find individual, partner, and corporate ownership of property and lists of business partners. A common method of bribery is to give someone property ventures. It is also wise to check property ownership records of relatives and in-laws of people you investigate as property is often hidden under relatives' names. To find names of in-laws, check the marriage license bureau.

TAX ASSESSOR

Tax assessors' records make possible other methods of checking land and property ownership and determining property values. Tax information is available and records will also indicate who pays the taxes on various parcels of property. Wouldn't it be interesting to find that some low-paid civil servant has title to property worth millions of dollars and the taxes are being paid by someone else?

VOTER REGISTRATION

Voter registration records will give you information on party affiliations, previous addresses, dates of birth, and social security numbers. In some investigatory work, knowledge of birth dates and social security numbers are necessary for computer searches.

POLICE DEPARTMENT

Police logs or blotters contain the daily activities of police departments. Police logs list people arrested or brought in for questioning and complaints filed. Since police logs are not privileged information, however, be very careful in using this information without verification. Police audio tape recordings of their radio transmissions can also be valuable sources of information. The audio tapes cannot be used on the air but in some states they are public records. WPLG Television's Clarence Jones says police audio tapes were valuable in his investigation into the death of Arthur McDuffie, a black insurance executive of Miami, Florida. Three police officers were charged and tried in connection with McDuffie's death. Police department audio tapes contained the radio transmissions from police officers chasing McDuffie, who tried to elude arrest on his motorcycle. Once McDuffie was stopped, police officers at the scene did not immediately request an ambulance. The police dispatcher even asked if an ambulance was needed; the reply from officers at the scene was "No." Two minutes later, according to the audio tape, officers at the scene requested an ambulance for McDuffie. What happened in those two minutes?

AMBULANCE PARAMEDIC REPORTS

Ambulance personnel and paramedics file detailed reports of their activities. These reports contain accurate times, locations, names of victims, and sometimes personal observations. In the Arthur McDuffie investigation, paramedic reports contained a notation that as the ambulance arrived one paramedic observed a police officer striking McDuffie's motorcycle helmet on the curb, apparently to simulate a motorcycle accident. That information was written in the report and available for public inspection.

FLIGHT INFORMATION

The Federal Aviation Agency also makes audio tape recordings of control tower transmissions. These tapes are public records and they can reveal information about air traffic, which planes were in the area, or accident situations. Many pilots file flight plans for trips, but flight plans are not required and they are not always accurate.

VEHICLE REGISTRATION

Determining vehicle ownership is easy in most states if you have vehicle tag numbers. Local vehicle registration offices can tell you who owns a particular car or truck by cross-checking vehicle tag numbers.

BOAT OWNERSHIP

Boat ownership can also be determined through departments of natural resources or similar state agencies. Ownership is cross referenced by boat registration numbers.

CORPORATE RECORDS

Secretary of State's offices list all state corporations and names corporation officers. Corporation records held by states do not normally contain stockholder information.

AIRPLANE REGISTRATION

Airplane ownership records are held by the Federal Aviation Administration (FAA) in Oklahoma City, Oklahoma. To find out who owns an airplane, simply obtain the N_____ number on the wings or body of the plane and call the FAA. Past history of airplanes can also be found through the FAA and specialized airplane title companies in Oklahoma City. After obtaining current ownership ifnormation from the FAA, the FAA will provide you with the names of airplane title companies which will trace the ownership history of aircraft.

HEALTH DEPARTMENTS

City, county, and state health department records are usually public records. Health investigation records concerning rabies, venereal disease, quarantines, health violations, and birth and death statistics are available for the asking. Sanitation reports on restaurants, hospitals and nursing homes are very important and quite revealing. Wouldn't it be interesting to find out that a fine local restaurant has serious health violations or a local hospital has been cited for having filthy operating rooms?

GOVERNMENT AGENCIES

Depending on state public records laws, most city, county, and state government agency reports are public records. This includes investigations, annual budgets, telephone logs, travel information, and salary scales.

A problem dealing with government agencies, though, is that they have so many records and files that, unless you know specifically what you want, you may not be able to find information through random record searches. Merely providing access to government records and files is not sufficient unless someone who knows the filing and records system is willing to help you locate specific materials.

FINANCIAL INFORMATION

Financial information on people, corporations, or non-profit organizations can be obtained through several sources. *Dun and Bradstreet*, found in library reference sections, will give overall financial pictures for business organizations. The Internal Revenue Service also maintains public records on non-profit organizations. Most radio, television, or cable television station sales departments are credit bureau members and may be willing to order a credit check to help out the news department.

PUBLIC SERVICE MONITORS

Various government public service agencies communicate over public service radio frequencies using codes or plain language. Much of their radio traffic is mundane but occasionally information of great news value is transmitted. The public and news agencies can monitor these public frequencies and listen to police, fire, sheriff, highway patrol, forestry department, weather bureau, marine patrol, Coast Guard, or paramedic radio transmissions. Every time a fire occurs or a crime is detected the report is telephoned into the fire or police radio dispatch rooms where the information is re-transmitted, over public service radio channels, to nearby police units or fire stations. If news departments monitor police and fire channels, newspeople immediately know of spot news events and can keep track of potential news stories by listening to the coded traffic. Minutes after hearing initial fire or police reports over the public service monitor, news crews can be sent quickly to scenes of the fires, accidents, crimes, or other breaking news events.

Those public service agencies that communicate frequently by radio or wish to keep messages confidential utilize numerical codes. Almost all police and sheriff's agencies use numerical codes and may even have scrambled or secure channels of communications not available to the general public or news departments. However, the numerical codes can be obtained so you can decipher standard police, fire and sheriff's messages.

NEWS BEATS

Many police departments around the country are finding that their officers do not have good contacts in the community or, in some instances, community support. Part of the reason for this situation is that police officers, riding around in patrol cars, are insulated from their communities and the people they are paid to protect. It is hard to trust or feel supportive toward someone you've never seen or talked with. Research is showing that a good way to cut crime and build community support is get police officers out of patrol cars and back on beats where officers can meet people in their communities and they, in turn, can learn to trust police. The same principle is true for broadcast journalists. Covering regular beats leads to increased knowledge of areas and familiarity with people and news events in the community. Reporters covering beats will quickly learn which government offices are regular suppliers of news and which people to go to for information or help. Covering regular beats involves reporters in their communities and leads to greater knowledge, better contacts, and more trust.

Some major criticisms of broadcast news are that few stations cover news in depth or break major news stories. Part of the reason for these criticisms is that many broadcast reporters do not cover regular beats, build good contacts, and have broad knowledge of an area.

On the national level, major news organizations have learned that assigning reporters or correspondents to beats leads to more in-depth news coverage. Wire services and networks assign reporters to cover the White House, Defense Department, State Department, Supreme Court, Department of Justice, and other major news-generating government departments. Beat reporters develop dependable contacts and over a time become specialized and extremely knowledgeable about their beats.

Locally, one news reporter can easily cover the police department and important city/county offices in a few hours. After a few months of covering the same beat the reporter will learn which offices need to be contacted daily and which departments can be covered less frequently. On a daily basis, the most productive departments will probably turn out to be police, sheriff, fire, courts and planning/zoning offices. Establishing good sources inside these departments will prove valuable. There are times when police or other officials may refuse to give out legitimate information and a personal source may confide that newsworthy information to you. Once good personal contacts are established you will not have to cover offices daily. You may decide to personally cover some less active offices weekly and telephone your personal contacts daily.

SUBSCRIPTIONS

News departments should subscribe to as many publications as possible and get on the mailing lists of all types of organizations. News ideas come from many sources, and magazines or newsletters can generate good story ideas.

NEWSPAPERS

News departments should subscribe to all local and county newspapers, major state newspapers, and all weekly or suburban newspapers in the station coverage area. Even though some surrounding newspapers will arrive a day late, news ideas can be clipped out and filed in future files.

Foreign language or minority targeted newspapers are found in most major cities with large ethnic populations. These newspapers can keep news departments aware of national or religious holidays and major issues facing minority groups. Even if the newspapers are in foreign languages, minority or ethnic newspaper editors can help you keep informed of news and social events concerning their readers.

Subscribing to local college and high school newspapers will help news departments keep in touch with important and large audience segments. Colleges and universities are important economic and social segments of communities, and college-based stories may have broad implications for the whole community. High school newspapers can also generate good story ideas. For example, a high school teacher retiring after forty years of service could generate a nice human interest feature. The retiring teacher would know thousands of former students who would have stayed in the community and would be interested in their former teacher.

Other possible newspaper subscriptions might be national or specialized publications, such as the New York Times or the Wall Street Journal. These two newspapers cater to specialized national audiences, and they try to have broad coverage of diverse events which might give you local story ideas.

JOURNALS AND NEWS MAGAZINES

News magazines such as Time, Newsweek and U. S. News and World Report are must reading for news people. These magazines go into great depth, provide newspeople with background information on many subjects and, at the same time, provide possible local story ideas. There are many national or international stories which can be localized. An example would be a national space program story which focuses on a local firm providing crucial parts for the space shuttle. Localizing national stories can be done with medicine, agriculture, crime, business and the sciences.

Trade magazines or specialized professional journals are also valuable sources of information. Even though much of what is in trade journals will not be of use, there are always those little items that provide good local story ideas. Almost all state government agencies publish monthly or quarterly magazines summarizing accomplishments, projecting future plans, and containing general stories of interest to people working in those specific departments.

NEWSLETTERS

Get on the newsletter mailing lists of civic and social organizations, professional groups, or state government departments. Much of the information in newsletters is highly specialized, but some information may have broad appeal and can be used in local stories. The Kiwanis Club, Jaycees, Chamber of Commerce, Rotary, Lions Club, and other important civic groups are constantly getting involved in charities or civic projects. These events generate good stories. Many civic organizations also sponsor speakers who have newsworthy things to say. For example, the Gainesville, Florida, police chief first announced at a Kiwanis Club luncheon that Gainesville's crime rate was among the top ten in the country. It took several days for that story to circulate and reach local newspapers, radio, and television stations that covered the story after the fact.

With all of these newsletters, journals, and newspapers flowing into newsrooms, it is impossible to assign one person to read and digest all the information. A good idea is to encourage reporters and writers to develop areas of interest and then channel specialized newspapers, newsletters, and journals to those people. This provides news departments with people who have specialized knowledge and it helps assignment editors keep track of stories which may interest the whole community.

The thing to remember is that you don't know where you will find ideas that lead to good local stories. Always evaluate newspapers, newsletters, magazines, and journals in terms of local situations and local audiences.

TELEPHONES

Novice broadcast journalists are always surprised at the amount of time spent talking with people on the telephone. The broadcast journalist's image is of someone who is "out and about" town gathering news. That image is true, but to avoid wasted time and effort, the telephone is used to set up interviews, confirm facts, and arrange meetings. Reporters spend a good deal of time talking on the telephone, and an organized approach to telephone use can help you be a better reporter and save hours of time. After beats and personal contacts have been established, reporters may personally cover their beat only two or three days a week and keep in touch with news sources on other days by telephone. In some instances, people will take reporter's telephone calls when they would refuse personal meetings or interviews. Telephone calls can fit into someone's busy schedule when personal interviews might be an inconvenience. Once someone takes a telephone call, a few quick questions between appointments might be stretched to a comprehensive interview.

A good way to save time and organize telephone use is to have several different newsroom telephone lists. Many news departments have daily telephone call sheets listing names and numbers that must be called daily or several times a day. Having the list organized and on a clipboard near the telephones saves time looking up numbers and makes sure that all important numbers get called. Sometimes a space is left on the call sheet for reporters to initial once calls have been completed. The most frequently called agencies might include police, fire, sheriff, city manager, county commissioners, city clerk, city and county attorneys' offices, and school board. These offices are usually called daily. Police or fire departments may be called two or three times daily.

Another important telephone list is of agencies or important contacts in city, county, and state government who are frequently in the news. The people on this list are not usually contacted daily but, because of their position, they generate news and are constantly being interviewed. This list could include area hospital telephone numbers and the names of hospital spokespeople; the weather bureau; city and county building officials in surrounding communities; and personal contacts. To supplement this list, some news departments also keep a comprehensive list of personal contacts cross-referenced by jobs or agencies of employment. This cross-referenced list helps newspeople locate contacts by job titles or agencies without actually knowing specific names.

Specialized cross-listed telephone directories of communities are valuable newsroom references. Telephone subscribers are cross-listed alphabetically by street and street number. For example:

2121 Baker Street	Marley, R.	275-5132
2122 Baker Street	Wilson, Ralph P.	275-3144
2123 Baker Street	Olsen, G. M.	322-4178
2124 Baker Street	Smeyak, G. P.	444-5921
2125 Baker Street	Morgan, D. A.	275-6198

Newspeople wanting to find out the name and telephone number of the person living at 2123 Baker Street would look up Baker Street and run down pages of consecutive

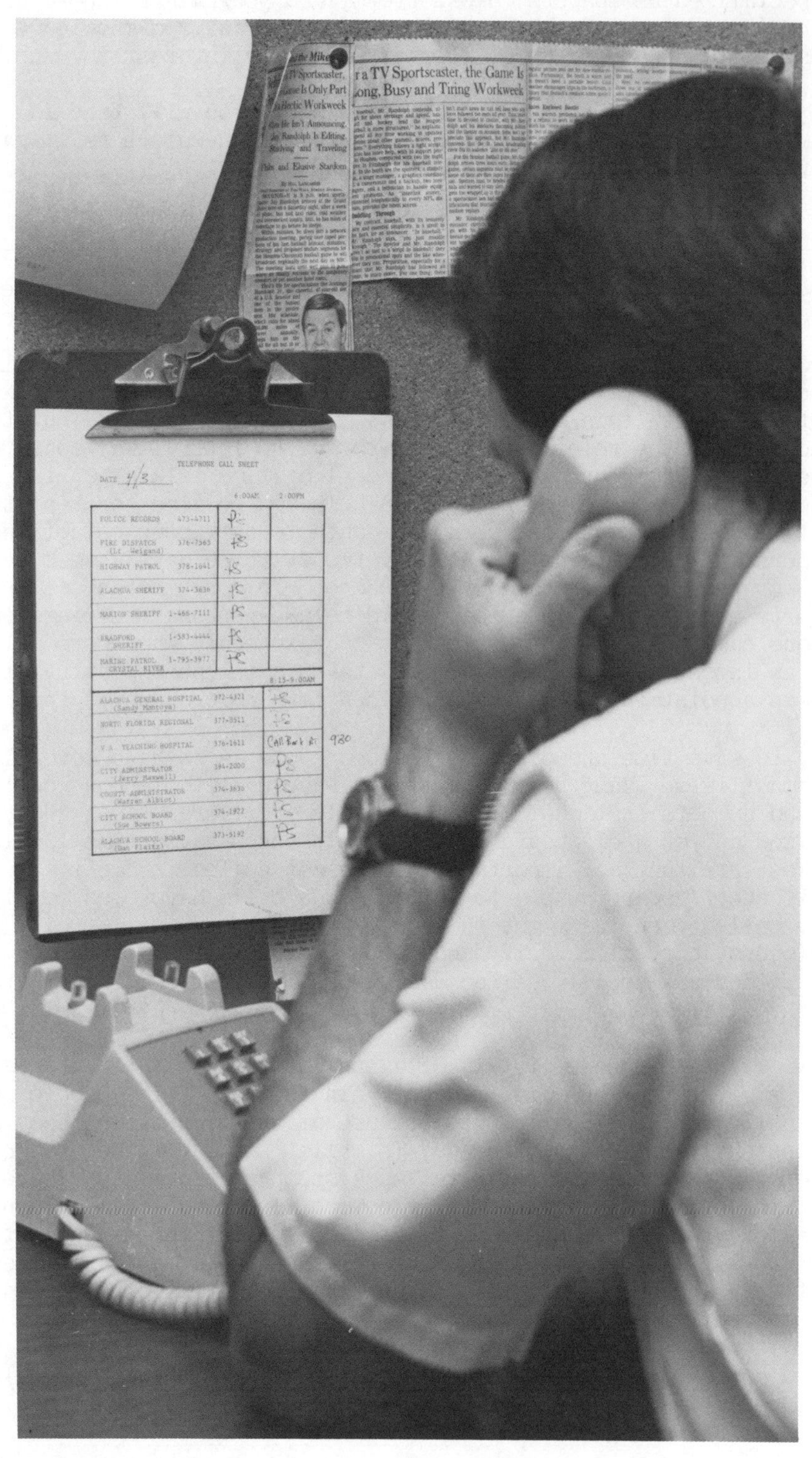

EXHIBIT 7-4. Telephone call sheet

street numbers until finding 2123. Proper use of cross-listing directories can save time and result in a great deal of information. For example, newspeople hearing reports of a fire at 211 Howard Street could use a cross-listed directory to telephone people living next door to 211 Howard Street and ask if there is a fire; how severe it is; and for an eyewitness account of what is taking place.

Telephones are powerful devices in news gathering if newspeople are creative and quick thinking. Some dramatic telephone interviews and audio tape actualities have been obtained by quick thinking reporters. In September, 1975, a group of Arab terrorists took over the Egyptian Embassy in France and held the Egyptian Ambassador hostage. The terrorists threatened to blow up the embassy and kill all hostages unless Egyptian President Sadat disavowed the Sinai peace agreement signed by his country and Israel. A reporter for one of the American networks telephoned the embassy and asked to talk with the Egyptian Ambassador. The terrorists allowed him to talk with the reporter and in a calm, British-accented voice the ambassador described the terrorists and the type of explosives they were planting in the embassy. He said there was no doubt in his mind that they would kill everyone in the embassy if police tried to rush the building. There are other stories of reporters calling banks or homes where armed people were holding hostages and talking with the hostages or their abductors.

PUBLIC RELATIONS DEPARTMENTS

The basic role of public relations departments is to gain good public relations for an organization and to minimize bad publicity. A stated goal is to present their side of an issue and to make sure their view is widely disseminated by the news media.

There are thousands of businesses, civic organizations, clubs, charities, political, and non-profit groups that feel their activities or views merit news coverage. Some of these groups employ public relations firms or have internal public relations departments to handle their public relations activities. Public relations specialists provide news departments with news possibilities and they do this in several ways. One PR function is to send news releases to media announcing plans, events, or activities which might draw news coverage. Examples of the types of events that are mentioned in news releases are major plant expansions, new products, promotions, charitable activities, or anything that might have some interest or impact on the community. Some news releases are too self-serving or not-too-subtle attempts to generate publicity, and they have little news value. However, other news releases may point out significant events that have an impact on the community. They could lead to good news stories.

Another function of the public relations specialist is to create or arrange events which generate publicity and draw news coverage. Some common public relations events that might gain news coverage are award banquets, open houses, news conferences, ground breaking ceremonies, and speeches. An example of a public relations event that would probably generate news coverage would be for the local blood bank to get the mayor to donate a pint of blood on the first day of a blood drive. Invitations announcing the event would, of course, be sent out to local newspapers, radio, television, and cable stations several days prior to the special event. The mayor's public relations specialist, of course, would be pleased with the special event arranged by the blood bank. The event would be a fairly good story on a slow day, and it would serve the public relations needs of the blood bank and the mayor.

Another function of public relations departments is to maintain good relations with local news organizations and to cultivate friendships with local reporters. This is done by assisting reporters who need information and by developing friendships with reporters. Public relations specialists can save newspeople time by helping them obtain information, check out facts, arrange private tours or interviews and, in general, gather favorable news about their clients or organizations. The thing that you must remember is that the basic role of public relations specialists is to project a favorable image of their clients and to make sure that bad publicity is kept to a minimum. Some public relations specialists find their role occasionally hard to accomplish because they feel that to maintain credibility with the news media they must be absolutely honest. During the early days of the Vietnam conflict, State Department Briefing Officer Robert McCloskey put his job on the line when he answered reporters' questions openly and affirmed that the United States' role in Vietnam had changed from passive to active. Other public relations specialists, though, may not have the same philosophy as Robert McCloskey. Reporters checking out negative aspects of a story should be wary of public relations specialists whom they do not know or trust.

Most radio, television, and cable stations, in addition to receiving written news releases, also receive audio tapes, video tapes, and public relations announcements. Public relations specialists know the value of audio and video stories to broadcast and cable journalists, and they supply visual or audio releases that can be included in newscasts. Some organizations providing audio or video news releases are public utilities, hospitals, universities, sports organizations, government agencies, armed forces, politicians, and businesses. Some video and audio news releases are blatant publicity gimmicks while others have legitimate news value and can be used in newscasts. These pre-packaged audio or video news releases do not have to be run intact and can be shortened or edited to fit formats and reduce promotional or propaganda aspects.

In dealing with publicity or public relations specialists, reporters must remember PR people are not paid to help reporters with negative stories about clients. Public relations specialists are paid to generate good images of their clients through a variety of methods. A school board, facing tough collective bargaining with teachers, may publicly present its side of the dispute and try to gain public support by arranging news interviews with the superintendent. By carefully orchestrating events and news releases, the school board might manipulate the news media into publicizing the school board's position. Prepackaged video or audio tape news releases are notorious for presenting biased views or trying to capitalize on the publicity value of events. Whenever contents of a video or audio news release are biased, you should name the source of tape or film and avoid favoring one side of a controversial issue. It is also against the law to air promotional material without stating the financial arrangements.

Another tape service offered by some public relations departments are audio call-in services. Some of these services have toll-free numbers to encourage radio stations to telephone and record voicers and actualities prepared by the public relations department. The National Aeronautics and Space Administration offers this service to radio and television stations during a space shot. Some politicians, especially during political campaigns, have regional offices offering audio reports or interviews with candidates.

Responsible journalists have a public duty to check information given to them and carefully evaluate sources of information. Newspeople must present accurate newsworthy stories and not abuse the trust placed in them by news consumers. While many public relations specialists would not lie to news reporters, they may refuse to answer or try to avoid questions. Newspeople may find themselves in situations where they have to aggressively ask questions; bypass low echelon people or even make enemies to effectively do their jobs. Being friendly with public relations people can be advantageous but it is not a priority when compared with the main responsibilities of being a journalist.

COMPETITION

Listen to the competition. Wear out radio dials and channel selectors listening to and watching all newscasts in town comparing your performance against all other news organizations. Ask yourself, "How do I stack up against other radio stations, television and cable operations and the newspapers?" Critically analyze the news situation in the community. Who is doing the better job of getting enterprise stories or following up on old stories and generating new and different angles to traditional types of news events? Are you being beaten on too many major stories; who are the competition's contacts and whom do they interview; what type of stories are they running? When you listen to the competition, don't hide the truth from yourself. Record the competition's newscasts and analyze writing style, content, length of stories and number of stories in newscasts.

Missing occasional stories happens in every newsroom. Those enterprise stories the competition develops add flavor to their news operation. What you cannot allow is consistently being beaten and being forced to play catch-up. If this is the situation, it is time to sit down and carefully analyze what you are doing and how you are doing it. Are competitors picking up city and county stories because they have city-county beat reporters or are their reporters at the city-county buildings better than your reporters? Determining the sources of your competitor's stories will help you analyze your performance and correct problems that develop.

When competitors beat you on a story, don't ignore the story as if it never happened. The other thing to avoid is playing catch-up by trying to do the same story that your competitors did earlier. Nothing sounds worse than having a station run an old story the day after the newspapers or competing radio and television stations. Trying to duplicate a competitor's story means you will never catch up because you have to cover the same ground they covered. Use the story as a starting point and try to update. For example, if the competition has an interview with the police chief announcing that crime in your community has increased 100 percent, don't redo the same interview. Try to find out causes for the crime increase by going to criminologists, psychologists, and sociologists. Find out what the mayor plans to do to halt the crime increase. Interview judges about the legal system and determine if it is contributing to the high crime rate. Do a series of stories on how to crime-proof homes, cars, neighborhoods. You can never catch up with the competition on the original story, so you must jump ahead and gain control of the situation.

STRINGERS

News stringers or correspondents are part-time people who work for news organizations. They can significantly increase news gathering abilities without a great deal of cost. A stringer normally gets paid by the story, with stations picking up expenses, mileage, and film, video, or audio tape costs.

Stringers are valuable because they provide coverage in areas outside the market or in fringe areas stations cannot afford to cover regularly, such as the suburbs, nearby small communities or the state capital. It would be impractical to assign newspeople to these areas daily, but stringers, who already live and work in the small communities, can provide news coverage on a part-time basis. Anyone whose job or schedule allows freedom to cover newsworthy events can be a stringer. Suburban newspaper reporters, college students, housewives, and self-employed people make good stringers because they have flexible schedules.

In most state capitals, some enterprising newsperson will set up a news bureau and sell stories to stations in the state wishing a capital correspondent. The newsperson may cover one major story and sell targeted reports of the event to four or five different stations. If stations wish individualized reports from the capital, the newsperson may charge more for the story because of the extra time and effort. This is a valuable service for stations outside the capital that wish to provide coverage of capital events that affect their audiences.

A surprising number of news stories are picked up by news departments from tips called in by news listeners. Listeners may call in and ask "Why didn't you run the story on the small plane crash?" and alert the news department to the plane crash. In small and medium-sized markets, where listeners strongly identify with stations and personnel, listeners regularly call in tips about news events. Some stations encourage this practice by offering cash awards or mentioning who called in tips. Paying for "news tips of the week" has proven effective in some markets because it keeps hundreds or thousands of regular news listeners looking for newsworthy events.

Some stations employ people as tipsters on a confidential basis. These paid tipsters usually do not want their relationships with stations made public because it might endanger their jobs. Examples of paid tipsters would be the night police or fire dispatcher. Anytime a major story occurs during the night the dispatcher, after sending police or fire units to the scene, would call local news reporters and tell them of the story. Other tipsters of value could be people in the prosecuting attorney's office or budget and auditing departments of city and county governments. Tipsters, unlike stringers, are not newspeople and do not cover stories. Tipsters report events to news departments and regular staff newspeople cover the stories.

QUIZ

1. What are the differences between AP's radio wire and AP's "A" wire?

2. What three services to television stations does APTV provide?

3. Which item is more important coming over the wire services, a "flash" or a "bulletin?"

4. What does "DEF" stand for?

5. Explain what the DEF does for local stations?

6. List two sources where you might be able to find financial records on someone who is still alive.

7. What is the difference between a "stringer" and a "tipster?"

EXERCISES

1. Create a daily telephone call sheet for your market. First use the local telephone directory to determine which organizations and telephone numbers should be included on the list. Then, as a class project, assign one person to contact each organization to determine who should be contacted for information. (Assigning one person will avoid the same person getting calls from everyone in the class.)

2. Have the class evaluate one full hour of Associated Press or United Press wire copy.

3. Have the class determine which state weather zone they are in so that they can use the correct weather forecasts from the wire services.

ASSIGNMENTS

1. Examine the open records/meeting laws in your state and determine what government records are available to news reporters.

2. List all of the broadcast and cable organizations in your immediate market and assign teams of students to determine which sources are available to stations and evaluate the sources. Also, have the teams evaluate how effective the day book or future file operation is for each station.

ENDNOTE

1. Information and photograph courtesy of Reuters.

8

NEWS ORGANIZATION, FORMATS AND FORMULAS

For most television and many radio stations news has become their single most important local production. Radio stations rely on record manufacturers or prepackaged music services for most programming. Television stations get the vast majority of their programming from networks or program syndicators. Aside from a few local public affairs or religious programs, news is the only major production of many radio and television stations.

The increasing importance of local news in program schedules can be attributed to the amount of money local stations can make off news programs and the importance of the station's image to viewers and advertisers. News has become an important profit center for stations and some stations make more money from news programming than any other production. This has not always been the case as, for years, news was viewed by some station managers as a necessary evil. News was something that had to be programmed to make sure that the Federal Communications Commission, every three years, renewed the station's license to broadcast. In the early 1960s many stations lost money on news and some managers carried news programs only because the FCC said it was in the "public interest, convenience and necessity." Because news was not profitable, some station managers had token news operations, and they put as little of their stations' resources into news as possible. Some of these stations had one-person news departments with miniscule budgets and no access to station resources. Other station owners and managers felt that news and public affairs programming was a major responsibility and, even if news lost money, it deserved first call on money, staff, and equipment.

Throughout the years, managers and station owners have found that there is more than a direct monetary reward for having a highly rated, prestigious news department. In many communities, a station's news image sets the overall feeling the audience has toward the station. Being the news leader creates a *halo* effect which carries over into other areas. This is due, in part, to the fact that more than sixty percent of the American public relies solely on radio, television, and cable news for their information needs. Electronic news is also considered the most unbiased and credible news source. Being the news leader in a market can make audiences and advertisers feel the station is the leader in all areas. This image carry-over increases the value of the station's public affairs and entertainment programs. A broadcast account executive has a better chance of selling marginal programs to sponsors if sponsors think highly of the station and want to be affiliated with the number one station in town. How audiences perceive stations, in large part, determines how advertisers feel and where advertising dollars will be spent.

People are becoming more and more concerned about the world around them and the things which affect them. One method people have of learning how to control their lives is by gaining information. This need for information has created growing news appetites that have been documented by researchers hired by the Associated Press, networks and various radio and television stations. People want news that keeps them informed of world and local events, helps them cope with life and lead a better existence.

In the largest broadcast markets, all-news radio or news-talk radio is one of the top five rated formats. All-news radio has trouble surviving in the smaller markets because it is costly to program and commercial rates are high for personnel and equipment.

The success of Cable News Network 1 (CNN1) and Cable News Network 2 (CNN2) are strong indicators that news appetites continue to grow. The American Broadcasting Company (ABC) and Westinghouse Broadcasting also plan an all-news cable channel designed to compete with CNN1 and CNN2.

Television networks have found that news programming outside the traditional 6:30 p.m. period gains wide audiences. All three television networks schedule one-minute news updates throughout the evening and many local stations also program local news updates. ABC's experiment with "NIGHTLINE" at 11:30 p.m. has created a highly rated, network news program in the late evening. CBS television has also expanded "Sunday Morning" from one hour to two hours. The three major television networks are also planning on starting overnight news programs during those times when the networks traditionally sign off the air. CBS plans a three hour newscast from 2:00 to 5:00 a.m. ABC plans a one hour newscast immediately following their late night entertainment program and "NBC Overnight News" will follow "Late Night with David Letterman."

PROGRAM CONSULTANTS

Because money and image are important to a station's economic survival, managers are constantly trying to improve local productions and increase ratings. In some major television markets, a single rating point can mean as much as $100,000 to $150,000 a year in commercial revenues. A competitive edge, no matter how small, can mean significant profits and improved image.

During the 1960s, periodic rating surveys told managers how their stations were performing against the competition, but ratings did not tell managers how to improve their programming. Most improvements or changes in local news productions came about through trial and error devised by news and production staffs. Low ratings over a period of time led to changes in announcers, news staff, news management and sets. However, no one was sure if changes were necessary or actually improved news programs. The situation was reminiscent of the advertiser who said that he was sure that half his advertising budget was wasted. The problem was he didn't know which half.

Sensing a void, several people founded research firms which specialized in news research and consulting. Researchers used questionnaires and interviews to find out what people thought about news and what people wanted to see or hear in news programs. The consulting firms evaluated all elements of radio and television newscasts, including talent, sets, formats, news content, competition, time of newscasts, and newscast lengths. Following the research and evaluations of news programs, consultants made recommendations to management which, they hoped, would lead to larger news audiences, higher ratings, and more money.

Initially, reception of news consultants by news directors ranged from total rejection to total acceptance. One of the most publicized criticisms came from WTVJ Television, Miami, Florida, news director Ralph Renick who calls the consultants "trojan horses." He claims they come into stations to research and recommend and end up dictating news policies and content to newspeople. Network newspeople--Charles Kuralt, Walter Cronkite, John Masterman-- have also been critical of the news consultants' power and ability to affect decisions these newspeople feel should be left to journalists. The primary complaints about news researchers and consultants appear to be that some news directors feel newscasts have been turned into entertainment programs catering to audiences rather than trying to educate and inform. News directors claim consultants become involved in news decisions and judgments and this charge seems to be true.

On the other side of the issue, some news directors say the consultants have been a positive force and have revolutionized broadcast news. Frank Magid, of Frank Magid Associates, feels that news directors who resist research and consultants are the older traditional news people who are afraid of change.

Whatever your personal feelings, news research and consulting has become common and researchers provide managers with information that is used in decision making. News consultants and researchers are a force in broadcasting because managers rely on them for information and trust their recommendations. The influence of news consultants on news formats, talent, sets, and content has increased significantly since the late 1960s. Station managers, looking at profit and loss sheets, are aware that news consultants have a better than average record of improving news ratings, which, in most instances, leads directly to increased station revenues.

Virtually all television and many radio stations have conducted news and program research or wish they had enough money to hire consultants. Research, if done correctly, can provide programmers and managers with important information about program concepts and audience likes, dislikes, hopes and desires. Research can help answer important questions such as "Why is my 6:00 p.m. news ranked higher than my 11:00 p.m. news?" or "Is the sports segment targeted to the available sports audience?" Research, if properly used, can be an important decision making tool for news directors and station managers. Research improperly used can result in newscasts looking like circuses where news content gets lost in flippant chatter or legitimate news stories are dropped for lurid stories stressing sex and violence.

RADIO NEWS

Television and radio coexist with each other; each medium assuming a unique communications role in industrialized nations. For the most part, television dominates the evening hours when families are together. During the day, however, radio remains the major news and entertainment medium. Most radio programmers, capitalizing on radio's strengths, have gone primarily to a music and news format. Radio listeners are busy people who are commuting during drive times (6:30:-9:30 a.m. and 4:00-6:30 p.m.) and who need to be entertained and informed. Millions of people wake up to clock radios and throughout the morning hours, until they get to work or school, radio is their companion. Radio does not demand full attention while people rush to work or school. Because the morning drive audience is constantly changing and on the go, news, headlines, weather, and traffic reports are programmed frequently. At night, during the evening drive time period, radio provides the same basic information and entertainment services.

The period between the morning and evening drive times is also important for radio program directors. Homemakers are encouraged to use radio for companionship while homes are cleaned, shopping is accomplished, and children are rushed to and from school. Entertainment and news are designed to appeal to homemakers who may use radio as a companion and steady source of information and entertainment. Disc jockeys and newspeople may try to appeal to homemakers by targeting news and entertainment. Newscasts during the day may take on a softer news approach by offering consumer news and tips, shopping guides or other information relevant to homemakers.

Radio programmers and news directors have been searching for the "right" answers regarding how much local news should be programmed and at what times. Many radio stations have hired research firms to help them find the right answers, but, all too often, at small stations these important decisions are made on intuition or faulty information. The Associated Press, to help its members, commissioned two national news surveys to determine radio news listener preferences. The AP studies confirm some prior research done on radio news, but the studies are comprehensive in nature and have explored some aspects of radio news that have previously not been researched. The studies cover three broad areas: the national radio audience; news presentation and content; and news scheduling and desires.

NATIONAL RADIO AUDIENCE

It is clear from the AP studies that the vast majority of people who listen to radio select stations because of specific music formats--Top 40, beautiful music, country western, blue grass, soul, classical, album oriented rock, etc. The exceptions to this are people who listen to middle of the road (MOR) music or all-news and all-news-and-talk radio. Specifically, people who listen to MOR music formats consider news just as important as the music, and news may determine which MOR station they ultimately listen to. In highly competitive radio markets with two or more MOR stations, a strong, aggressive news operation may be a determining factor in which MOR station gains the largest audience. People desiring music formats other than MOR are less concerned with news, however, the overall attitude of people listening to all radio stations is generally positive towards news. Eighty-six percent of the people questioned in the AP studies indicate that either news is very important or that when news comes on they pay attention. Only ten percent of the people questioned indicate that news means very little to them and only three percent say they turn off their radios when news come on.

NEWS PRESENTATION AND CONTENT

The Associated Press studies tried to determine what type of stories appeal to radio listeners and how writing style, delivery, and actualities affect audience perceptions of news.[1]

The AP studies show that people are interested in news which affects them--local news that deals with "health, heart, and pocketbook" issues. Exhibit 8-1 lists audience interest in various types of stories.

The AP studies also indicate that straight writing and delivery styles are the most effective. Writing in present tense or personalizing stories by using "you" or "we" does not substantially raise the level of interest in stories. Personalizing and writing in present tense does increase the level of interest of stories already interesting and relevant to radio audiences. However, if stories are not interesting to people, personalizing, writing in present tense, or using celebrity names has very little impact and can actually make stories less interesting.

What really makes news interesting to radio listeners is content and/or the answer to the question *"What's in it for me."* In other words, most people listening to radio news want to hear news that is useful and pertinent. The AP stresses the *"health, heart, and pocketbook"* approach.

Use of taped actualities is extremely important in news. Those people responding to the AP study tend to feel newscasts containing actualities are more professional or interesting than newscasts that do not utilize actualities. More than seventy percent of the people surveyed said they liked to hear the voices of people in the news as opposed to just newscasters reading. Tape actualities are desirable if:

1. They enhance stories and make them interesting

2. The stories are technically clean

3. The tapes are used to inform rather than entertain

Exhibit 8-1

RADIO AUDIENCE INTEREST IN VARIOUS TYPES OF NEWS STORIES*

	Very Interested	Total Mention Somewhat Interested	Not Very Interested
Taxes story	63.6%	28.0%	8.4%
Environment story	62.6%	27.9%	9.5%
Weather story	62.0%	31.4%	6.6%
Energy story	58.2%	29.9%	11.6%
The economy story	57.5%	30.7%	11.7%
Medicine and health story	55.8%	34.5%	9.7%
Personal financial growth story	55.6%	31.5%	12.9%
Labor story	53.1%	32.9%	14.1%
Parenthood & child rearing story	51.9%	27.0%	21.1%
Consumer information story	50.6%	37.3%	12.0%
Crime story	48.6%	37.7%	13.7%
Education story	48.3%	40.7%	11.0%
State and government story	45.8%	38.1%	15.8%
Security and protection story	43.3%	39.5%	16.8%
Science story	42.8%	39.4%	17.7%
Recreation and vacation story	40.8%	35.8%	23.1%
Politics story	39.4%	37.7%	22.7%
Food story	34.3%	35.1%	30.4%
Political morality story	34.2%	42.4%	23.4%
International relations story	33.9%	45.8%	20.2%
Interesting people story	32.3%	42.2%	25.3%
Business news story	29.1%	44.4%	26.5%
Agriculture story	27.6%	43.7%	28.6%
Television story	27.3%	40.8%	31.9%
Sports story	25.1%	37.0%	37.5%
Self-improvement story	24.2%	37.3%	38.5%
Movie story	22.0%	42.7%	35.3%
Love and sex story	19.4%	32.4%	47.5%
Music and musical arts story	18.3%	33.3%	48.4%
Fashion and beauty story	17.0%	31.4%	51.4%
The arts story	16.7%	35.1%	48.1%
Entertainment story	13.6%	32.1%	54.3%

*Courtesy: Associated Press

NEWS SCHEDULING AND DESIRES

The AP studies tried to determine when people wanted to hear radio news and how long newscasts should be. In general, people want news available on the hour throughout the day but the biggest demand for news occurs during the morning drive times (6:00-9:00 a.m.); noon; afternoon drive times (5:00-6:00 p.m.); and in the late evening at 10:00 p.m.

Overall, the most desired length of newscast is five minutes and the least desired newscast length is two or three minutes. A surprisingly large number of people indicated they wanted longer newscasts, ten to fifteen minutes in length, especially during the morning and afternoon drive time periods and at 10:00 p.m. In effect, during the morning and afternoon drive time period, there is strong demand for longer newscasts that go into detail.

MUSIC FORMATS AND NEWS TARGETING

Radio has become a highly competitive medium with radio stations trying to find and attract narrow target audiences. In some medium or major sized markets, it is not unusual to have thirty to forty radio stations seeking out specialized audiences and programming to attract people in the target group. Target audiences are analyzed, researched, probed, and poked for differences which might give a station a programming advantage over other radio stations trying for the same audience.

Mass appeal programming for radio audiences is no longer viable and radio stations are trying for specific audience groups. The key to finding and reaching specific audience groups is understanding their demographics (age, sex, income, and education) and programming music, news and other material which interests the specific group. Advertisers and radio programmers have found that age seems to be a major determinant in buying habits and radio listening habits. Certain products tend to appeal to people in certain age groups. Music formats also appeal to people in certain age groups. These two facts have created modern radio formating and targeting. For example, young people who listen to album oriented rock (AOR) music or contemporary hit music (CHM) tend to frequent certain types of fast food restaurants and purchase specific types of clothing. Cadillac ownership, on the other hand, tends to appeal to a certain age/social group which listens to MOR, classical, or beautiful music. Both of these age/social groups tend to have certain demographic similarities and radio listening patterns which programmers can appeal to through music selection and news programming.

The most common music formats have certain similarities which must be considered when deciding how to reach a specific target audience.

ALBUM ORIENTED ROCK (AOR)

Album oriented rock music appeals mostly to people in the 18 to 24 year old age group who want high fidelity and stereophonic sound. AOR music formats fit best on FM stations which provide greater fidelity. AOR audiences tend to have very low news desires or a commitment to standard types of news. Many AOR programmers believe that news is a "turn off" for their audience and would prefer to delete news or keep it to an absolute minimum. Any news presentation should be targeted to the interests and desires of the 18 to 24 year old age group. AOR programmers prefer a combination of straight news and targeted life style features delivered in a low key conversational manner.

If AOR stations are network affiliated, they prefer affiliation with ABC's American FM Network, ABC's Contemporary or NBC's "The Source." These networks program youth-oriented music features and news designed to fit into a youth-oriented music format such as album oriented rock.

ALL-NEWS OR NEWS-TALK

All-news radio or news-talk radio appeals primarily to the 55+ age group with a secondary audience between 25 and 54 years of age. These age groups are expanding as the population steadily gets older. It is estimated that during the 1980s, eleven million people will be between 35 and 44 years of age, which is right in the middle of all news radio's secondary audience group.

All-news or news-talk audiences tend to be more affluent and better educated than average. The older demographics of all-news radio listeners makes this a good format for AM radio.

People who listen to all-news radio or news-talk radio want standard news and straightforward writing and delivery. All-news radio audiences are concerned with news content and news credibility. Happy talk or joking about news events hurts station credibility and should be avoided. A good blend of national, international and local news appeals to this audience along with "health, heart, and pocketbook" news items.

Radio networks which fit in well with all-news or news-talk formats are CNN RADIO, CBS, MBS, NBC, and ABC's Information Network. These networks offer traditional news emphasizing politics, economics, foreign and domestic news geared to the needs of an older, more traditional audience.

BEAUTIFUL MUSIC (BM)

Beautiful music attracts 25 to 54 year old listeners who want the greater fidelity of FM radio. Many BM listeners use beautiful music as background throughout the day.

Beautiful music audiences tend to have fairly low news desires or commitments except during drive times. They prefer standard news styles stressing content and straightforward writing and delivery styles.

Most beautiful music stations prefer not to be network affiliates because they want to avoid network news and features hourly breaking their music formats. However, if beautiful music stations are network affiliates they prefer the networks which appeal to older audiences such as MBS, NBC, CBS and ABC's Information Network.

ADULT CONTEMPORARY

Many radio music programmers consider adult contemporary as encompassing a wide variety of cross-over sounds from country and western, middle of the road, and top 40 music formats. Adult contemporary can be shifted to appeal to different audience demographics by music selection. Adult contemporary formats, for the most part, appeal to the 30+ age group.

Because adult contemporary appeals to the 30+ age group, news can be an important programming element. As people get older, they seem to want more news and information. News styles should be traditional with straightforward writing and delivery.

Adult contemporary stations, if they are network affiliates, tend to join networks appealing to older demographics such as MBS, NBC, CBS, and ABC's Information Network or ABC's American Entertainment.

CONTEMPORARY HIT RADIO

Contemporary hit radio, sometimes referred to as urban contemporary, is targeted to younger listeners under 30 years of age. This young audience is very transitory and has very little station loyalty. It is not uncommon for contemporary hit radio listeners to switch radio stations during commercials or newscasts.

Contemporary hit radio listeners have low news desires and commitments. News is considered a "turn off" by many contemporary hit radio programmers who want to keep music interruptions to a minimum. If news is programmed on contemporary hit radio stations, news must be short and deal with issues with which young listeners can identify. Some news topics are music groups, clothing styles, entertainment trends, and youth oriented politics and issues.

COUNTRY AND WESTERN (C&W)

There are actually two country and western music formats: country rock music and country blue grass music. Both country formats are often programmed on AM radio stations because country music listeners tend to be older and more conservative. However, country-rock has been programmed successfully on FM stations.

Country music listeners have greater news desires and commitments than AOR listeners. They prefer standard news with a strong emphasis on local and regional events. Straightforward writing and delivery are the most acceptable.

If country and western stations are network affiliates they tend to prefer the traditional networks of NBC, CBS, RKO II, MBS, and ABC's older targeted networks: American Information or American Entertainment.

MIDDLE OF THE ROAD (MOR)

Middle of the road music formats have broad target audiences in the 25 to 54 age group with secondary listening groups between 18 and 34 years of age. MOR listeners have older audience demographics and MOR formats are generally on AM stations, although some MOR formats are programmed successfully on FM stations.

Since MOR listeners are older and somewhat traditional, they have high news desires and commitments. News, for some MOR listeners, may be the deciding factor on which station they select. MOR audiences tend to want standard news with international and domestic content. Straightforward writing and delivery styles are preferred.

MOR stations which are network affiliates tend to join NBC, CBS, RKO II, and ABC Information networks. UPI audio and AP radio are also common on MOR stations.

RADIO NEWS FORMATS

Devising radio news formats depends on a number of station and competitive factors. The major factors which will affect news policies will be the station's music format, network affiliation, and length of newscasts.

As was discussed earlier in this chapter, music formats will affect news style and presentation. Music formats are designed to attract specific demographic groups, and most station managers demand that their news programming fit with the music policy and be targeted to the station's desired audience. Presenting national political and economic news in a straightforward writing style and delivery would probably turn off young adult contemporary hit music listeners. News selection, writing and presentation must fit with the station's overall sound, which is designed to attract certain demographic groups.

Network affiliated radio stations generally avoid covering national or international news unless there are local angles. Network news departments have vast resources and provide excellent national and international coverage, leaving local affiliates free to concentrate on local and regional news. Network news also adds a strong degree of credibility for some listeners and this provides a halo effect for local news departments.

Being network affiliated also creates some problems for local news departments, and local managers must decide where to position their own news and how much local news is needed. If network news is taken at the top of the hour, one solution is to offer five minutes of local news at the bottom of the hour.

:00
:05
NETWORK NEWS
MUSIC
MUSIC
LOCAL NEWS
:35
:30

This format balances news at the top and bottom of the hour with two identical music segments following network and local news. However, some programmers do not like to break their music format twice an hour and prefer to have two- or three- minute local newscasts immediately following network news.

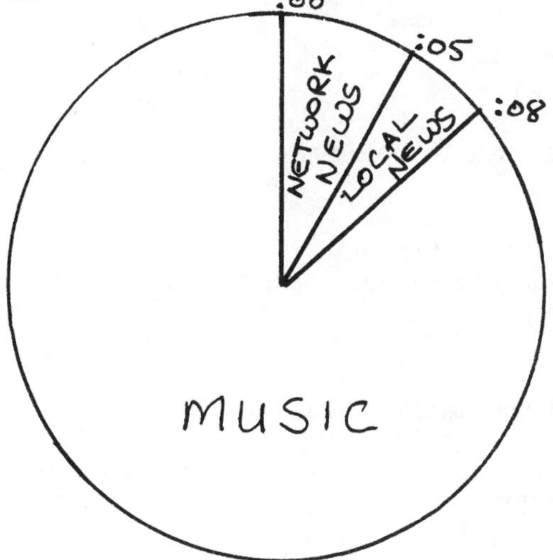

Research has shown that most radio news listeners want news at the top of the hour and find it irritating to have to search for news at other times. Keeping news lumped together at the top of the hour fits in with most news listeners' wishes, but it does create a seven- or eight- minute break in music which can lead other people to get news-weary and tune to other stations.

The most widely used radio news format presents news in order of importance rather than by particular category, such as national/international or local/regional. Except at all-news radio stations, most newscast lengths are five minutes or less and stories are organized by importance. It would not be unusual to lead with a major weather story if that happened to be the major story of the hour. Analyze the organization of the following five- minute CBS network newscast, in example 8-1.

Most newscasts are put together in approximately the same way. Using the CBS radio newscast as an example, newscasters or producers would first determine how much time is available for news--commonly called the *news hole*. This is done by determining how much

EXAMPLE 8-1

CBS RADIO NEWS
(2:00 p.m. News, January 17, 1982)

Story	Time	Lines
Open and Audio tape story of recovery of Air Florida victims in Washington, D.C.	:40	11
Britain announces increase in Boeing 737 jet takeoff speed in icy weather	:15	4
COMMERCIAL	1:00	
Record cold in upper midwest	:20	4
Audio tape story of Colorado winds knocking down power lines	:40	12
Poland and martial law	:30	8
COMMERCIAL	1:00	
Singapore starts compulsory religious training in schools to reduce crime	:25	7

time will be deleted from the allotted five minutes for commercials, open and close. In the CBS news example, time deleted for an open, close, and commercials would be approximately 2:10, which leaves a 2:50 news hole. At a standard reading rate of 15 lines per minute, newscasters can use 45 to 46 lines of newscopy. The CBS newscaster or producer probably considered ten to twenty different stories before finally settling on the six stories used. The producer probably first decided to use the two audio tape stories and then fit the remaining stories into the newscast. The combined time of two tape stories is 1:20, which leaves 1:30 remaining for other copy stories. The producer then probably assigned various times or line counts to each copy story to make sure that their total time would not exceed two minutes. Each copy story was then written and edited to fit the allotted number of lines. Each story's potential interest and the amount of information available dictated the number of lines assigned and the serial order of presentation. Another factor which would affect the order of presentation was the attempt to keep related stories together, such as the Air Florida crash and Great Britain's action increasing the take-off speed of Boeing 737's in icy weather. The tie between the stories is that the Air Florida jet which crashed into the Potomac River on take-off from National Airport because of ice buildup on the plane was a Boeing 737. Two other related stories are cold temperatures in the upper midwest and warm winds in Colorado which blew down power and telephone lines.

RADIO NEWS FORMULA

News consultants often deny they have a set formula for radio news. They say each market is different and market research dictates what is recommended to each client. This is true because each market has different characteristics which are found through research. However, examining the recommendations of news consultants indicates there is a radio news formula with three basic elements. The three elements are: (1) use many short stories, (2) use many short audio tape actualities and voicers, and (3) use human interest stories that will get listeners emotionally involved.

In an average five minute local newscast, minus time for open, close and commercials, the news hole is only 3:30. Some consultants recommend this time be filled with a minimum of ten to twelve news stories, each story no longer than twenty seconds. Consultants say research shows that people who listen to radio news want to hear headlines about what is happening without much detail. If greater depth is wanted, consultants say listeners will turn to television or read newspapers for the complete story.

Most newspeople argue that a twenty-second time limit leads to a series of shallow headlines without sufficient background information to explain why. They say that twenty seconds is not enough time to tell stories about city council actions or rezoning hearings.

Despite the disagreement between newspeople and news consultants, the argument seems based more on principle than practice. Most radio news stories are short. They range in length from twenty to forty-five seconds and rarely run longer than one minute unless they are breaking stories of great interest. The argument comes down to whether or not radio news consultants should set arbitrary time limits on stories. Newspeople say they should make news decisions based on their knowledge of the community and importance of news stories and not by arbitrary time limits set by researchers or consultants who are not familiar with the community.

Few newspeople would argue against the radio news consultants' second recommendation calling for the use of audio tape. Radio newspeople have known for years that news listeners like to hear news being made through actualities and voicers. Audio tape also adds a professional sound to newscasts and builds strength and credibility in news operations if used correctly. Some stories are important enough to warrant actualities or voicers and the use of audio tape enhances the immediacy and importance of news events. Problems occur when pressure is put on news departments to get voicers and actualities even if stories do not warrant the use of audio tape. The pressure to come up with audio tape has led to instances where stations have run poor quality tapes or have used interviews which were garbled or incomprehensible. One station put together a story about a newsperson making a long distance call and getting a wrong number. The newsperson taped the wrong number interview and put together a forty-five second story that had limited news value. (The tape also clearly indicated the newsperson was recording before getting permission, which is against the law.) Some questions asked in the no-news-value story were:

How's the weather?

Do you often get people making wrong number calls?

Other news managers, feeling pressure to get voicers and actualities, encourage their newspeople to cheat. To add an "on the scene" flavor to stories, newspeople inside the station telephone the newsroom and have their copy stories audio taped so they sound like voicers called in from the scene of a news event.

Every day news editors face decisions on whether or not to run marginal actualities and voicers in place of copy stories. As the Associated Press studies indicate, the correct decision is to use audio tape only if it is technically good and enhances the story. The AP studies give news editors a basis for arguing against using audio tape just to use audio tape. Unfortunately, some newspeople under great pressure from management and consultants feel forced to run marginal audio tape stories just because it fits into the radio news formula.

The third element of the radio news formula is the use of humor and human interest stories. Humor and human interest can be used for a change of pace or to end newscasts in an upbeat mood. Most people like to laugh or hear of an amusing story with human interest. Humor and human interest stories provide welcome breaks when all of the news seems grim and newspeople and news listeners need to smile or recognize the importance of the human spirit. Humor and human interest stories have a definite place in news but these stories should not be allowed to dominate or replace legitimate news. Some news directors say researchers and consultants forget the purpose of news and want to insert too many human interest stories in newscasts.

TELEVISION AND CABLE NEWS

While radio news has contracted to short newscast formats, local television and cable news must be considered the growth area of broadcasting because of major time and personnel expansions. Newscasts continue to get longer (usually in thirty-minute increments) and television news departments continue to get larger to keep up with the demand for more television and cable news programming.

The expansion of cable and television news is closely allied to the creation of new electronic technologies and the use of program research by managers. The mechanical television news process inhibited television news innovation and growth. The cumbersome, slow mechanics of film production, graphics, teleprompters and alphanumeric presentation of information limited what television news could do. Film, for example, is a mechanical process that requires processing time; editing is slow and there are constant problems synchronizing sound and visuals. The mechanics of television news took so much time that story deadlines were two or three hours prior to airtime to allow time for film processing, graphics, and slide preparation. Electronic newsgathering (ENG), electronic editing, time code editing, electronic graphics, and information processing are making news departments more productive and better able to handle greater amounts of information and visuals.

Program research into television news has brought about several newsroom changes. The first change was that programmers and managers realized the untapped need for news programming. The other thing research did was provide news directors and program directors with information about the needs and desires of television news viewers.

This information, if properly used, helped news managers tailor news, sports, and weather to fit audience needs. Better targeted newscasts attracted greater audiences and, as audiences grew, so did station commercial rates until news has become the primary local profit center for most television stations. To meet this growing demand for local news, many stations have increased newscast lengths from thirty minutes to sixty, ninety, and even 120 minutes. As more program time is devoted to news, news department staffs grow proportionally in size, to keep up with increasing news programming responsibilities. Research has also shown the growing demands for softer types of news stories and news programs. News magazine programs are popular on the network and local levels. CBS News' "60 Minutes" continues to be one of the top ten rated television programs. Other networks have tried to copy the successful "60 Minutes" format with news magazine programs of their own. Locally, the syndicated "PM Magazine" program continues to be quite popular and highly rated in many American television markets. "PM Magazine" has a unique format that allows participating local stations to use their own announcers to host the program, making it appear to be a local production. Participating stations also produce segments on a regular basis which are inserted into the program.

The second change is that program consultants and researchers have become an integral part of many television and cable news operations. Sometimes the relationship between researchers and newspeople is good and at other times it is strained with hostility. Some stations and television groups have hired their own researchers to assist news directors and managers in program decision making. Most television news operations have used researchers or program consultants and many stations retain consulting firms on an annual basis. The highly competitive nature of television and cable news and the large profits which can be made with news programming has created a climate where researchers and program consultants are very important to managers.

The third change brought about by consultants was the creation of integrated television newscast formats which replaced the old block format. Integrated newscasts are complex and need to be carefully coordinated. This resulted in the need for local television news producers who became responsbile for organizing and constructing sophisticated *Eyewitness* and *Action* news formats.

BLOCK FORMATS

The simplified block formats in television news were rigidly organized into content blocks of sports, weather, national/international news and local/regional news. See Example 8-2. The *15-5-10* segmented blocks were relatively easy to put together and, in most instances, there was no need for a producer or format sheet. The three blocks, fifteen minutes of news, five minutes of weather, and ten minutes of sports were divided by commercial breaks. Commercials also divided the fifteen-minute news block into six minutes of national/international news and six minutes of local/state news. Block organization also led advertisers to sponsor various blocks inside newscasts. For example, an advertiser sponsoring the weather block would get an opening billboard, closing billboard and one commercial. Advertisers usually got reduced commercial rates for purchasing the total weather block and there were added inducements of full sponsorship and recognition and free commercial mentioned in the opening and closing billboards.

Because newscasts were blocked out by commercials, news, sports and weather segments were produced individually and newscasts were not treated as one cohesive unit. News, sports and weather people wrote and produced their own particular segments without consulting each other because there was no particular need for close coordination. Each person knew how much time needed to be filled in each block. Television studio directors coordinated transitions from each block to another and monitored time to make sure newscasts ended on time.

The block or segmented newscasts were not designed to hold viewers throughout newscasts and about halfway through, just after most viewers heard the weather, a significant number of people turned off their sets and went to bed. This tune-out obviously reduced the value of commercial time in sports segments and in programs following late

EXAMPLE 8-2

TELEVISION BLOCK FORMAT

START TIME	EVENT	EVENT TIME	TOTAL TIME
11:00:00	Commercial	1:00	1:00
11:01:00	NEWS - national/international	6:00	7:00
11:07:00	Commercial	1:00	8:00
11:08:00	Commercial	1:00	9:00
11:09:00	NEWS - local/state	6:00	15:00
11:15:00	Commercial	1:00	16:00
11:16:00	WEATHER	2:00	18:00
11:18:00	Commercial	1:00	19:00
11:19:00	WEATHER FORECAST	1:00	20:00
11:20:00	Commercial	1:00	21:00
11:21:00	SPORTS	4:00	25:00
11:25:00	Commercial	1:00	26:00
11:26:00	SPORTS	3:00	29:00
11:29:00	Commercial	1:00	30:00
11:30:00	TONIGHT SHOW, NIGHTLINE, or LOCAL PROGRAMMING		

evening newscasts. For years, NBC-affiliated stations had a definite advantage because the "Tonight Show" with Johnny Carson had a loyal audience that watched through the sports block. The other networks tried to combat tune-out problems with various programs, but ABC's "NIGHTLINE" is the only other successful late night network program following late news.

INTEGRATED NEWS FORMATS

One method devised by local stations to combat viewer tune-out was to go to an integrated newscast format which was less rigid and not organized into specific content blocks. Newscasts are carefully organized so that commercials do not segment sports, weather, national/international news and local/state news. News, sports and weather segments are organized to flow into each other without giving viewers logical places to tune out. And news, the common denominator which draws most people to newscasts, is carefully organized throughout the newscasts. There is even a short news segment between weather and sports and a short news segment following sports to close out the newscast. A simplified integrated newscast format would look like the following:

NEWSCAST OPEN

NEWS (major news segment)

SPORTS

NEWS (short segment transition from sports to weather)

WEATHER

NEWS (short segment to close out newscast)

Integrated newscasts are designed to flow together as one tightly constructed program instead of three separate units divided by commercial breaks.

The NEWS 5 FORMAT sheet uses abbreviations or television news production jargon common in broadcasting.

FONT Font is the abbreviated term for vidifont, which is a type of character generator. Font has come to mean alphanumeric information, such as names, locations, or telephone numbers superimposed over the television picture. See for example, Exhibits 8-2 and 8-3.

FIB Font in Box. This newscast uses a television monitor to present visual information rather than chromakey. The monitor is commonly called a box. FIB means fonted visual material in the box or television monitor.

LOGO Logo traditionally means the newscast logo. See, for example, the NEWS 5 logo in Exhibit 8-2 which is fonted over the long shot of the news set.

BUST Bust is the term for head and shoulders shot (a bust shot) of a person.

2-C Is a production direction to the studio director for a two shot of the two people sitting in the center of the set in preparation for a transition between news announcers.

2-L Is a production direction to the studio director for a two shot of the two people sitting on the left side of the set in preparation for a transition between the news announcer and the weather announcer.

EXAMPLE 8-3

DAY/DATE Nov 17, 1981 NEWS 5 FORMAT PRODUCER ZUCKER

PAGE # ONE DIRECTOR LEENDERS

PAGE	ANCHOR	VISUAL	FONT	FIB	STORY SLUG	TIME	SOURCE	BACKTIME
1	STEVE	LOGO			HEADS			
1A	THERESA	LOGO			HEADS			
1B	2-C	LOGO			HEADS END			
					PSA/ID/OPEN ROLL		V/B OPEN ROLL	
2	2-C	LOGO			HELLOS	:05		
3	STEVE	CITY HALL	X		CITY COMM/UTILITIES	:15/	1:55 PKG SCHRACK	
4	STEVE	ADMIN BLDG	X		COUNTY COMMISSION	:20/	:30 VO/BITE	
5	STEVE	BUST	X		GHETTO RAPIST	:15/	1:30 PKG ODONNELL	
6	THERESA	BUST			EMERGENCY SPENDING	:20		
7	THERESA	BUST			FARM BILL	:20		
8	THERESA	LOGO	X		ARMS LIMITATIONS	:20/	:30 BITE	
9	THERESA	LOGO			TAG	:10		
10	STEVE	STOCKMAN			REAGAN ON STOCKMAN	:20		
11	STEVE	AFL-CIO			AFL/CIO CONVENTION	:20		
12	THERESA	USSR	X		TECHNOLOGY SALE	:15/	2:00 PKG	
13	THERESA	REAGAN			VENEZUELAN PRES.	:20		
14	THERESA	RICHARD ALLEN			ALLEN INVESTIGATION	:20		
15	SET		X		SET TEASE	:05	BUMP SET	
					PSA	1:00	FILM	

EXAMPLE 8-3, continued

DAY/DATE Nov 17, 1981 NEWS 5 FORMAT PAGE 2

PAGE	ANCHOR	VISUAL	FONT	FIB	STORY SLUG	TIME	SOURCE	BACKTIME
20	THERESA	LOGO	X		CROSSROADS CHURCH	:15/2:25	PKG	
21	THERESA	BUST			SCHOOL PRAYERS & LUNCHES	:20		
22	2-L				WEATHER INTRO	:15		
23	NORA	WEATHER	X		WEATHER	2:30	CUR, SAT, LOWS, SL, VIDEO	
24	2-L				WEATHER PITCH	:15		
25	STEVE	TAXES			STATE SALES TAX	:20		
26	STEVE	FLA			FLA BUDGET CUTTING	:20		
27	VIDEO		X		VIDEO TEASE	:05	BUMP VIDEO	
					PSA	1:00	FILM	
30	STEVE	ANDERSON	X		ANDERSON PRESS CONF.	:20/:30	VO/BITE	
30A	STEVE	"			TAG	:10		
31	STEVE	BUST	X		SLEEPING	:20/:40	VO/BITE	
31A	STEVE	"			TAG	:10		
32	2-R				SPORTS INTRO	:14		
33	BRUCE	SPORTS	X		SPORTS	4:30		
34	2-R				SPORTS PITCH	:15		
35	THERESA	PRISON	X		PRISON MEDICAL CARE	:15/1:30	PKG	
36	2-C	LOGO			BYES/CREDITS	:35		

2-R Is a production direction to the studio director for a two shot of the two people sitting on the right side of the set in preparation for a transition between news and sports.

BUMP Bump is the term for fonted material which bumps or promotes a story coming up in the news.

TEASE Tease is a term for verbal material presented by one of the studio announcers promoting some story coming up in the newscast.

TIME This particular news operation uses a method to indicate script and video tape time. In Example 8-3, page 35, the time is listed :15/1:30. This means the package is 1:30 long and the studio announcer's live opener script is :15 long. Total story time is 1:45.

News stories are presented in order of importance rather than in clearly defined national/international and local/regional news blocks. Some stations also use an organization with two news segments; one at the beginning of the newscast and the other at the end of the newscast. In effect, weather and sports are surrounded by news. To keep viewers throughout the newscast, the two news segments are carefully balanced with content and visuals. The end news segment contains major stories, although there is usually an emphasis on human interest or feature material. In the first news segment, newscasters tease or promo upcoming visual stories in other news segments, hoping to hold viewers and reduce tune-out after weather.

Integrated newscast organization also means more money for stations because nonsegmented newscasts do away with full sponsorship of news, sports, and weather segments. Commercials are sold individually and advertisers cannot get reduced rates for second commercials. Commercial lead-ins are eliminated and if advertisers want billboards they are sold as separate commercial positions. Because national/international and local/regional news is not segmented, participating commercials can be inserted at any point. From a strict profit and loss sheet view of news, integrated newscast formats are the ultimate commercial vehicle. Commercials can be inserted anywhere without breaking newscast flow (except, of course, between news, weather, and sports segments) and the number of commercial minutes in the newscast can be increased by as much as twenty or thirty percent. Some stations have been known to run as much as eleven commercial minutes in a thirty-minute newscast.

The decline of full sponsorship for news, sports, or weather segments has been a positive move for most news departments. Some advertisers felt that full sponsorship gave them some editorial control over news content and an occasional news story about their business or product was demanded. This frequently led to confrontations between sales and news departments which could only be settled by the general manager, who traditionally came from sales. Reporter-writers quickly learned to avoid certain types of stories that might create problems. For example, writers in one news department, where one newscast was sponsored by a natural gas company, avoided referring to the causes of fires or explosions where natural gas was suspected.

Integrated newscast formats also demand greater organization and planning for transitions to avoid places where tune-out can easily occur. See Example 8-4. Transitions must be done quickly, naturally and maintain audience interest. The theory is that by getting into stories quickly before people have a chance to tune out, their interest will be piqued and they will remain viewing.

NEWSCAST FORMATS

The specific integrated newscast format that a news department adopts has broad ramifications for writers, reporters, talent, editors, production staff, and audience.

EXAMPLE 8-4

TRANSITIONS (PITCHES) FROM WEATHER TO NEWS
AND FROM NEWS TO SPORTS

WEATHERCASTER ON CAMERA--TURNS AND PITCHES TO NEWSCASTER	<u>WEATHERCASTER</u>: .....AND SO BOB, YOU DON'T HAVE TO WEAR YOUR RAINCOAT OR CARRY YOUR UMBRELLA TOMORROW. WE'LL ALL HAVE A NICE DAY.
NEWSCASTER ON CAMERA	<u>NEWSCASTER</u>: THANKS RAY. THAT NICE WEATHER WILL PLEASE COUNTY FAIR OPERATORS WHO NEED GOOD WEATHER. THE COUNTY FAIR COMES TO TOWN TOMMORROW...
	(VO county fair story)
	<u>NEWSCASTER CONTINUES</u>: ...A SPELL OF
NEWSCASTER TURNS TO SPORTSCASTER AND PITCHES TO SPORTS	BAD WEATHER COULD HURT FAIR ATTENDANCE. MICHELLE...I UNDERSTAND LOW ATTENDANCE IS A PROBLEM FOR BASEBALL OWNERS AFTER THE STRIKE.
SPORTSCASTER ON CAMERA	<u>SPORTSCASTER</u>: YES BOB...ATTENDANCE IS THE BIG PROBLEM FOR BASEBALL TEAM OWNERS. PEOPLE ARE FINDING IT HARD TO GET BACK INTO THE SWING OF THINGS AND SUPPORT THEIR LOCAL TEAMS. THAT MEANS BIG MONEY LOSSES FOR...

The format will, in some manner, reflect the prevailing news philosophy at the station. This philosophy will affect the writing style, amount of time devoted to stories, types of stories covered, use of reporters live-on-set, and the type of anchors the station employs. A newscast format is the visual representation of a news philosophy and how the station management perceives its news viewers. Research has shown that certain writing styles, talent delivery, and newscast pacing have an effect on the type of people who watch various newscasts.

The major integrated television newscast formats are:

TRADITIONAL

Traditional or formal newscasts start with the assumption that news is serious and should be presented in a serious, straightforward manner. The CBS Evening News with Dan Rather is an example of a traditional newscast format. A formal writing style is used, although human interest or humor is not avoided. Traditional news formats have newscasters and reporters sitting in front of a studio camera reading scripted news without adlibs or "chatty transitions" between announcers. Newscasters maintain a business-like manner and keep themselves and personal comments out of the newscast.

The traditional newscast format was quite common during the 1950s and up through 1968. It is associated with block formats and is virtually obsolete in most local markets.

EYEWITNESS NEWS

Eyewitness news formats stress using reporters live-on-set or visually identified in video packages shot in the field. Eyewitness reporters are expected to be able to come on set and deliver live reports about various stories they covered. The eyewitness news philosophy is to show that reporters were at the scene of news events and are now telling you what they witnessed. Reporters often use personal pronouns in telling what they saw and how it affected them. Most eyewitness news sets have regular positions on set which are used by reporters who come on set live for a story.

Eyewitness news formats stress lively writing styles and some verbal interplay between reporters and newscasters. After reporters finish live reports on set it is not unusual for newscasters to ask questions about some aspect of the story.

ACTION NEWS

Action news formats are exactly what the name implies. News is fact paced, visual and action oriented. Most video news stories are between 15 and 40 seconds in length and stress eye appealing subjects. Action news formats are noted for heavy use of flashy electronic graphics and fast paced production. Video stories follow each other separated only by eye-jarring video transitions or electronic effects.

The action news writing style mirrors the fast pacing and upbeat production techniques. Writing is very crisp, stressing action words, present tense, and not much story detail. Most action news departments concentrate on action type stories and avoid local government stories because they demand detailed reporting and they are visually slow moving.

Because action news formats are fast paced, there is little time for idle chatter between announcers. Transitions are friendly but businesslike, and announcers do not insert their personalities into stories or make personal comments.

WARM AND FRIENDLY

Warm and friendly or informal formats create the image that news teams are composed of warm people who enjoy their work and working with each other. Newscasters chat with each other between stories and make personal or joking remarks to each other. A definite attempt is made to allow personalities to develop. An easygoing atmosphere is created on set.

Most consultants say this is a good format to use because their research indicates audiences want newscasters to be warm and friendly people who get along with each other.

Because of the relaxed set atmosphere, warm and friendly formats do not go well with action news formats. However, a warm and friendly atmosphere can be used quite effectively with an eyewitness news format.

TABLOID NEWS

Tabloid newscasts sensationalize news and stress lurid details of sex, crime, violence, deviance, and human interest. Tabloid formats follow the lead established by tabloid newspapers such as The Tattler or The National Enquirer.

The delivery and writing style is very upbeat and jokes, humor and double entendre are common elements. Even serious stories are treated in an offhand or tabloid manner.

Tabloid news formats do not appear to have the same broad appeal as other formats, although, initially, tabloid newscasts can draw large audiences.

TOTAL ELECTRONIC NEWS

Total electronic formats stress live coverage and have nearly all news presented live from the field. Studio announcers take on the role of electronic traffic officers directing and co-ordinating live field reports, as a network newscaster does during space shots or political conventions.

Reporter-writers, working with electronic news gathering (ENG) equipment and portable microwave units, present live reports from the scene of news events. Studio based news announcers read some stories but the majority of news is presented by reporters in the field.

Research shows the electronic format has great audience appeal and may eventually replace the warm and friendly format as being the most preferred. The excitement of live reporting is a strong audience attraction.

Total electronic news sets stress electronics. Television monitors and other electronic devices are prominently displayed. To enhance the electronic aspect of the format, monitors in the background may show reporters getting ready for live reports or count down leader.

NEWS SETS

Designing the correct news set to fit specific newscast formats and news departments needs has become a complex production problem. Several firms specialize in building news sets for news departments. There are many important things to consider when designing and constructing a television or cable news set, such as color combinations, station's use of graphics, newscast formats,and the image or mood of the newscast.

The news set must match the news format. For example, an eyewitness news set will always have a position available for reporters to use when they come on set for live reports. A stark color combination would not fit with a warm and friendly news format, which stresses a leisurely pace and a warm atmosphere.

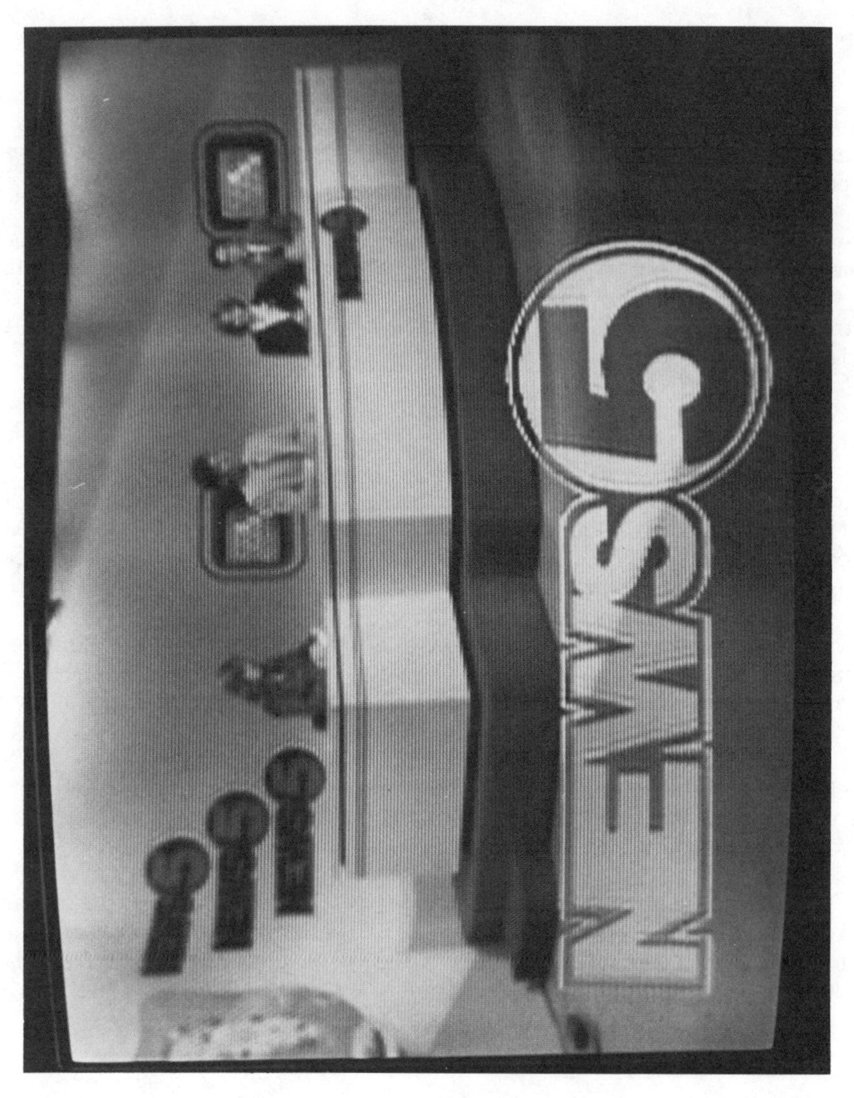

EXHIBIT 8-2. WUFT-TV news set. Note positions for tandem news anchors, sports and weather announcers.
Photograph: Courtesy of WUFT Television, Gainesville, Florida

There are three basic set designs commonly used, although the *standard news set* is preferred by most news organizations. The standard news set is designed to be a set for news productions and not give the feeling announcers are in living rooms, NASA space control, or newsrooms. See photograph 8-1. Designing a standard news set is not a simple project. Most news set designs take months of planning and may result in several models being built and examined in detail. Standard news sets must meet the needs of several station departments and an external news audience. Sets must be simple, visually pleasing, seemingly comfortable, and easy to light. Sets must support the news format and news philosophy. Sets must also accommodate the electronic news production process and the studio production process. Studio staffs must be able to easily light the news sets, get proper camera angles, and insert chromakey or electronic graphics.

NEWSROOM SET

The newsroom set has newscasters and reporters sitting in a newsroom setting during newscasts. This set emphasizes the news process and the activities and excitement of newsrooms. News viewers can see and hear wire machines, reporters typing, and police monitors in the background.

This news set has lost a great deal of appeal because it creates production problems and limits the use of chromakey which needs a blue background behind announcers. One other problem with a newsroom set is that most news functions in the newsroom have to stop shortly before and during the newscast. Studio technicians have to set microphones, get audio levels, check lights, and move in cameras. Television production people also say the newsroom format is too "busy" and may overpower newscasters or distract audiences.

NEWSCENTER OR ELECTRONIC SETS

Electronic news formats stress television and cable technology, even if the technology on set has no real purpose. Most people are fascinated by the television and cable production process, and electronic sets let people have a tantalizing glimpse of behind-the-scenes television and cable. NewsCenter and electronic news sets try to create an atmosphere of being the electronic center of the news process. Announcers on set coordinate live reports from the scene. Small monitors and other electronic devices on the set let viewers see these live reports being set up and finally introduced on the air.

It would not be unusual to hear and see the studio announcer introduce a live report from the field and simultaneously, in the background, see the reporter on a monitor. In some instances, there is verbal interplay between studio announcers and reporters in the field, emphasizing the electronic gadgetry being used.

NEWS PRODUCERS

Integrated or nonsegmented news is profitable for stations, but it is complicated to produce. Instead of news, sports, and weather people working independently of each other, they must be closely coordinated. People put in charge of organizing newscasts into desired formats are news producers. The background, power, and role of news producers vary from station to station. In some stations, news producers may have the authority to exercise news judgments as well as make production decisions. In most stations, however, producers are specifically involved with organizing or formatting newscasts into predetermined formats. News assignment editors, on the other hand, are involved with making news judgments about what is news and what will be covered by staff reporters. Producers take the stories generated by news editors and package them into cohesive news programs by making production decisions and judgments.

EXHIBIT 8-3. NewsCenter or Electronic News Set. Courtesy of WESH Television. Orlando Florida

EXHIBIT 8-4. NewsCenter 4 KOA TV, Denver, Colorado. Courtesy of KOA Television. On set, from left to right are: Sam Allred, Janet Zappala, George Caldwell and Ron Zappolo.

Good news producers have skills or abilities in three areas: news, production, and management. News producers work with news content, and they must have a strong feel for news and the importance of stories in their particular market. News producers rely on news decisions made by news editors, but they must also have news judgment, because production decisions ultimately affect news content. Producers must, by the very nature of their jobs, have solid production skills and understand what can technically be done. Along with technical production skills, producers must have a "feel" or instinct for pacing, mood, and organization. Producers must also be managers, because they bring together and manage the people and technical resources that make up newscasts. They are responsible for blending the talent, commercials, news, sports, and weather into complete newscasts. The hardest part of any management job is dealing with people, especially talented people who have large egos. Producers must be superb negotiators to get what they want without destroying important working relationships.

Despite the seemingly great latitude of producers, they work within confining circumstances. Many constraints within which producers work have already been predetermined by news and production managers. For example, the length and time of newscasts, styles of delivery, specific formats, news philosophies, production equipment, and personnel available are all predetermined and producers must work within these confines. Within these predetermined elements, though, producers do have exciting and creative jobs.

Most producers start their days out in pretty much the same way. Producers for early evening newscasts usually start working three to four hours before airtime by obtaining a copy of the daily station log. The log indicates exactly what time the newscast goes on the air and the number and length of commercials scheduled for the newscast. These two elements allow producers to figure out exactly how much time they have for news, sports, and weather. Even though newscasts generally go on the air daily at exactly the same time, there are certain minor time differences caused by special network programs or the number and length of commercials scheduled immediately prior to news. The commercial load inside newscasts can vary from day to day. Since weather and sports are already short segments, commercial loads have the most direct bearing on the news hole, or amount of time available for news.

Once producers determine how much time is available for newscasts, their next step is to become familiar with the day's news. Producers read wire copy, examine assignment boards and discuss news assignments with news editors. At this point, producers should have a pretty good idea of which stories will be packages, voiceovers, soundbites, or readers. With help from news editors, a tentative story order can be roughed out and decisions can be made about which stories can be paired because of similar content, geography, or visuals. Sometimes two or three reader stories can be paired with a video package and the result is one major strong story with three different angles rather than three individual news stories with moderate importance. These tentative decisions must be made before scripts are written and video tapes edited, because story order and pairing can affect content. For example, a reader news story may be written differently if it is part of a video package. Tag lines for one story may also serve as transitions or lead-ins to other stories. Writers can also coordinate scripts to reduce unnecessary repetition. If the lead to one story explains something, then leads or scripts of related stories do not need to contain the same information and can be cut down or used to relay other important information.

Producers next evaluate packages, voiceovers, soundbites, and readers to determine how much air time should be allotted to stories to be included in newscasts. These are always tense moments, because some reporters will feel their stories are more important than other stories and should be placed higher in the newscast to get more air time. Many reporters fail to get an overall view of newscasts and they tend to rate their stories as more important than they really are. Producers and news editors must retain an overall view, and, through negotiation, arrive at a firm story order with specific times allotted to each story. Because television is a visual medium, visual stories will get the greater percentage of air time. Producers must also pace and visually balance newscasts. Visual stories are balanced against readers to avoid stacking all visuals or readers together causing the newscast to move very quickly and then dragging through the nonvisual or reader stories.

Deciding on exact story placement does not totally depend on respective story importance or strength. Producers may change story order to avoid production problems, balance pacing, group together related stories, or strengthen the end segment of the newscast. It is not uncommon to take the second or third strongest story and move it to the second news segment or end of the newscast. Placing strong visual stories throughout the newscast can reduce viewer tune-outs if stories are strongly promoted during the newscast with bumps and/or promos.

Once story order and times are determined, producers construct format sheets following predetermined policies. Format sheets vary from station to station and producer to producer. Format sheets must, however, carry enough information for production and news staffs to do their respective jobs. Once a format sheet is completed, it becomes the program log for the newscast and everything done during the newscast is coordinated by the format sheet. Most format sheets list events, anchors, visuals, fonts, story slugs, event times, sources, and total times or backtimes.

The NEWS 5 television news format sheet (Example 8-3) is for a standard integrated newscast. Copies of the format sheet are distributed to news and production staffs. Film chain operators use format sheets to load slides and commercial films in order. Video tape operators will make sure their news video tapes are stacked in correct order for playback. When all news scripts are finished, producers and studio directors compile their scripts in order according to format sheets. Errors occur when someone deviates from the format sheet order or makes changes without making the changes on all the format sheets. Everything is carefully checked and rechecked against format sheets to prevent such production disasters as out-of-order scripts, video tape, or slides.

There is one major difference between numbering radio news stories and television news stories. Television news stories, no matter how many pages long, are given unit or page numbers that correspond to numbers on format sheets. No matter how many pages the story actually runs, the page number remains the same. In Example 8-3, page 3 on the format sheet, the CITY COMM/UTILITIES story, actually runs three pages long. Pages are numbered 3-1, 3-2 and 3-3. This page or unit numbering system ensures that everyone has the same number on every news story, and it also makes it easier for producers to keep newscasts on time. Toward the end of newscasts, when time is getting critical, producers will start deciding whether or not to cut news stories so the newscast will end on time. If the newscast is running longer than it should, producers will wait until the studio director gets into commercials or video packages and tell everyone on the intercom to delete a specific story. To avoid confusion, producers refer to stories by page or unit numbers. For example, if the NEWS 5 newscast was running 1:30 long, the producer would tell everyone to delete page/unit 35. Everyone would pull page 35 even if page 35 is a three or four page story (page 35-1, 35-2, 35-3) and there would be no confusion.

ENG CO-ORDINATORS

Working closely with producers and news editors, in stations with live capabilities, are ENG co-ordinators. The live capabilities of news teams in the field have expanded both the producer's and news editor's jobs beyond most people's capabilities. Hard-working news editors or producers simply do not have the time to co-ordinate live coverage.

The ENG co-ordinator's job is between production and news editing, because the job involves news judgments and production skills. If there will be live reports inside newscasts, producers will block out necessary time for the report and leave the details to ENG coordinators who act as assistant producers. ENG co-ordinators arrange and organize microwave equipment, personnel, timing, communications, and backup for the live insert.

ENG co-ordinators also become involved with content when news crews in the field send video material back to stations via microwave. Throughout the day, crews in the field obtain interviews and cover video for various stories. To avoid everyone arriving at the station at 4:00 and six or eight crews trying to write and edit stories at the same time, material can be microwaved back to the station throughout the day. Writers and video editors in the station can start writing and packaging stories earlier in the day and reduce traditional "air time" panic and confusion two hours prior to air time.

TELEVISION NEWS FORMULA

NEWS ANNOUNCERS

The television news formula is more complex than the radio news formula and it is heavily weighted toward news announcers or air personalities. The dominant news station will have dominant air personalities in the news, weather, and sports.

Researchers interview news viewers in markets about their preferences in news, weather, sports, sets, formats, news content, time of news presentation and, most importantly, news talent. Results of the interviews are analyzed and news, weather, and sports announcers in the market are compared and contrasted. Consultants may recommend replacement of certain personalities and will, in most instances, be able to recommend replacements who are available in other markets. If station managers refuse to replace air personalities, consultants may video tape the competition's air talent and show the video tape to station managers in other markets who need announcers. Consultants work in many television markets and one way of improving a bad competitive situation is to find the competitor's successful announcer a job somewhere else. A number of news, sports, or weather announcers have had good job offers come in when they were not actively looking for other jobs.

Another way of improving talent situations is to get training or coaching for air personalities who need help. Several consulting firms coach studio announcers on stage presence or dramatic techniques.

There are several other factors in the television news formula, but dominant announcers can overcome weaknesses in set design, writing, or editing. All elements in the television news formula are important but, by far, the most important decision is the choice of news announcers.

TANDEM ANCHORPEOPLE

Consultants generally recommend using tandem news anchors in newscasts. Tandem anchor formats utilize two news announcers who provide viewers with visual and personality changes. Some stations make definite attempts to balance sex, race, and age of tandem news anchorpeople. Tandem use of announcers should not lead to segmented news content with one person doing national/international and the other person doing local/regional news. Newscasts should remain integrated with newscasters alternating every two or three stories. Despite tandem formats, there can be only one dominant newscaster and this person should handle major stories and dominate the team by being psychologically heavier or more aggressive.

NEWS FORMAT

The warm and friendly format is usually recommended by most news researchers or consultants. Consultants say it is important to develop a warm and friendly team atmosphere by having announcers engage in casual conversation between stories or transitions between news, weather and sports segments. The ability to act spontaneously during transitions and carry off transitions is very important in establishing a warm and friendly mood.

Other recommendations include making greater use of field reporters for "in studio" live reports or live reports from the field. Using live reports builds credibility. Such reports stress immediacy of news events and the fact that the station has the electronic capabilities to cover live news anyplace in the community. Live capabilities and helicopters can be important news gathering tools and they also have promotional value with audiences.

Bringing reporters on set for special reports also creates possibilities for initiating regular consumer or news product features, environmental reports, or an action reporter. Not only does this provide visual change but news viewers feel the person knowing most about the story is doing the reporting. This also has the added advantage of allowing stations to groom potential air personalities by giving them constant exposure to news audiences and building credibility and viewer recognition.

WEATHER

Many television news consultants recommend using radar weather and meteorologists as weather announcers. Aside from its utilitarian aspects, radar weather is highly visual and it holds fascination for most viewers. Audiences also perceive radar weather programs to be more accurate than weather segments not using radar weather, because radar clearly shows rain squalls, thunderstorms, and/or turbulent weather. Radar weather should be aggressively promoted because of its strong audience appeal.

Meteorologists who generate their own weather predictions have great audience credibility. This is probably quite important to people in areas of the country where major storms, tornados, or dangerous weather occur frequently. However, even in moderate climates, trained meteorologists doing weather have strong promotional value.

NEWS SETS

Another important element in the news formula is the news set. Most consultants say news sets should be distinctive and modern looking. Sets should also be able to show all announcers interacting and give the feeling that the news team is together and not separated, which promotes the team atmosphere. Stark colors should be avoided. Commonly used colors are tans and beiges, which tend to be softer and more relaxing.

Consultants also recommend that stories be kept short, with video package stories rarely running longer than ninety seconds. Most voiceover or soundbite stories should run fewer than forty-five seconds and readers should not be longer than twenty seconds.

Other promotional aspects of the formula include a short news break during prime time which will promote the station's strongest video stories. During newscasts, consultants recommend an aggressive use of bump material, promoting stories through commercial breaks, news and sports commentaries, and editorials. Consultants also recommend a series of headlines at the beginning of the newscast and humorous or human interest stories at the end of the newscast.

QUIZ

1. Define the term "demographic." ______________________________

____

2. What are the two main reasons stations are devoting more time and resources to news operations?

____

____

3. The AP studies indicate that most listeners/viewers want more news about three areas of concern. What are these areas?

____

____

4. What is a "news hole?" How would you determine the "news hole" for a normal five-minute radio newscast?

____

____

____

5. The radio news formula that most consultants use has three elements. What are the elements?

____

____

____

6. What are the major differences between a television block news format and an integrated news format?

____

____

____

____

7. What are the major differences between an eyewitness television news format and an action news format?

____

____

____

____

____

8. What does an ENG co-ordinator do?

EXERCISES

1. Assume that you have just been employed as the news director for an album oriented rock station (or contemporary hit radio station). Your general manager wants you to make suggestions regarding news philosophy, newscast length, and newscast scheduling. Your manager also wants you to block out what a typical newscast might look like, showing types of stories you think would fit in with station philosophy.

2. For the station you selected in exercise # 1, write a three-minute targeted newscast. Try to target your writing style and content to the music listeners.

3. From wire copy of newspaper stories, select five local stories. Targeting your writing style, write the stories for an action news format and an eyewitness news format. Assume that the stories are readers and will be read by the newscaster in the studio.

ASSIGNMENTS

1. As a class project, have students do an analysis of all of the 11:00 p.m. local newscasts received in your market. Divide the class into groups and assign groups to view, time, analyze, and psychoanalyze the different newscasts and write a major report on their findings.

   From viewing the newscasts, class groups should be able to write a narrative about the station's news philosophy and format. The analysis should try to determine which audience the station is trying to attract with its news through the use of format, anchorpeople, news and weather announcers, reporters, pacing, writing, and graphics. Students should also write narrative comments regarding all of the elements and indicate whether or not they are being used to the station's best advantage.

   Reports should cover:

   Amount of time devoted to news
   Amount of time devoted to sports
   Amount of time devoted to weather
   Amount of time devoted to commercials
   Number and length of packages
   Number and length of readers
   Number and length of voice-overs
   Amount of local news vs. national/international

   In class, have people give brief summaries of their findings and chart on the chalkboard the statistical information students obtained on news, sports, weather, and commercial times.

ENDNOTES

1. Information quoted from both Associated Press studies is reprinted with permission of the Associated Press.

2. Copyright 1981. Columbia Broadcasting System. All rights reserved. CBS News-On-The-Hour format of January 17, 1982, 2:00 p.m.

9

LEGAL JUDGMENTS

Newspeople work in a legally hazardous profession. Every day, newswriters deal with stories that involve politics, controversial issues, personal attacks, defamation, invasion of privacy, trespass and constitutional rights. Newspeople, out of self defense, become well versed in mass communications law and Federal Communications Commission rules and regulations. If you are going to work in news, you had better learn the legal ground rules before some angry person teaches you right from wrong in a court of law. However, even cautious newspeople who know mass communications law and FCC rules and regulations get into trouble. They make a mistake, trust a source who had wrong information, or just get involved in a legal issue that is undergoing change in the courts. The law is a living thing that changes with the times and what is legally correct today may be changed by the courts next month. The state and U.S. Supreme Courts are constantly reviewing laws and redefining their intent and scope. For example, in the past thirty years, the laws of libel have changed significantly because the Supreme Court has redefined, on numerous occasions, what is libelous behavior on the part of the news media.

FIRST AMENDMENT

Journalistic freedom in the United States rests on First Amendment guarantees. However, First Amendment applications to broadcast news are confusing and contradictory even though the First Amendment seems rather specific in its intent. The First Amendment reads:

> Congress shall make no law respecting an establishment of religion, or prohibiting the free exercise thereof; or abridging the freedom of speech, or of the press; or the right of the people peacefully to assemble, and to petition the Government for a redress of grievances.

Strict constitutionalists say the First Amendment is very specific and means exactly what it says. It means that Congress or the courts should have no say over speech or the press. Throughout the years, though, the strict constitutionalists have lost ground and, in a series of U.S. Supreme Court decisions, First Amendment freedoms have been narrowed and defined.

There are certain First Amendment legal fundamentals about which broadcast journalists should be knowledgeable.

MARKETPLACE OF IDEAS

The real reason for the First Amendment, according to Supreme Court Justice Oliver Wendell Holmes is to ensure a "marketplace of ideas." The people who framed the Constitution and Bill of Rights, following the American Revolutionary War, were very sensitive about having their ideas suppressed. They wanted to make sure that no one in the future would be able to ban speech, press, or the right to gather in groups. The people who wrote the Bill of Rights wanted to make sure that all ideas, no matter how repulsive, would have a chance to be heard and evaluated, so people would get sufficient information on which to base their decisions.

FREEDOM OF PRESS IS NOT ABSOLUTE

The courts have ruled, throughout the years, that freedom of speech and press is not absolute and must be examined in relation to national circumstances at that moment. Justice Holmes first enunciated the "clear and present danger" test for free speech and press. It simply means that the community has the right to protect itself in the face of internal or external danger. The community or nation has a right to stop people or the news media from inciting riots or violence, divulging troop movements or classified information during war time, purveying pornographic materials, defaming individuals or groups, or violating an individual's privacy or right to a fair trial.

FIRST AMENDMENT PROTECTION EXTENDED

The courts have ruled that the First Amendment applies equally to all media. People who pass out handbills or use a loudspeaker have the same rights to First Amendment protection as does the publisher of the New York Times. There is only one exception to this extension of rights.

THE EXCEPTION IS BROADCASTING

Broadcast and cable journalists do not have the same rights or First Amendment protections enjoyed by newspaper or magazine reporters. There is a double standard and electronic journalists must contend with certain restrictions or requirements that members of other news media do not.

In 1975, Chief Justice of the United States, Warren Burger, was asked in a United States Information Agency interview if freedom of the press is equally applicable to radio and television. His answer was that the First Amendment is not equally applicable. His explanation followed traditional U.S. Supreme Court thinking on this issue. Anyone can start a newspaper in any location without special permission. However, to start a radio or television station you would first need to secure a federal license to use "part of the public domain" or the airwaves. Using "public property" places the broadcaster under government regulations "which would be found unacceptable with respect to the print media."

Many of the regulations to which Chief Justice Burger referred are in the *Communications Act of 1934*, as amended. The statutes most directly affecting broadcast journalists are the "Fairness Doctrine," "Section 315," and regulations dealing with obscene and indecent language and news staging.

Most stations employ attorneys to handle legal questions or interpretations. However, in the day-to-day operations of a newsroom, newspeople are generally expected to be able to handle routine legal questions. If every time a news-related legal question arose, you called your station attorney, you would have a huge legal bill and your news would never get on the air. As a newsperson, you should be very familiar with the following aspects of mass communication law and FCC rules and regulations. Even though Congress and the FCC are considering deregulating some aspects of broadcasting, the following regulations are currently being enforced.

POLITICAL BROADCASTING

"Section 315" of the *Communications Act of 1934* is a broad provision that actually concerns political broadcasting, the "Fairness Doctrine," and "Personal Attack" provisions. The "Fairness Doctrine" and political broadcasting, while not the same, are sometimes hard to separate because politics can become a controversial issue and stories about candidates or election issues could fall under the "Fairness Doctrine."

The part of "Section 315" which deals with politics reads:

> (Sec. 315.) (a) If any licensee shall permit any person who is a legally qualified candidate for any public office to use a broadcasting station, he shall afford equal opportunities to all other such candidates for that office in the use of such broadcasting stations: provided, that such licensee shall have no power of censorship over the material broadcast under the provisions of this section. No obligation is hereby imposed upon any licensee to allow the use of its station by any such candidate.

"Section 315" is designed to prevent a station from favoring one candidate with free time or access to commercial time while denying other candidates for the office the same rights. If one candidate for office uses station facilities, all other legally qualified candidates for the same elective office must have the same opportunity to use the station.

LEGALLY QUALIFIED CANDIDATE

During election periods, many news departments try to obtain broadcast time outside regularly scheduled newscasts to present candidates talking about political issues. For example, the news department at station WXXX obtains program time to allow the incumbent Republican mayor and the Democratic opponent each ten minutes of free air time to present their platforms to the public. Another person, hearing of the proposed broadcasts by the Democratic and Republican candidates, demands air time under "Section 315" saying he is also a candidate for mayor. Does the third person get free air time along with the two other mayorality candidates? Not necessarily.

People in the news department must first determine if the third person is a "legally qualified candidate" for the office. Legally qualified candidates are people who have publicly announced they are candidates for the office; can legally serve if elected; and can get on the ballot or be legal write-in candidates for the office.

A person who walks into your station or cable operation and asks for equal opportunity under "Section 315" must act like a candidate; that is by making public announcements of candidacy. If there are specific requirements for the office the person must also be able to meet those requirements. For example, if it is a requisite that the mayor be at least 21 years old, not a convicted felon, and a resident of the city, then the person must meet those requisites to be a legally qualified candidate. The last hurdle for prospective candidates is whether or not they can get on the ballot or be legal write-in candidates. Some stations have requested that people claiming to be legally qualified candidates obtain statements or certificates of candidacy from the Secretary of State before the stations allow use of their facilities.

USE

Questions about "use" always arise in trying to understand "Section 315." The Federal Communications Commission (FCC) has determined that use means "any candidate's personal appearance by voice or image" on the station's facilities. Your station, WXXX, has an afternoon show targeted to homemakers. On the set wall are autographed photographs of prominent people who have been on the program. The incumbent mayor's photograph is one of those on the set wall. The mayor's political opponent notices the photograph and demands equal opportunity. Does the opponent get equal air time? Not necessarily, unless the incumbent mayor has personally appeared on the program, or the show host has been giving "on the air" political plugs for the mayor or the photograph has been highlighted in some manner.

Use has come to mean any personal appearance, no matter how brief or in any capacity, except for four specific exclusions. These exclusions are:

Appearance by a legally qualified candidate on any

(1) bona fide newscast
(2) bona fide news interview
(3) bona fide news documentary (if the appearance of the candidate is incidental to the presentation of the subject or subjects covered by the news documentary), or
(4) on the spot coverage of bona fide news events (including but not limited to political conventions and activities incidental thereto)

News coverage is exempted from the "equal opportunity" provisions if the political candidate appears in a newscast, regularly scheduled news interview, documentary, or on the spot news coverage in a role incidental to his or her candidacy. The mayor being interviewed about a local police strike and the actions he or she intends to take would not provide political opponents with grounds to get equal opportunities. The mayor is acting outside the candidate's role and responding to a legitimate news event as the mayor. Interviewing the mayor about campaign plans, however, would mean that other mayorality candidates could ask for and receive equal opportunity on your station.

These exclusions in "Section 315" give the incumbent office holder a distinct advantage in getting news coverage. The incumbent mayor makes news by appearing at events and has more opportunity to get news coverage because what the mayor does is news. It is not uncommon, during election times, to have incumbent office holders show up at news generating events such as important banquets, fires, accidents, or meetings and be willing to make comments about the event.

Originally, "use" did not apply to a candidate's supporters, friends, family, or campaign officials. In 1970, however, the FCC expanded "Section 315" to cover political supporters in the *Letter to Nicholas Zapple*. The *Zapple letter* enunciated what is now termed the Zapple Rule and gives political supporters of a candidate access to a station's facilities. The *Zapple Letter* says that if a station sells time to supporters of a political candidate, the station cannot deny supporters of opposing candidates the sale of "comparable" time. The letter did not take up the issue of free time for political supporters but it can be assumed that the Zapple Rule would also apply here.

EQUAL OPPORTUNITIES

"Section 315" is often incorrectly referred to as the "equal time rule" but equal time is not really required. "Section 315" calls for political candidates to receive "equal opportunities" which means a great deal more than equal time. Equal opportunities means that political candidates should get approximately the same amount of time in the same time period. Giving the incumbent mayor ten minutes of free time at 8:00 p.m. following a highly rated program and allowing the mayor's opponent nine minutes immediately after the 5:00 a.m. sign on, would not be considered to be granting "equal opportunities." The amount of time you allocated to each candidate would probably not be questioned by the FCC, because it would appear that each candidate was given approximately the same amount of time. The sticky part would be over the time period each candidate was given. "Equal opportunities" means amount of time and also the same approximate time period which would also reach approximately the same audience.

"Section 315" provides that candidates must request "equal opportunities" within seven days after the original use by another political candidate. If the mayor's opponent approaches station WXXX for equal opportunities on the ninth day after the mayor appeared on a program, the station can legally refuse the request. The station does not have to notify candidates that time has been given to political opponents; the burden falls on the candidates.

CENSORSHIP

"Section 315" forbids stations from censoring what political candidates say when candidates are using station facilities. However, the prohibition against censorship does not apply to candidates who are involved in bona fide newscasts, news interviews, news documentaries, or on the spot news coverage. For example, if a candidate for office curses or defames someone during a bona fide news interview, the station has the right to edit out the offending words. However, if the station provides candidates with free time and the candidate swears or defames someone, the station does not have the right to edit or censor the remarks. Station personnel can ask to review scripts or make suggestions to the candidate about possible legal problems, but the station cannot censor the candidate's remarks. In every instance, except political use, the station licensee is held strictly accountable for what is broadcast over the facilities.

POLITICAL DEBATES

In October, 1975, reversing earlier rulings, the FCC decided that political debates and presidential news conferences did not fall under "Section 315." Debates and presidential news conferences, according to the FCC, were "on the spot" news coverage of an event under certain circumstances. The circumstances are that to be considered "on the spot" news coverage, debates must be organized and controlled by groups or people other than the candidates and broadcasters. In other words, candidates or broadcasters cannot organize debates and then have radio, cable, or television stations provide "on the spot" news coverage and be exempted from "Section 315." But the news or programming department of your station could cover political debates sponsored by the League of Women Voters or some other political group as long as the group was not affiliated with the candidates. The station could not cover debates sponsored by the candidate or supporters without providing equal opportunities for other candidates not included in the debates.

FEDERAL ELECTION CAMPAIGN ACT

Prior to 1971, station licensees did not have to allow candidates for public office free time or the opportunity to purchase commercial time. With the passage of the *Federal Election Campaign Act*, "Section 312" of the Communications Act, was amended, and now requires "reasonable access" to broadcasting and cable by political candidates. Stations cannot ignore political races and refuse to give or sell time. Under "Section 312" stations can either sell time, give free time, or do both. If the station allows reasonable free time to candidates then commercial time does not have to be made available to candidates, and vice versa. The option is available to the station as long as political candidates have "reasonable access" to broadcast and cable facilities on a paid or free basis. What is reasonable? Although not tested in the courts, reasonability probably depends on a number of factors. What will probably affect the FCC's determination of what is reasonable is how many races are going on, how many candidates there are for each office, total number of candidates, specific political issues, and importances of individual races in each market.

Stations are also required, under the *Federal Election Campaign Act* of 1971, to charge the lowest unit price in a time period for political commercials. The station or cable operation is forbidden from charging higher prices for political commercials than they would normally charge for other commercials.

What is strictly legal and how news departments operate may vary significantly. Some stations have, for various reasons, become highly partisan in political campaigns and have even violated various aspects of "Section 315" or "Section 312." However, most stations, conscious of their public responsibility, news image, and credibility, are highly sensitive to charges of political partisanship. Strictly speaking, the mayor's opponent may not be entitled to "equal opportunity" to respond to a mayor's comment in a bona fide news interview, documentary, newscast, or on the spot news coverage. The station, however, may have internal news department policies which provide for giving each political candidate equal opportunity no matter what the circumstances or legal exclusions. Some stations even keep a political log in the newsroom with an up-to-date record of how many news minutes each candidate has received. The political log book can take the wind out of angry political candidates who charge the news department with favoring one candidate over another. The newsperson can quote the exact number of minutes and number of stories devoted to each candidate, and turn an angry candidate into an apologetic candidate.

ELECTION PERIODS

"Section 315" deals with political candidates who are running for office. If no candidates have announced that they are running for an office then "Section 315" does not apply. This is why during presidential election years there are a number of "non-candidates" who travel the country mending political fences and getting high visibility. They avoid declaring their candidacies because once they announce they are candidates then "Section 315" comes into force and equal opportunities must be given to their opponents.

THE FAIRNESS DOCTRINE

The "Fairness Doctrine" requires media access for controversial issues of public importance. It is designed to make sure that broadcasters do not become partisan and refuse to allow the broadcasting of controversial issues with which they disagree. The "Fairness Doctrine" is often treated separately from "Section 315," because "Section 315" deals with media access for politicians while the "Fairness Doctrine" deals with access for controversial issues. Even though the two concepts have different intents, in 1959 Congress amended "Section 315" to include the "Fairness Doctrine."

Historically, the idea for a "Fairness Doctrine" for broadcasters goes back to the Radio Act of 1927. The Act contained a statement that stations must broadcast in the "public interest, convenience and necessity." This statement has been interpreted to mean that a station licensee must be fair. In the 1940 Mayflower Decision, which was in response to complaints about a station editorializing, the FCC banned stations from editorializing, saying that stations did not have the right to become partisan and advocate causes. Nine years later, in 1949, the FCC reconsidered its earlier decision banning editorials and said that broadcasters did have a right to editorialize as long as the station provided time for opposing points of view. In fact, the 1949 decision put a positive burden on broadcasters, saying not only did they have a right but they had an obligation to get involved and seek out and air all sides of controversial issues in the community. Then, in 1959, Congress legislated the "Fairness Doctrine" into the Communications Act as part of "Section 315."

In "Section 315," following the exclusions of bona fide newscasts, news interviews, news documentaries, and on-the-spot news coverage, the "Fairness Doctrine" states:

> Nothing in the foregoing sentence shall be construed as relieving broadcasters, in connection with the presentation of newscasts, news interviews, news documentaries, and on-the-spot coverage of news events from the obligation imposed upon them under this Act to operate in the public interest and afford reasonable opportunity for the discussion of conflicting views on issues of public importance.

In effect, even if the broadcaster sells and/or gives free time to politicians, there is a positive burden to allow reasonable opportunity for the discussion of controversial issues. Complying with the political aspects of "Section 315" does not relieve the broadcaster of the responsibility to broadcast conflicting views on issues of public importance.

CONTROVERSIAL ISSUES

Broadcast journalists report on many issues in their community. Which ones are controversial? This is generally a simple question for newspeople to answer. Newspeople are in the community daily becoming sensitized to important controversial issues. There are probably more controversial issues in a community than there is time for broadcasting them. To determine which issues should be presented, newspeople and station representatives should be in contact with community leaders, business leaders, civic leaders and government officials. National, state or local government actions will also give broadcasters a clue to what the government feels is controversial. Local groups or organizations may contact station personnel asking for time to discuss a problem and this will bring controversial issues to your attention. What the FCC looks for in "Fairness Doctrine" compliance is a good faith effort to ascertain controversial issues of public importance. An attempt to ascertain community problem areas and air all sides of controversial issues will probably satisfy the FCC that the station acted in good faith.

PUBLIC IMPORTANCE

Part of the key to determining which controversial issues should get attention is the phrase public importance. Many issues are controversial but not all of them are of public importance. Neighbors may have a controversy over a boundary matter, pets, or maintenance of yards but these are not of public importance. Public importance implies a common interest in the matter. Determining public importance also means dealing with issues that are pertinent to your broadcast area. A rural station, covering an area with virtually no welfare recipients, might decide that welfare was not a controversial issue of public importance for their area. However, a pesticide question might be a valid issue of public importance. An urban station, however, might ignore the aspect of pesticides and concentrate on welfare fraud or some other problem that is germane to their area. Market size, economy, mix of professions and demographics of the audience will ultimately determine what issues are controversial, of public importance, and deserving of reasonable time for balanced discussion.

BALANCED COVERAGE

The aspect of balanced coverage in the discussion of controversial issues provides some interpretation problems for newspeople. The courts have ruled that balanced coverage or balanced discussion means that significant groups or populations in the community are not ignored and have a reasonable opportunity to be heard. Again, the specific population mix in the market will determine what is balanced coverage or programming. An urban station, with a forty percent black population, should be careful to reflect this significant population group in the amount of time devoted to discussing controversial issues of public importance. A rural station, with a large Hispanic population, must take care to reflect Hispanic issues of public importance in their programming.

Balance also refers to the way broadcasters provide discussion on controversial issues of public importance. The broadcaster does not have to balance every program with the pros and cons of a specific issue. However, balance must be achieved in overall programming. So a program discussing the pros of an issue should, within a reasonable period of time, be followed with a program covering the cons of the issue.

For example, Station WXXX presents a news documentary on the growing costs of defense spending and what it is doing for the regional economy and how it affects local people. The documentary does not present interviews or summarize the positions of those demanding cuts in defense spending. The program obviously presents one side of the issue. The station, however, would not be in violation of the "Fairness Doctrine" if they are planning on presenting or had presented the other sides to the issue.

Most news departments, though, are very careful to present individual programs that provide balanced coverage of controversial issues. It defuses possible complaints if each program contains balance. For example, if a newsperson obtains interviews expressing one side of a controversial issue, it does not take much time or effort to obtain opposing interviews or summarize alternative viewpoints. The presentation of opposing viewpoints sets up a conflict between people and it provides for better news coverage if differing viewpoints are expressed at the same time.

Station licensees are not exempted from providing balanced coverage of controversial issues even if one side refused to speak out. The station still has the responsibility to present balanced coverage and make sure that all sides to the issue are presented. If, for example, station WXXX presents a documentary on welfare and is unable to get a welfare recipient or social worker to respond, the station would have to use its own staff to present the opposing point of view. Failure of one side of an issue to respond cannot halt debate or discussion on the issue.

The Federal Communications Commission has usually started out with the assumption that stations are living up to their obligations under the "Fairness Doctrine" unless there is a history of violations or complaints. The FCC allows broadcasters a great degree of latitude in dealing with controversial issues and the burden of proof usually falls on the person or group complaining about unbalanced or inadequate coverage. If the FCC receives a complaint, it usually sends a letter of inquiry to the station licensee asking for a response. A full and open response to the FCC assuring the Commission that the station is providing reasonable opportunity for the discussion of the issue, with some specifics to back up your statements, will probably end the matter. Unless the individual complaint is very specific and substantiates charges that the station is not presenting balanced dicussion, the FCC will not act.

In "Fairness Doctrine" situations, the station staff does not have to turn over station facilities to advocates of controversial issues as they must do with politicians. The station licensee is responsible for what is broadcast during the presentation of controversial issues and must retain control. If newspeople feel the presentation of spokespeople is too risky for live coverage, because the event is too sensitive or emotional, they may record and edit interviews expressing each side of the issue. Staff members may decide that a particular interview is not airworthy and delete the interview as long as someone summarizes the particular position. There is no requirement that advocates must appear on the air; there is only a requirement that all sides of controversial issues of public importance are discussed; the FCC is not concerned with how or even who presents the issue.

REASONABLE OPPORTUNITY

What is reasonable opportunity to discuss controversial issues? The FCC generally allows newspeople to determine what is reasonable opportunity in the discussion of controversial issues. Reasonable opportunity does not mean equal opportunity; it means a reasonable effort to discuss all points of view of a controversial issue. It is quite common for newspeople not to give equal time to advocates on an issue. If station WXXX presents a half-hour documentary on welfare, a subsequent ten- or fifteen-minute discussion of opposing views might be sufficient. The licensee may also determine that the station has given enough coverage to an issue and decline to allow the debate to go on indefinitely. Many times, advocates feel that licensees or newspeople have prematurely cut off debate, but this is the prerogative of the station staff.

SPONSORSHIP

One other problem that has confused broadcasters is the sponsorship of controversial issues. Even if the WXXX welfare or defense spending documentaries are sponsored and a sponsor for the opposite views cannot be found, WXXX must still present programs expressing other views. Failure to find sponsorship cannot affect the discussion of controversial issues of public importance.

To this point, the "Fairness Doctrine" discussion has evolved around issues that the newsperson or licensee has chosen to discuss. Sometimes newspeople or licensees find themselves in "Fairness Doctrine" cases without any idea that they were dealing with a controversial issue. An example is the cigarette advertising controversy. Licensees never dreamed they were presenting only one side of a controversial issue by allowing cigarette advertising. The FCC ruled that, in this particular case, presenting cigarette advertising without giving time to non-smokers was a violation of the "Fairness Doctrine." Another example is the presentation of military recruiting public service announcements during the Vietnam War. Some people felt that this was presenting only one side of a controversial issue and alternative views should be presented. The lesson from both of these situations is that newspeople or licensees should not be insensitive or closed-minded about "Fairness Doctrine" complaints. Issues should be carefully examined and weighed for validity before requests for air time are accepted or rejected.

Are politics controversial issues of public importance? Yes, they are. During election periods "Section 315" governs a licensee's coverage of candidates and their supporters. During other times, the "Fairness Doctrine" may govern some of your political reporting.

PERSONAL ATTACK

When Congress legislated the "Fairness Doctrine" in 1959, it provided access for ideas. The FCC, however, became aware that there was a fault in the existing regulations that provided access for politicians and ideas but not to individuals attacked during the presentation of controversial issues. In 1967, the FCC enacted the personal attack and political editorializing rules. Specifically, when the "honesty, character, integrity or like personal qualities of an identified person or group" are attacked during the presentation of a controversial issue , the licensee has an obligation to the person attacked. Within seven days of the attack, the licensee must transmit to the person attacked notification of the date, time and place of the broadcast, a script, tape or summary of the attack and an offer of reasonable opportunity to respond to the attack.

Station WXXX covers the county fair live and during one segment of the broadcast a newsperson interviews people walking by the broadcast booth. One of the people interviewed makes remarks about the police chief's honesty and the way the police department handles drug cases. Does the police chief have a legal right to respond to the charges under the "personal attack" rules? Probably not, because the attack was not made during the presentation of a controversial issue, unless, for some reason, the county fair is a controversial issue in the community. Although the station is not legally bound to give reasonable time to answer the attack, the licensee would be wise to do so. The licensee should contact the police chief and offer time to respond in return for a written commitment absolving the licensee from responsibility in any possible defamation action. Even though the comments made about the police chief were not a personal attack, the charges might constitute defamation and the station could be held liable. A public apology by the station would not hurt, and it might mitigate damages if the police chief later files a defamation action against the station and the person who made the charges.

When licensees provide time to an individual or group to answer a personal attack, they have the legal right and responsibility to edit the response to avoid defamation or obscenity. The licensee maintains control over the broadcast and is held responsible for anything aired, since the "Section 315" political regulations are not applicable.

EXCLUSIONS

Two exclusions to the personal attack regulations are for foreign public figures or groups. Personal attacks made by legally qualified candidates, their spokespeople or supporters do not come under the personal attack section. Candidates attacking each other fall under "Section 315." Also excluded are people attacked during a bona fide newscast, bona fide news interview, and on the spot news coverage of a bona fide news event. While not required to allow access to respond in these exclusions, most news departments are only too happy to allow an individual to respond to a personal attack. In many instances the attack and the response will be run in the same newscast. This controversy or conflict not only generates interest in the news story but it also avoids favoritism charges.

Editorials and news documentaries are not excluded. If an attack is made during an editorial or news documentary the person being attacked must be warned of the attack and given reasonable opportunity to respond. The assumption is that in editorials and news documentaries, the licensee has greater editorial control than in bona fide news coverage, news interviews, or on the spot news coverage.

SEVEN DAY REQUIREMENT

The FCC enforces the seven day notification requirement very strictly and fines have been levied against stations for not meeting the deadline. The licensee should also act quickly in marginal cases because the FCC will not accept a claim that an attack was not made if there is contrary evidence. If the licensee thinks that charges or statements may have been a personal attack, it is wise to follow the notification guidelines and offer reasonable opportunity to respond.

POLITICAL EDITORIALS

There is a difference in notification requirements when a licensee endorses or opposes a legally qualified candidate. The licensee must notify the candidate opposed in the editorial within twenty-four hours of the broadcast. The notification must include the time and date of the editorial and an offer of reasonable opportunity to respond over the licensee's facilities. If the political editorial is made within 72 hours of the election, the notification must be made far enough in advance to allow the candidate time to prepare and present a response before the election.

TELEPHONE RECORDING

This legal section is crucial for radio reporters because the telephone is an important tool for obtaining interviews which will be used in the news. The FCC has specific rules for recording telephone conversations for rebroadcast:

> Before recording a telephone conversation for broadcast, or broadcasting such a conversation simultaneously with its occurrence, a licensee shall inform any party to the call of the licensee's intention to broadcast the conversation.

BEFORE

Before is the key word in this regulation because it requires newspeople to notify the other party and obtain consent before a tape recorder is used to record the conversation. This means that if you called the mayor to obtain a recorded audio tape statement for use in the newscast, it would be against the law to have the tape recorder operating before the mayor picked up the telephone and you asked for permission to record. You must inform the person you wish to record of your intent before you turn on the recorder. A good way to stay on the right side of the law is to ask for permission twice. For example:

MAYOR: HELLO.

REPORTER: MAYOR, THIS IS SUSAN CALL FOR WXXX RADIO NEWS. WE ARE DOING A STORY ON THE ZONING HEARING AND I WOULD LIKE TO RECORD YOUR COMMENTS ON THE HEARING FOR USE IN OUR NEWSCAST.

MAYOR: OKAY, GO AHEAD WITH YOUR QUESTIONS.

REPORTER: JUST A MINUTE, SIR, I HAVE TO TURN ON THE TAPE RECORDER.

(RECORDER TURNED ON AND RECORDING)

REPORTER: OKAY, MAYOR, THE TAPE RECORDER IS ON AND WE ARE RECORDING THIS CONVERSATION FOR REBROADCAST IN OUR NEWS, IS THAT OKAY WITH YOU?

MAYOR: SURE, IT'S OKAY, GO AHEAD.

The reporter requested the mayor's permission to record the conversation before the tape recorder was turned on. Once the mayor gave permission, the reporter turned on the recorder and, while the tape was recording, again asked for permission to record. Now the request and the mayor's answer will be on audio tape and provide legal backup for the reporter. The reason for backup is that occasionally people say too much during an interview (face-to-face or telephone) and later deny they gave permission or knew they were being recorded for use in a newscast. Having the request and response on audio tape would defuse this problem.

The old "beeper" warning system that required periodic warning beeps on the telephone to warn people the conversation was being recorded has been discontinued. Instead of electronic beeps, now the FCC only requires a verbal warning and obtaining permission before the conversation is recorded for broadcast.

Another aspect of the FCC telephone regulation is that you cannot telephone someone and broadcast the conversation live without first getting permission. This means that you must telephone the person first and inform them that you will call back and that you intend to broadcast the conversation. Telephone talk show hosts who occasionally telephone someone while they are on the air violate the law, because they do not warn the person and get permission beforehand.

The requirement to inform people before recording or broadcasting a conversation does not apply to station personnel or people who call into a program expecting to have their comments broadcast during a talk show. So, if newspeople at the scene of a report telephone, you need not notify them and request permission as you would have to do with someone who did not work for the station.

WIRETAPPING AND EAVESDROPPING

Occasionally during the course of a news investigation, reporters want to record information or conversations (audio or video) to provide themselves with backup material for their investigation. The material will not be broadcast but if the reporter is challenged the film or tape would provide legal support for the story. The U.S. *Omnibus Crime Control Act* of 1968 forbids wiretapping or electronic eavesdropping. Violations can result in a fine of up to $10,000 or imprisonment for not more than five years. However, the law does have a relevant exception for news investigations:

> It shall not be unlawful under this chapter for a person not acting under color of law to intercept a wire or oral communication where such person is a party to the conversation or where one of the parties to the communication has given prior consent to such interception....

In effect, the federal law makes allowances for newspeople who audio tape telephone conversations or make concealed recordings of conversations (audio or video) as long as one party to the conversation gives prior permission. Despite this federal exclusion for newspeople, at least nine states have passed laws which ban this type of recording, claiming it is an invasion of privacy. These states are California, Delaware, Florida, Illinois, Massachusetts, Michigan, Montana, New Hampshire and Pennsylvania.

NEWS STAGING

The Federal Communications Commission has been concerned with news staging and news slanting since 1939, when Orson Welles scared several million people with his news format broadcast of "War of the Worlds." People were so outraged at being duped that the FCC was pressured into obtaining a verbal agreement with the networks forbidding dramatic recreation using a news format. Both The FCC and the networks wanted to end the "War of the Worlds" controversy quickly for different reasons. The networks did not like the bad publicity and the FCC was getting into First Amendment areas where it probably had no business. Charges of news slanting and staging surfaced again in the 1960s during urban rioting. Investigations of the news staging charges exonerated newspeople of most of the charges, but the fear is still present that seemingly responsible newspeople would falsify or stage an event to get a better news story. There have also been FCC investigations into management policies which dictate biased reporting or news slanting.

The Federal Communications Commission's concern about news staging and news slanting is understandable. The problem, however, is that the guidelines on news staging and slanting are vague. Some legal experts contend they are unconstitutional and could not stand up to a First Amendment court test. Whatever the case, the FCC looks at three factors when trying to determine if news staging/slanting charges are valid.

DELIBERATE DISTORTION

The FCC is not going to get involved in matters of news judgment unless there has been a deliberate distortion. Editing a news tape or film is not slanting the news unless there is a deliberate attempt to twist the content of an interview and give a false impression and deceive the audience. The courts have consistently held that, in matters of news judgment, editors are for editing.

MATERIAL SIGNIFICANCE

The FCC is also concerned about distortion of material significance or significant matters. Twisting facts or deleting material which would change the thrust of a story would be matters of material significance. Asking demonstrators or rioters to restage something would be considered news staging because the event was significant. However, if you arrived at an event late and missed a photo opportunity with the mayor presenting a check to the United Way chairperson, it probably would not be considered news staging to have the mayor do it again so you could record the event. The event was not significant and redoing it for the cameras would not materially alter anything.

Having a radio newsperson go to another room in the station and telephone a report to the newsroom to add an "authentic" telephone audio quality would not be news staging as long as the reporter did not say the report was telephoned from the scene of the event. If, however, the reporter in the station lied and said the telephone report came from the scene, then it would be a deliberate distortion of material significance. Even though the first example was not news staging, it denotes shoddy journalistic practices and ethics.

Indicating a report was "live", when in fact it was taped or filmed, is deceptive. This is not news staging, but it is illegal under another section of the FCC regulations, which requires announcements to be made if material is recorded.

EXTRINSIC EVIDENCE

The third criteria the FCC looks for to determine if it should investigate a news staging or slanting charge is "extrinsic evidence" that the charge is true. In otherwords, the FCC, treading carefully, wants substantial outside proof that news staging or slanting has occurred. A simple charge that someone was misquoted is not substantial evidence because this charge is frequently made. An example of "extrinsic evidence" would be if newspeople at a station complained to the FCC that they were forced by the management to slant or stage news. Charges that newspeople were slanting news in return for favors, money, or jobs would also be extrinsic evidence and probably warrant an investigation.

The penalty for being found guilty of news staging or slanting is extreme: license revocation or denial of license renewal. The penalty is aimed at the licensee, not individuals in the station. If the licensee is responsible for news staging or rigging, then the FCC can deny license renewal because one of the criteria for holding a broadcast license is good character. Being found guilty of news staging or slanting would denote a lack of good character. If news slanting or staging is done without the licensee's knowledge, the FCC still has recourse if they desire to pursue the issue. The licensee is responsbile for everything that is broadcast, and the FCC can question the licensee's ability to adequately manage a station and supervise employees.

DEFAMATION

Many news events deal with controversy, crime, possible misdeeds, or unethical activities, and news reporters trying to write these stories are constantly skirting defamation. This discussion on defamation is not designed to terrify prospective newspeople, but to sensitize them to their rights and responsibilities when they deal with information which could be defamatory. Defamation can be considered a narrow line and, in some instances, to cover news adequately the newsperson has to be able to find the line and go as close as possible without stepping over. The easy way to handle stories that could lead to possible defamation actions is to ignore them. This timidity, however, will result in news audiences' not getting information they should legitimately receive. Going too far, however, can result in a law suit, and, what can be as disturbing, severe damage to a person's character or reputation. Once a defamatory attack is made on a person or group, those charges may follow them forever. There are always people who remember the charges of misconduct or illegality but not the retraction.

DEFAMATION

Defamation is injuring a person or group's good name or reputation by holding them up to hatred, contempt, or ridicule. Defamation also involves the idea of a loss of respect or confidence in which a person or group is held.

LIBEL AND SLANDER

Defamation is classified as either oral (slander) or printed (libel). Slander, or oral defamation, is usually considered a less serious offense than libel. This is because the human voice has a limited range. The slanderous remarks have a transitory quality because words, once said, are gone. Slander may also indicate words spoken in haste without real intent to do lasting harm. Libel, on the other hand, is considered more serious because people give greater credence to the written word. Printed defamation has greater circulation and words, once written down, will not disappear. There is also a lasting quality about written defamation. Libel also indicates some degree of premeditation, because of the editing and production aspects of the publication process.

Defamation over broadcast and cable facilities has been ruled, in most states, to constitute libel. The reasoning behind this decision is the wide circulation of radio, television, and cable. Even though broadcasters communicate orally, the impact of the broadcast word is much greater than that of slander uttered in a bus, office, or meeting. Research has also shown that most people hold broadcast news in high regard and consider broadcast and cable journalism credible. A few states, however, make the distinction between a defamatory ad lib and defamation read from a script, which places great weight on premeditation. The defamatory extemporaneous ad lib of a broadcaster in New York is considered slander while written defamation is considered libel.

For broadcast and cable journalists, scripted defamation will probably be considered libel and carry a greater financial penalty than slander. Defamation in a audio tape, film, or video tape may also constitute libel. Even though the courts have not ruled on this situation, evidence indicates that as long as the journalist has the legal or editorial right to edit film, audio tape, or video tape, the defamation would be considered libel. To this point, courts have not had to consider defamation in a live field news report and this legal question has still not been resolved. In the case of defamation by politicians, covered by "Section 315" regulations, broadcasters do not have the power to censor political material and are relieved of responsibility.

Newspeople should investigate and become familiar with the libel laws of the state in which they work. Even though states differ in libel definitions, there are some national guidelines. As was previously stated, libel is written defamation that injures the good name or reputation of an individual or group. Nearly all states add that the defamatory attack must be malicious or have malicious intent. To be more specific, libel is falsely accusing someone of committing a crime, having a loathsome disease, low mentality, bad motives or morals, being unchaste or dishonest, and so on.

LIBEL PER SE AND *LIBEL PER QUOD*

There are two types of libel: libel per se and libel per quod. Libel per se means libelous on the face of it. In other words, there are certain words which are clearly libelous. Examples of libel per se are criminal, pervert, common-law-wife, syphilitic, communist, Nazi, murderer, drunkard, alcoholic, drug addict, embezzler, bastard, prostitute, pimp, homosexual, etc. These words, if related to an identifiable person, would clearly damage or lower a person's good name or reputation if what is said is not true or does not fall under one of the legal defenses for libel.

Libel per quod means libel due to special circumstances; the words are not libelous on their face. Examples of libel per quod would be mixing up television visuals and reading a story about a women charged with murder while showing the visual of a local beauty contest winner. Not fully identifying a person charged with a crime could result in a libel suit from someone with the same name who is mistaken for the person named in the story. A libel suit in Kansas occurred when a station aired a birth announcement based on information released from a local hospital. An unwed mother filling out the hospital admissions forms listed a local bachelor as the father of the child. The woman's reputation was not good; she was unable to prove the identity of the father and the local bachelor sued the station for damage to his good name and reputation. Even statements made in jest can be libelous and result in libel suits.

ELEMENTS OF BROADCAST LIBEL

There are three elements that must take place before something is libelous. The elements are *publication, defamation* and *identification*. Publication, in this discussion, is used in the broad sense and means published, broadcast, or widely disseminated in some manner. The second element, defamation, is obvious because without defamation there is no basis for action because no one was damaged. Identification, however, is a fine line which can offer newspeople protection while allowing relatively wide freedom in covering and presenting news. For example, a WXXX newsperson obtains a video taped interview with the deputy director of the state's Wildlife Management Bureau about a drug related investigation. During the taped interview, the deputy director, who is in charge of 31 regional offices, says:

> WE'VE GOT A REAL PROBLEM IN TWO OF OUR OFFICES IN THE STATE. THE DRUG ENFORCEMENT PEOPLE HAVE FOUND THAT TWO REGIONAL DIRECTORS HAVE BEEN PAID OFF BY DRUG SMUGGLERS TO MAKE SURE THAT CERTAIN COASTAL AREAS WERE NOT PATROLLED WHEN DRUGS WERE SMUGGLED IN TO THE COUNTRY. THE D-E-A SAYS THESE TWO MEN GOT HUNDREDS OF THOUSANDS OF DOLLARS TO LOOK THE OTHER WAY. (He angrily shakes two files at the camera) NEXT WEEK WE'RE GOING TO FILE CRIMINAL CHARGES

AGAINST THESE TWO MEN. I'M GOING TO PERSONALLY MAKE SURE THAT RALPH JONES AND PHIL SMITH GO TO JAIL. IT'S AN OPEN AND SHUT CASE.

The statements, if not provable, are clearly defamatory. The problem the WXXX news director faces is that criminal charges have not been filed against the two men and the deputy director is saying it's an "open and shut case." If the news department runs the story and the charges are not filed, the station could be sued for libel. Even if the charges are true but for some reason the men are not arrested, tried, and found guilty, the station could be in serious trouble. In a libel action, the station does not have to prove that the interview was valid, but it must prove that the charges made in the interview are true or fall under one of the defamation defenses. The burden of proof in a libel action falls on the journalist to prove what was said was true.

Probably the best solution to this problem, until formal charges are filed against Phil Smith and Ralph Jones, is to run the taped interview but edit out the sentence identifying both men. As long as identification cannot be made, a libel action cannot be filed. Newspeople should be aware, though, that successful libel actions have been filed by individuals not specifically named in a story. If identification can be deduced or made from information in the story, the station could be sued successfully.

The problem of identification also applies to groups, businesses, or organizations. For example, the WXXX news department runs a story accusing police officers in town of being crooked and taking bribes. If the WXXX community has a large police force, individual police officers cannot sue for libel, even though they are part of the group libeled. If the police force consists of four or five people, then individual police officers may be able to bring a successful libel action. If the group is small and individuals are able to prove identification, a successful libel suit may be brought against WXXX. The size of the group does make a difference if members of the group try to prove the damaging statements affected their reputation or good name.

DEFAMATION DEFENSES

Most states recognize three defenses in a defamation action: *truth, qualified privilege*, and *fair comment and criticism.*

All state laws consider truth as a valid defense to a defamation suit. Nearly half the states also require that the charges, even if true, were made without malice. Truth is a defense if the statements are made "with good motives and justifiable ends." This means that digging up someone's past and holding the person up to possible ridicule, without justifiable ends, could still result in a successful suit being filed. (The suit might be for invasion of privacy rather than defamation.)

Courts have agreed that the literal truth of all charges need not be proven for a defense of truth. Accusing a person of stealing $3,000 might not be libelous even if later you could not prove the person took the entire $3,000. If you could prove the person took $800 and the charges were substantially true this would probably be sufficient for a defense of truth.

Absolute privilege is based on the theory that some things of public interest are more important than a person's reputation. Absolute privilege or immunity from defamation actions are extended by law or constitution to people participating in federal, state and local judicial, executive, legislative, or administrative proceedings. This protection is also extended to the official reports, records, and communications of these organizations.

Qualified privilege is granted to newspeople reporting on these judicial, executive, and legislative proceedings as long as reporting is "fair and impartial." For example, the mayor is absolutely protected from defamation actions if he slanders a person during a city council meeting. The broadcast journalist has qualified privilege if the report of the event is fair and impartial. Following the session, if the mayor makes the same statement to the news media in the hallway, the situation is no longer privileged. The mayor and the journalists who report the story may have to account for their actions without using privilege as a defense.

Many states do not extend qualified privilege to the news media in certain situations. Police blotters or daily logs may not be privileged, and reporting information directly from the police blotters may be nothing more than hearsay. A person taken into police custody may not have been charged with a crime. Reporters should be careful to distinguish among being charged with a crime, being taken into custody, and being questioned about a crime. Most state laws say that a suspect can be held for a specified period of time without charges being filed. It is permissible to report the person is being held or questioned in connection with a crime, but never report that charges have been filed until after they are filed. Report only what can be proven.

Guilt or innocence is determined by the courts, not by police, news media, or prosecutors. After a person has been charged with a crime, you can refer to the person as a "suspect," "person charged with the crime" or the "alleged burglar," etcetera. Only after a person is found guilty by the courts should you refer to the person as a burglar, bank robber, murderer, etcetera. In relation to guilt or innocence, some news departments have a policy of writing only "guilty" or "innocent" in news scripts. The news management in these departments feel that using "not guilty" can lead to errors because news writers, in a hurry, have been known to delete the word *not*, which changes the whole complexion of the story.

A defense of fair comment and criticism can only be used with public officials and public figures. This defense is intended to encourage newspeople to comment on and criticize the public actions of officials and public figures. As long as malice is not involved, newspeople can criticize plays, novels, products, sports events, discoveries, unions, government officials, businesses, demonstrators, and everyone who places themselves in the public view. Fair comment and criticism, though, stops at the private life of an individual. Calling actor Frank Jones' latest play an "atrocity commited [sic] in the name of art" is legitimate criticism of his public performance; referring to Frank Jones as an unfit father intrudes into his personal life and would not be fair comment and criticism.

PARTICIPATION

One other libel defense, not universally recognized or interpreted in the same manner, is getting the defamed individual to participate in the defamation. For example, the mayor, standing outside the council chambers after the meeting, defames a city council member during a taped interview. This information is not privileged and does not fall under a defense of fair comment and criticism. If the newsperson goes to the council member and obtains a rebuttal to the mayor's remarks this is called participation. The council member, by rebutting the mayor's defamatory remarks, gives implied consent to using the mayor's defamatory remarks as part of the story and participates in the libel. Participation is not only a good legal move, it is good news judgment to present both sides of a controversy.

RETRACTION

While not a complete defense, retraction can mitigate the amount of damages collected in a defamatory action. If a story is in error and the error is retracted and corrected immediately, this may indicate malice was not intended. However, retracting a story does acknowledge that an error was made and this may damage your legal position. A good rule is to consult your station attorney before making a retraction which might weaken your legal position. Another factor that will mitigate damages is the reputation of the plaintiff. Courts have ruled that people with bad reputations, criminal records, or low moral character may not be entitled to sue for defamation because their character cannot be damaged.

PUBLIC AND PRIVATE LAWS OF LIBEL

Since 1964, the laws of libel have been going through a continuing process of redefinition. Two libel standards have evolved based on whether or not the person involved is a private person or public person as defined by the courts.

The public laws of libel have made it nearly impossible to defame a public official or public figure as long as "actual malice" is not involved or cannot be proven. This public law of libel, sometimes referred to as the *New York Times Rule*, has extended the defense of fair comment and criticism; set national standards for libel of a public official/figure; and defined actual malice.

The *New York Times* decision expanded fair comment and criticism when journalists deal with public officials and public figures. The Supreme Court feels that erroneous statements are inevitable in free and public debate and that journalists should not be penalized for errors about public officials/figures as long as malice is not involved. Initially, the decisions only concerned public officials, but this has been expanded to include all public figures. The courts have ruled that journalists are protected if stories deal with judges, police chiefs, college students, senators, county commissioners, clerks of courts, city and county administrators, county attorneys, and candidates for public offices on all levels. When the public laws of libel were extended to public figures this opened up a new problem for journalists who had to define who was a public figure. The courts have defined two types of public figures. The first type of public figure is someone who voluntarily thrusts himself or herself into the public eye and who occupies a position of such "persuasive power and influence" as to be deemed a public fugure for all purposes. The other public figure is either voluntarily or involuntarily thrust into a public controversy and becomes a public figure in regard to a limited range of issues. These latter public figures must be treated with care because they are public figures only in specific instances. For example, someone who is socially prominent is not necessarily a public figure who is open to comment and criticism in other areas.

A public official, to sue for libel, even if the story is factually incorrect, must prove malice was present. Malice is extremely difficult to prove. Some public officials and public figures claim that the malice standard makes them fair game for flagrant abuses by irresponsible reporters. Recently, though, some public figures have sued major publications and won by proving that there was an extreme departure from normal journalistic standards or that there was "reckless disregard for the truth."

Private figures are people who have not voluntarily thrust themselves into public controversies or tried to influence matters of public policy. A private figure has no special social prominence, fame, or notoriety in the community. However, even private figures lose their protection or right to privacy if they get involved in a newsworthy event or matter of legitimate public concern. Speaking out during a city council meeting, attending a public rally, or witnessing a crime may propel a private figure into the public eye.

A private figure does not have to prove actual malice in a defamation action against a radio, television, or cable reporter. The private person need only prove that the reporter did not exercise "reasonable care" in reporting and simple negligence occurred. In other words, when reporting about private figures, you must be extremely careful and avoid any mistake which would injure a person's name or reputation.

MALICE

The 1964 *New York Times* decision defined a perplexing legal term related to defamation -- malice. The courts have ruled that malice or actual malice means the newsperson went ahead with the story with "reckless disregard of whether it was false or not." Knowing that statements are false or entertaining "serious doubts" about the validity of information or sources would constitute "reckless disregard." If a newsperson can prove that he or she exercised reasonable investigative journalistic standards and believed the information was correct, this would be a sufficient defense, because malice was not present. The plaintiff would have to prove that the journalist's actions were an "extreme departure" from normal journalistic standards to prove malice was present. In recent cases, the courts have ruled that people lodging defamation suits must have access to reporters' notes and private papers relating to the story, and can even question a reporter about private thoughts in an effort to determine the reporter's state of mind when the story was produced.

INVASION OF PRIVACY

Privacy has been defined as the "right to be let alone." Most courts will allow an individual to recover damages for a serious invasion of privacy by the news media. Privacy is invaded if a journalist publicizes an individual's private affairs with which the public has no real concern; gives a false public impression of the person; generally invades a person's right to solitude or publicizes a person's likeness or name.

Privacy, though, is a fragile commodity in an age known for quick and easy communication. Our names, bank accounts, credit background, criminal records, and other personal items are in computer storage systems waiting to be retrieved by anyone with the right computer codes. To protect some classes of citizens, some states have laws protecting the privacy of rape victims and juvenile offenders. Some of these privacy laws have been challenged by journalists who feel the public's right to know outweighs a juvenile offender's privacy. Even if there are no state laws about rape victims or juveniles, many news departments have policies against using the name of rape victims. The general feeling is that rape victims have enough problems without the news media adding to their burden by publicizing their identity.

NEWSWORTHINESS

The formulation of the *New York Times* doctrine in the area of defamation has also affected the laws of privacy. Most of the *Times* doctrine has been applied to privacy cases and courts have ruled that, if a person becomes involved in a newsworthy matter, the person loses his or her right to privacy. In effect, the public's right to know outweighs an individual's right to privacy. Even people unwittingly involved in public events lose their right of privacy. For example, a California man grabbed a woman who tried to shoot President Ford. Media attention focused on him and it was revealed that he was a homosexual. His being involved in an event of public importance opened up his private life to public scrutiny by journalists. Another example would be if WXXX television camera operator Fred Jones shoots video of a major hotel fire and shows people being evacuated from the hotel. Among the evacuees is a local businessman escorting a young woman who is married to someone else. The video tape is run in the news and it causes business and family problems for both people. Despite the damage to their private lives, becoming involved in a newsworthy event reduces their chances of successfully claiming invasion of privacy. Where newsworthiness or the public's interest is involved, truth is a defense unless actual malice is proven. Courts have ruled that even factual errors will not result in successful invasion of privacy actions if the story is newsworthy and malice cannot be proven.

Even public officials and public figures who thrust themselves into the public eye can retain a private life. Courts have held that private sexual relations, homes, bank accounts, and private letters can remain private unless they somehow become involved in a newsworthy event and the public's right to know outweighs privacy.

TRESPASS

In some instances, trespassing on private property can be an invasion of privacy. For example, a television crew taking a camera into a restaurant is asked to leave, and if the crew refuses, it could be an invasion of privacy. The television crew may go onto public property and shoot video of the restaurant from the street or sidewalk, but they can be barred from entering the private premises. Courts have ruled, however, that journalists can enter private homes or buildings as long as no one objects and they do not cause any physical damage "under common custom and usage." The "common custom and usage" phrase means that it is common for journalists to enter private premises where news is taking place, to provide a fair and accurate story, as long as nobody objects and they do not cause damage.

Generally, news reports based on public records are protected from invasion of privacy actions even if the matter is sensitive or considered private. For example, marriage, birth, divorce, court, and legislative records are public and can be used in news stories.

Television stations have gotten into trouble by using file video or general video used to provide generic types of visuals for news stories. For example, WXXX news editor Sally Reed has a controversial Equal Rights Amendment story from the state legislature but she does not have any visuals to use with the story. Reed decides to pull some file video of previous legislative hearings and uses it with the ERA story. When the story is run that night, the newscaster reads the story and mentions that a lesbian group was at the hearing supporting the passage of the Equal Rights Amendment. At that point in the story, though, the video showed Mrs. John Smith who attended a legislative session several months previously with her Women's Flower Club. Mrs. Smith, outraged at the use of her image and false impression caused by the story, decides to sue. She may have legitimate grounds for a successful legal action.

A similar problem occurred for a television station in the midwest. A major drug arrest occurred and more than sixty local people were arrested and charged with various drug related violations. A local television station sent a crew to the police station to obtain video of the arrests. Later that day, the story concerning the drug arrests was used in a newscast and the newscaster's script identified the people as being charged with various drug offenses. One of the shots, however, showed a man and his son who were at a police station to file a stolen bike report. The problem was solved with a retraction later that night but the situation could have become quite serious for the station.

OBSCENITY AND INDECENT LANGUAGE

The obscenity laws are confusing, vague, and constantly changing.

OBSCENITY

The Supreme Court, in a series of decisions indicating its frustration in trying to decide what is obscene, passed this question back to local courts. However, in doing that, the court set three criteria to help local communities evaluate potentially obscene material.

The key to two of the criteria are local standards. The work, as a whole, judged by local standards, must appeal to prurient interests and it must describe in an offensive manner sexual conduct specifically described in the obscenity statute. These criteria, sure to be redefined through court challenges, set local standards up as the determinant for what is considered obscene. A film, magazine, video tape, or book declared obscene in Boise, Idaho, might not be considered obscene in New York City.

Obscenity in broadcasting, however, is not determined by the same standards as obscenity in other media. Obscenity in broadcasting also comes under the United States Criminal Code.

Section 1464. Broadcasting Obscene Language. Whoever utters any obscene, indecent, or profane language by means of radio communication shall be fined not more than $10,000 or imprisoned no more than two years or both.

What is obscene will still vary from area to area, but broadcasters also have to deal with the Federal Communications Commission which applies different obscenity and indecent language standards. The FCC applies different standards noting that broadcasting comes directly into the home. There are four points which the FCC considers in regulating obscenity and indecent language:

1. Children have access to broadcasting and, in many instances, are without parental supervision.

2. Radio receivers are in the home where people's privacy interests deserve extra care.

3. Unconsenting adults may tune in to programs containing obscenity or indecent language without warning.

4. Scarcity of spectrum space leads to government regulation.

Recently, the FCC has stopped trying to prohibit indecent language in broadcasting. Their effort has been to channel indecent language into time periods when children are not using radio, television, or cable.

INDECENT LANGUAGE

The interpretation of what is indecent language has undergone significant changes throughout the past thirty years. As we become a more permissive society, our values change and what was not acceptable language is now commonly used by large segments of the population. In the past, the FCC has ruled that sounds of a commode flushing were "vulgar and offensive." Courts have also held that referring to a person as "damned" or the irreverent use of "by God" were profane. Double entendre or language with "indecent connotations" has resulted in convictions under Section 1464. The FCC defines indecent language as language which:

> describes in terms patently offensive as measured by contemporary community standards for the broadcast medium, sexual or excretory activities and organs at times of the day when there is reasonable risk that children may be in the audience.

The FCC has indicated that it recognizes the right of a station to present provocative or unpopular programming as long as reasonable efforts are made to protect children.

Most radio and television operators, however, will never come into conflict with FCC or courts regarding obscenity or indecent language. For the most part, broadcasters are extremely conservative about programming and avoid offending audience segments. Most broadcasters and advertisers are more afraid of public reactions to programs which might be perceived as obscene than they are of FCC actions.

However, newspeople do have to make decisions in this legal area. For example, Station WXXX covers a four alarm fire in the downtown area of the community. At one point, the fire threatens to get out of control and destroy a whole block of stores and offices. A WXXX camera operator recording natural sound picks up the fire chief yelling to his assistants, "if we can't stop it here the whole Goddamn town is going up in flames." Later, back in the newsroom the news director must decide whether to run the statement intact in the 6:00 p.m. news, edit the tape, or delete the statement altogether.

The news director has a tough decision because there are a number of areas requiring news judgment. The judgment made in the heat of the moment may not look as good several days or weeks later.

The safest decision is to obviously edit out the words "Goddamn" or not use the statement at all. The news director decides, though, that the emotion of the situation justifies using the tape. The news director decides that the statement, taken in context with the rest of the tape, is crucial to the intensity of the story. In effect, the decision is that the statement, although profane, will be used as part of the tape and will not overly sensationalize the story. Cutting out "Goddamn" would destroy the intensity of the moment.

The decision to run the tape has been made and community standards will provide the judgment on whether it was a good decision.

The news director can help mitigate the situation by having the script warn the news audience of what they will hear on the tape. Putting the comments in perspective will help the audience understand the emotions in the situation and what the fire chief was going through at that moment. A specific warning, in the fire story, would probably not be necessary if the script prepared the listener for the intensity of the situation and the seriousness of the fire.

One other important aspect of carrying a story which contains violence, nudity or indecent language is the time period in which it will be used and what audience is available to see or hear the tape. What might arouse protests at 6:00 p.m. might not even create a ripple at 11:00 p.m. For example, a late night show with an adult audience, like the "Tonight Show," has relaxed standards on what is considered obscene or indecent. Playing to an adult audience of some sophistication, Johnny Carson and his guests engage in double entendre and say things which would not be tolerated on programs run earlier in the evening.

FREE PRESS-FAIR TRIAL

The issue of Free Press-Fair Trial is the result of two constitutional protections colliding head-on. We have the First Amendment guaranteeing freedom of speech/press and the Sixth Amendment guaranteeing, in criminal prosecutions, the "right to a speedy and public trial, by an impartial jury." Over the years, the conflict has resulted in narrowing First Amendment protections for journalists wishing to report on criminal trials. In some criminal cases, such as the Bruno Hauptman, Billy Sol Estes, or Sam Sheppard trials, the news media acted in such a manner that many people seriously doubted the ability of the defendants to get a fair trial by an impartial jury. The media's reporting or broadcasting of the trial contaminated the defendant's right to a fair trial and presented a clear and present danger to the administration of justice.

CAMERAS IN THE COURT

Because of past excesses by the news media, the American Bar Association's Code of Judicial Review [Canon 3A (7)] bans radio broadcasting, television, and film cameras from courtrooms. Despite arguments that broadcast technology has improved to the point where cameras or tape recorders would not be noticed, the ABA continues to follow Canon 3A (7). The grounds are that broadcasting or recording a trial might somehow affect or inhibit witnesses, judges, jurors, and attorneys in their courtroom duties.

Despite Canon 3A (7), Florida, Colorado, Alabama, Georgia, Nevada, Kentucky, Texas, New Hampshire and Washington allow cameras and electronic recording devices in their courts under certain circumstances. In some states, coverage is dependent upon consent of all parties or the judge's discretion, on a case-by-case basis.

The Supreme Court has ruled that each state should have the option of deciding whether or not to allow cameras in the courts. The Court, though, has left a lot of questions unanswered, but it has opened up the way for states to experiment. Many states have committees composed of judges, journalists, and attorneys who formulate guidelines for trial coverage. These committees will probably help formulate guidelines for the use of cameras and electronic coverage in trials.

TRIAL REPORTING

Despite the relaxation of the ban on cameras in the courts by the Supreme Court, the Court still maintains reporting guidelines. Following the 1964 reversal of Sam Sheppard's conviction for murder, the Supreme Court ruled the original trial judge did not "fulfill his duty and protect Sheppard from inherently prejudicial publicity which saturated the community and to control disruptive influences in the courtroom. ..." The Supreme Court then set down judicial guidelines which, if not followed by judges, will result in reversal of convictions.

Judges must:

1. Sequester the jury during the trial, as well as during deliberations if broadcast or newspaper coverage might affect their decision making;

2. Limit the number of reporters in the courtroom at the first sign that their presence would disrupt the proceedings;

3. Adopt and enforce strict rules regulating the conduct of newspeople in the courtroom;

4. Insulate the jurors and witnesses from the news media;

5. Forbid extrajudicial statements by any lawyer, party, witness, or court official;

6. Consider a change of venue when news media publicity may interfere with a defendant's right to a fair trial.

Newspeople or court officers who violate the judge's rules can be held in contempt of court. You should note that most of the six guidelines apply to court officials; not newspeople. The guidelines do not affect what you can report or what interviews you can obtain. If, for example, an attorney or court officer violates the judge's guidelines and talks with you about the case you can use the information in a story without fear of getting in trouble.

GAG RULES

Over a period of years, the Supreme Court has consistently refused to let stand judicial orders gagging the press from reporting on trials. In effect, the Supreme Court says gag rules are a form of prior restraint and courts should exhaust other methods of controlling pre-trial and trial coverage. The problem, though, is that a gag order stands until it is overturned and by that time the trial may be completed.

FEDERAL TRIAL GUIDELINES

Since the 1964 *Sheppard* decision, the U.S. Department of Justice has formulated guidelines on what specific information federal investigative agencies and attorneys can release to journalists. Although these rules apply only to federal agencies, some state or municipal police and prosecutors have also adopted the rules. The rules go into effect once a person becomes the object of an investigation. The news media can be told:

1. The defendant's name, age, residence, employment, marital status, and similar background information;

2. The substance or text of the charge, such as a complaint, indictment, or information;

3. The identity of the investigating and arresting agency and the length of the investigation;

4. The circumstances immediately surrounding an arrest, including time and place of arrest, resistance, pursuit, possession and use of weapons, and a description of items seized at the time of arrest.

Department of Justice personnel are warned about making any statements during the trial and the period leading up to a trial because of possible prejudicial statements. Information about a defendant's prior criminal record cannot be volunteered, but this information can be given to newspeople if they ask. Justice Department personnel are specifically warned about:

1. Observations about a defendant's character;

2. Statements, admissions, confessions, or alibis attributable to a defendant;

3. References to investigative procedures, such as fingerprints, polygraph examinations, ballistic tests or laboratory tests.

4. Statements concerning the identity, credibility, or testimony of prospective jurors.

5. Statements concerning evidence or arguments in the case, whether or not it is anticipated that such evidence or argument will be used at the trial.

Department of Justice personnel are also specifically forbidden from taking actions encouraging or assisting news media in photographing or televising a defendant.

Since the adoption of the Katzenbach-Mitchell rules for Department of Justice employees, many states have tried to set up voluntary news media-bar association rules to protect the rights of defendants and the news media. While the states differ on their rules, most guidelines include bans on publicizing prior criminal records of defendants, confessions, testimony stricken from court records, names of juveniles, or interviews with trial witnesses.

PRIVILEGE

Journalists have claimed the right of privilege to protect the identity of confidential sources and, in some instances, the information they received from the sources. Reporters claim if they are forced to reveal sources of information to police and courts, other sources of information will dry up and this will hinder the news media's ability to report the news. The problem of confidentiality became acute during the turbulent days of the Black Power and Vietnam peace movements. News reporters were able to cultivate sources inside these movements and obtained information about the activities of various underground and militant groups. Prosecutors and police were unable to find their own information sources, and they subpoenaed news reporters demanding to know the reporters' sources and gain access to the reporters' notes and tapes of interviews. Some newspeople refused to cooperate with the police, claiming the relationship between a reporter and source was protected by the First Amendment.

The question of privilege, however, is not as clear cut as journalists would like to believe. Nowhere in the First Amendment is the right of privilege specifically granted to newspeople. To the contrary, the courts have consistently ruled that journalists are not exempt from the same legal obligations as any other American citizen. Those obligations specifically include the duty to testify or report information about a crime or conspiracy to commit a crime.

The Supreme Court and United States Congress have consistently refused to recognize a journalist's privilege claim nationally. The only nationally recognized privileged positions are between husband and wife, doctor-patient, attorney-client, and priest-confessor. Congress has considered several shield laws which would grant journalists some form of privilege, but at this time a newsperson's claim to privilege is not recognized nationally. Various state legislatures, however, have enacted shield laws for journalists that give varying degrees of protection.

The point about privilege that should be remembered is that in states without shield laws you could be held in contempt of court and sentenced to jail for withholding information from the court. If you are asked to guarantee confidentiality for a source, this should be carefully considered and you should obtain legal advice from an attorney.

Journalists' claims that confidential sources must remain privileged was severely weakened during Watergate and investigations into the Central Intelligence Agency. President Nixon claimed executive privilege to protect what he termed private material or information pertaining to national security. The Supreme Court ruled that the President's claim of executive privilege was not valid and subpeonas issued for papers and tapes would have to be honored. It is safe to say, in the light of recent decisions, that the Supreme Court and Congress are not in the mood to grant journalists a right denied to the President of the United States.

PRIVACY PROTECTION ACT

Despite the reluctance of Congress to grant privilege to reporters who refuse to reveal information, Congress has given newsrooms some protection from searches by police and prosecutors. The problem was that newspeople were able to cultivate sources and gain information that police and prosecutors were unable to obtain. Police and prosecutors obtained search warrants and legally searched newsrooms to obtain reporters' notes and tapes.

As of January 1, 1982, a federal law provides some protection from federal or state searches of newsrooms. The *Privacy Protection Act* requires prosecutors and police to obtain subpoenas instead of search warrants. A search warrant is issued in private by a judge and served on you when the law enforcement officials arrive to conduct the search. There was little opportunity to legally defend against search warrants. A subpoena, on the other hand, is issued by a judge or grand jury and the subpoena is served upon you requesting that you deliver information or testify at a certain time. You have the time to obtain an attorney and fight the subpoena.

The Privacy Protection Act does not totally eliminate the use of search warrants to gain access to newsroom files or information. However, law enforcement officials, in the future, will have to prove to a judge that a search warrant is needed because:

There is probable cause to believe the person in possession of the materials has committed or is committing a crime to which the materials relate, or

there is reason to believe that seizure of the materials is necessary to prevent death or bodily injury

when there is reason to believe that issuance of a subpoena instead of a search warrant would result in the destruction, alteration, or concealment of the materials, or

the materials have not been produced in response to a subpoena... .

Despite the exclusions, the Privacy Protection Act does place a burden of proof on the law enforcement official to convince a judge that a search warrant is necessary instead of a subpoena.

FREEDOM OF INFORMATION

Freedom of Information (FOI), or Sunshine Laws, have been passed in every state in an effort to open government actions to the news media and public. All states have some type of open records law and nearly all states have an open meetings law. The degree of access these laws provide journalists depends on individual state law. Some laws are fairly restricted while other state laws open up virtually all meetings and all records to public scrutiny.

On the federal level, the Freedom of Information Act provides journalists with a mechanism to try to get information from federal executive agencies and the military. An example of a federal executive agency would be the Federal Bureau of Investigation, Department of Labor, Federal Trade Commission, Central Intelligence Agency, Federal Communications Commission, and the Cabinet posts. Excluded from the act are Congress and the courts.

The federal FOI does not provide journalists with free information. Journalists can request access to or copies of agency records or files as long as journalists "reasonably describe such records." The federal FOI is not a fishing tool for journalists, because you must have a fairly good idea of what you are looking for and be willing to pay a reasonable charge for finding and duplicating the records. In some instances, where a search might be complex, the agency may require you to put up a cash deposit. Record searches normally cost under $10.00 per hour and duplicating costs are generally 25¢ per page.

To request federal information under FOI, you should send a registered letter to the specific federal agency outlining the material you want. Even though there is a ten-day limit on the agency to respond, most requests take more than ten days because of the FOI backlog. Since there is no penalty for not answering within ten days, most federal agencies do not put on extra help to answer FOI requests. If you are denied access to the material you request, the letter of denial must outline the appeals procedure that you can follow if you desire.

There are nine exemptions to the federal FOI Act. Exempted are:

1. National security information

2. Internal personnel rules and practices

3. Information specifically exempted by law (atomic energy information)

4. Trade secrets on file with Federal Trade Commission. This would include financial and commercial information received in confidence for government reports.

5. Inter- and intragovernment-agency communications designed to keep government functioning

6. Personnel and medical files of other people

7. Investigation records compiled for law enforcement purposes

8. Information on the supervision of financial organizations

9. Geological information concerning oil and gas wells

QUIZ

1. Define "malice." ______________________________

2. What is the difference between libel and slander? ______________________________

3. If you wish to record a telephone interview, when should you turn on your tape-recorder?

4. What is a "legally qualified candidate"? ______________________________

5. What are the three elements that the FCC looks for in determining whether or not news staging has taken place?

6. Even private people lose their right to privacy occasionally. When is that?

7. Briefly differentiate between the purpose of "Section 315's" political broadcast rules and the "Fairness Doctrine."

8. What does "equal opportunity" mean?

____

____

____

____

EXERCISES

1. Based on the following information, write a 30-second radio story for the 11:00 p.m. news.

10:09 PM Police monitor carries report of serious two car accident at intersection of Main Street and NW 44th Avenue.

Police unit in the area, a paramedic wagon and fire unit sent to scene.

10:17 PM Paramedic unit reports that they are taking a male and female to University Hospital.

10:32 PM You telephone the police department and talk with the radio room dispatcher. She tells you that the accident investigation team has been sent to the accident. She does not have names of injured, but she can tell you that the woman was driving one car and the man was driving the other car.

You have talked with this dispatcher on numerous occasions and have gotten somewhat friendly. So, you ask her what assumptions the accident team is working on. Her response is that this is not official, but the man just swerved slowly into the oncoming lane. People driving behind the man say he was swerving back and forth prior to the accident and they say he was drunk. Charges will probably be filed.

10:33 PM You call the hospital and get names and conditions.

Male - 27 years old
Ralph Powers
17773 Northwood Towers

Checking him for bruises, contusions and head lacerations. He will be treated and released.

Female - 47 years old
Mrs. Violet Williams
2451 NW 33rd Street

Severe chest injuries. She has been admitted in critical condition. Will probably undergo surgery.

While you are on the telephone with the hospital, the late night disc jockey comes in. He is a solid person not prone to exaggerations. He passed by the accident just after it happened and he says the place smelled like a "brewery." The guy was obviously drunk. He was staggering around after the accident talking incoherently.

Okay, write your story.

ASSIGNMENTS

1. Determine what protection you have in your state regarding a reporter's privilege or reporter's shield laws.

2. Determine what open meeting or open records laws your state has and how much access they really give reporters to records and meetings.

3. Discuss with local reporters their view of your state's open meeting and open records laws. Do these reporters feel the laws are sufficient?

TABLE OF CASES

Associated Press v. United States

Associated Press v. Walker

Banzhaf v. FCC

Branzburg v. Hayes

Capital Broadcasting v. Kleindienst

Curtis Publishing Co. v. Butts

Estes v. State of Texas

Farmers Ed. and Co-op. Union of America, North Dakota Division v. WDAY, Inc.

FCC v. Pacifica Foundation

Gannett Company, Inc. v. DePasquale

Gertz v. Welch

Herbert v. Lando

KFKB v. FCC

Landmark Communications v. Virginia

Miami Herald Publishing Co. v. Tornillo

Miller v. California

Near v. Minnesota

Nebraska Press Association v. Stuart

New York Times v. Sullivan

New York Times v. United States

Red Lion Broadcasting Co. v. FCC

Rideau v. Louisiana

Rosenbloom v. Metromedia

Roth v. United States

Schenck v. United States

Sheppard v. Maxwell

Time, Inc. v. Firestone

Time, Inc. v. Hill

United States v. Zenith Radio Corp.

Zurcher v. The Stanford Daily

GLOSSARY OF TERMS: APPENDIX A

Action News - A television news format stressing action oriented video, upbeat writing and quick pacing.

Alphanumeric - Letters and numbers.

Anchor - Abbreviation for anchorperson. An anchor is one of the primary newscast talent who appear regularly. For example, news anchor, sports anchor, or weather anchor.

A-Roll - One of two film reels used in a multiple chain or double projection film story. The A-Roll carries the primary picture and audio (see B-Roll).

A-Wire - The primary press wire service offered by the Associated Press and United Press International. The A-Wire is written in newspaper style and it emphasizes national and international news.

Air Talent - Anyone performing before a television camera or radio microphone on a regular basis.

Associated Press - One of the two major United States press wire services, it is owned and controlled by its associated members.

Audio - Sound.

Actuality - An audio tape interview or sounds of a news event which are played in a radio newscast.

B-Roll - The secondary film reel in a double projection or multiple chain film story. The B-Roll normally carries only silent film because the audio portion of the news story is taken from the A-Roll.

B-Wire - A secondary press wire service offered by the Associated Press and United Press International. The B-Wire is written in newspaper style and carries feature stories, full texts of speeches and reports, and other news not important enough to be transmitted on the A-Wire.

Backtiming - Planning the end of a newscast by timing the last few stories to insure the newscast closes exactly on time.

Balance - Presenting both sides of a controversial issue as required by the "Fairness Doctrine."

Beat - A regular assignment covered by a newsperson. Beats are normally covered by telephone or in person.

Billboard - A short announcement that portions of the program or newscast are sponsored by a particular advertiser.

Block Format - A newscast format which is rigidly organized, or segmented by content.

Bridge - In news writing, a bridge is the portion of a script between two sound films or audio tapes which is read by the announcer. The script provides a connection or bridge between the two sound cuts. In film, a bridge can be a silent or sound film used between two sound film segments. Sometimes, the reporter in the field will do a standup bridge which will later be edited between two sound film segments.

Bulletin - An important news story transmitted by the press wire services and which should probably be aired immediately.

Bumper Slide - A slide that promotes upcoming news stories and is flashed on the television screen for a few seconds before a commercial break.

Bust - Refers to the term bust shot. This is a close-up shot showing a person from mid-chest upwards.

Call Sheet - A list of regularly called telephone numbers.

Character Generator - An electronic word processing/graphics machine which allows the insertion of high resolution alphanumeric information into the television production process.

Chromakey - An electronic process that mats two television pictures together without a loss of picture quality. The most common use of chromakey in a newscast is to have film, video tape, or a still visual appear behind the newscaster.

Copy - A news script either typed out or printed by the press wire services.

Cover Shot - A wide film shot showing the whole scene and the relationship between different elements in the shot.

Cut - In news, this refers to the specific portion of a sound film, video tape, or audio tape selected for use in the newscast.

Cutaway - A film shot which is not part of the main action but is, in some way, related to the main action.

Dateline - The geographic location of a story transmitted by one of the press wire services.

Double System Sound - A film recording process in which sound and picture are recorded separately and synchronized in the editing process.

Drive Time - Those times when large segments of the population are driving to and from work and have the opportunity to listen to their car radios.

Dub - Transferring sound and/or video from a film, VTR, or audio tape to another film, VTR, or audio tape.

Echoing - When the first or second sentence of a sound cut is identical, or nearly identical, to the scripted lead-in.

Extreme Close Up - (ECU) a very close shot. For example, a film shot framing only the mouth, nose, and eyes of a person being interviewed. The shot would crop off the forehead and chin.

Electronic News Gathering - (ENG) Portable video tape recording equipment used in news gathering.

Establishing Shot - The same as a cover shot.

Eyewitness News - A television news format stressing the use of reporters live-on-set or in the field.

Field Recorder - A small format, portable, video tape recorder. Referred to as part of an electronic news gathering (ENG) unit which includes camera and field recorder.

Fill Copy - Extra news stories carried into the studio by air talent to fill time in case the regular timed portion of the newscast runs short.

Film Chain - A series of film projectors and a slide projector which feed their sound and/or audio into a vidicon television camera.

Film Line-up/Rundown - A list showing news films in the order in which they will be presented in the newscast.

Flash - The highest priority news story transmitted by the press wire services. A story of extreme importance that should be broadcast immediately.

Flip Card - A television still graphic. The same as a studio card.

Font - An abbreviation of the word Vidifont. Vidifont is a popular character generator trade name. Font has come to mean alphanumeric information or the command a studio director gives to a character generator operator to insert alphanumeric information.

Free Lance - A self-employed person who sells film or news stories to various radio or television stations.

Freeze Frame - Using one frame from a film as a still visual.

Front Screen Projector - A device that projects an image on a screen from the front similar to a 35 mm slide projector.

Future File - A file, organized by individual days of the month, which contains information about upcoming news events.

Handout - A press release or public relations film which is sent to a newspaper, radio, or television station.

Hard News - A news story which stresses news values as opposed to human interest or humor. In many instances, a hard news story loses its value if not reported immediately.

Inverted Pyramid - The term applied to a rigidly organized newpaper story which contains all essential information in the lead.

Key - see Chromakey.

Kicker - In news, this usually refers to the last story in a newscast which is either humorous or human interest.

Lead - Usually considered to be the first sentence of a news story.

Lead-in - The term applied to the scripted portion of a news story leading to an audio tape or sound film.

Lead-out - The sentence or two read by the newscaster after an audio tape or sound film. Tag lines usually reestablish the identity of the person in the sound bite.

Library Film - News film which is saved and filed and can be reused if the particular story should again become newsworthy.

Live Opener - The introductory portion of an audio or sound film story which is read by the newscaster on camera or on mike.

Localizing - Stressing the local portion of a national or regional news story.

Logo - A visual or audio identification.

Magnetic Sound - Sound which is recorded on a magnetic strip which runs along the edge of film. Most news film is shot magnetic sound because it is easier to edit than optical sound.

Mini Cam - A small portable television camera used as part of Electronic News Gathering equipment.

Monitor - A television receiver used in the television station on a closed circuit system.

Natural Sound - The actual sounds or background noise at a news event. This does not include narration or a standup.

Network - The interconnection of two or more broadcast stations for the purpose of carrying programs simultaneously.

News Hole - A term which applies to the amount of time in a program available for news. A program time may be five minutes in length, but after deleting time for billboards, commercials, open and close, the news hole may only be 3:30.

O & O - (Owned and operated) A network station owned and operated by the parent firm or network.

Out takes - (Outs) Segments of film which are not used in the final edited film story.

Package - A term which applies to news stories which contain soundbites, cover video and reporter narrations. The story has been edited together as a complete package for playback in newscasts.

Pad Copy - Extra news stories carried into the studio to fill time in case the regular timed portion of the newscast runs short. Same as fill copy.

Parroting - When the first or second sentence of a sound cut is identical, or nearly identical, to the scripted lead-in.

Producer - The person in charge of the program's production.

Promo - A promotional announcement.

Public Service Monitor - A radio monitor tuned to a frequency utilized by a public service agency, such as the police department.

Radio Wire - The press wire service association's news wire written in broadcast style.

Reader - A reader is a short radio, television, or cable news story read by the announcer without accompanying audio or visual support.

Rear Screen Projector - A device that projects an image on a screen from the rear while the picture is viewed from the front.

Real Time Coverage - Live coverage of an event.

Roll Through - Letting the film projector or video tape machine continue to run without being shown.

RTNDA - The Radio Television News Director's Association.

Sequence - A series of film or video tape shots.

Shot - A continuous run of the film or video tape camera from when the camera is turned on to when it is stopped.

Shot Sheet - A sheet of paper listing all of the shots taken by the photographer for a particular news story.

Sil - A Silent film.

Single Chain - A film story using only one film projector.

Single System - Film which has sound (optical or magnetic) recorded on the film alongside the picture.

Slide - A 35-mm still transparency.

Slug - Identifying information placed in the upper right or left portion of the news script. The slug usually contains the writer's name, a brief description of the story, and the date.

SOF - Sound on film.

Soft News - News which has a featurish angle.

Sound Cut - A segment of sound film, video, or audio tape selected for use in the newscast.

Sound Bite - A segment of sound film, video, or audio tape selected for use in the newscast.

Sound Reader - A device used by a film editor to hear the sound track on a film.

Sound Track - The audio portion of a sound film or audio tape.

Splice - Physically joining two segments of film, audio tape, or video tape.

Splits - Various time periods throughout the day which are left open by the national press wire services for the transmission of news by regional offices.

Spot - A commercial announcement.

Standup - A film or live report by the newsperson.

Stringer - Someone who works for a news department on a part-time basis and is paid by the story.

Super - (Superimposition) Electronically superimposing one image over another. Unlike a chromakey, the superimposition results in a lessening of quality of each image.

Sync - (Synchronization) In news, the relationship between the script and the various film shots.

Tabloid - A television news format which stresses a quick pace and lurid news of sex, deviance, crime, and violence.

Take - A shot. Also the point when a television director shows (takes) a film, video tape, or camera shot on the air.

Tag Line - The sentence or two read by the newscaster after an audio tape or sound film. Tag lines usually reestablish the identity of the person in the sound bite.

Talent - Someone who appears regularly on radio or television.

Tandem Format - The use of two anchorpeople in the news segment of the newscast.

Tease - A statement or sentence promoting news stories coming later in the newscast. A tease is designed to create interest in upcoming stories and keep the viewer/listener tuned in to the newscast.

Time Base Corrector - An electronic device which can correct time and base errors on a video tape.

Time Code Editing - A sophisticated video tape editing system where time number referenceds are placed on video tapes and are later used for accurate editing. The time number references cannot be seen on home receivers.

Update - The latest or most up-to-date information.

UPI - United Press International. One of the two major press wire services in the United States.

V-Cass - Abbreviation for video cassette.

Video - Picture.

Visuals - All of the visuals (film, video tape, or slides) used in a television newscast.

Video Tape - A magnetic tape which can record both sound and picture.

Voice Over - (VO) The scripted portion of a news story read over a visual, such as a film or video tape.

Voicer - An audio tape news report made by a newsperson.

VTR - Video Tape Recording or Video Tape Recorder.

COMMON WRITING ERRORS: APPENDIX B

There are certain writing errors that occur frequently in broadcast news scripts. Even expert writers make these mistakes occasionally. The Associated Press and others concerned with writing quality have compiled a list of common writing errors. The following are some of the problems a broadcast journalist should be aware of:

FURTHER refers to additional, while FARTHER is used to denote distance.

Children are REARED and pets, animals, and gardens are RAISED.

AFFECT means to influence, while EFFECT means to bring to pass.

Something is PROVEN not PROVED.

He DIVED not DOVE into the water.

Something is compared WITH something else not TO something.

Do not add an "S" to AFTERWARD, TOWARD and other words with the same suffix.

OVER refers to space relationships and should not be used with numbers. It would be MORE than 100 attended the meeting.

PEOPLE refers to the whole population and so a definite number would be 50 PERSONS.

People do not HEAD UP committees, they HEAD them.

People are UNIDENTIFIED not UNNAMED.

A person is HANGED, while animals and pictures are HUNG.

HEART FAILURE is the cause of death. HEART DISEASE is an ailment and not the cause of death.

People die OF a disease not FROM a disease.

DATUM is singular and DATA is plural.

A person cannot SUSTAIN a fatal injury because sustain means to withstand.

A person is INJURED in an accident but WOUNDED by another person.

IT'S is the contraction of IT IS and ITS is the possessive of IT.

A WIDELY-KNOWN person is not necessarily WELL-KNOWN. WELL-KNOWN means to know well.

A HOUSE can be sold, while a HOME cannot.

A GROOM works in a stable and a BRIDEGROOM gets married.

A person is RED-HAIRED not RED-HEADED.

The speaker IMPLIES, while the listener INFERS.

UNIQUE means one of a kind so something cannot be VERY UNIQUE or RATHER UNIQUE.

TEMPERATURES go up or down; they do not get colder or warmer.

INJURED refers to living things, while DAMAGE refers to inanimate objects like house, car, etc.

FUNERAL SERVICE is incorrect. A FUNERAL is a service.

Things are different FROM each other, not different THAN each other.

A Mass is CELEBRATED and a Rosary is RECITED.

AUTOPSY means to determine the cause of death. Performing an AUTOPSY TO DETERMINE THE CAUSE OF DEATH is redundant.

An autopsy is PERFORMED, not HELD.

On land, flags are flown at HALF STAFF and at sea they are flown at HALF MAST.

Universities GRADUATE students, while students ARE or WERE GRADUATED.

A COLLISION takes place only when the two or more objects were moving.

ECOLOGY refers to the study of an organism in relation to its ENVIRONMENT.

DEMOLISH and DESTROY mean to do away with completely. Something cannot be PARTIALLY DEMOLISHED or PARTIALLY DESTROYED. It is also redundant to say TOTALLY DEMOLISHED.

The person was CONVICTED, found INNOCENT or ACQUITTED. Do not use NOT GUILTY because this can lead to error.

DECIMATE means to reduce by one-tenth. So it is incorrect to say something was TOTALLY DECIMATED.

THAT refers to animals, things, or persons. WHICH refers to animals, ideas, and things, not to people.

WHO and WHOM refer to people. WHOM usually refers to someone who is the object of an action. THE WOMAN, WHOM POLICE QUESTIONED, WAS CHARGED WITH THE CRIME.

THE RADIO CODE: APPENDIX C

The Radio Code, published by the Code Authority of the National Association of Broadcasters, Twenty-Third Edition, July 1981.

I. Program Standards

A. News

Radio is unique in its capacity to reach the largest number of people first with reports on current events. This competitive advantage bespeaks caution--being first is not as important as being accurate. The Radio Code standards relating to the treatment of news and public events are, because of contitutional considerations, intended to be exhortatory. The standards set forth hereunder encourage high standards of professionalism in broadcast journalism. They are not to be interpreted as turning over to others the broadcaster's responsibility as to judgments necessary in news and public events programming.

1. *News Sources.* Those responsible for news on radio should exercise constant professional care in the selection of sources--on the premise that the integrity of the news and the consequent good reputation of radio as a dominant well-balanced news medium depend largely upon the reliability of such sources.

2. *News Reporting.* News reporting should be factual, fair and without bias. Good taste should prevail in the selection and handling of news. Morbid, sensational, or alarming details not essential to factual reporting should be avoided. News should be broadcast in such a manner as to avoid creation of panic and unnecessary alarm. Broadcasters should be diligent in their supervision of content, format, and presentation of news broadcasts. Equal diligence should be exercised in selection of editors and reporters who direct news gathering and dissemination, since the station's performance in this vital informational field depends largely upon them.

3. *Commentaries and Analyses.* Special obligations devolve upon those who analyse and/or comment upon news developments, and management should be satisfied completely that the task is to be performed in the best interest of the listening public. Programs of news analysis and commentary should be clearly identified as such, distinguishing them from straight news reporting.

4. *Editorializing.* Broadcasts in which stations express their own opinions about issues of general public interest should be clearly identified as editorials.

5. *Coverage of News and Public Events.* In the coverage of news and public events broadcasters should exercise their judgments consonant with the accepted standards of ethical journalism and should provide accurate, informed and adequate coverage.

6. *Placement of Advertising.* Broadcasters should exercise particular discrimination in the acceptance, placement and presentation of advertising in news programs so that such advertising is clearly distinguishable from the news content.

B. Controversial Public Issues

1. Radio provides a valuable forum for the expression of responsible views on public issues of a controversial nature. Controversial public issues of importance to fellow citizens should give fair representation to opposing sides of issues.

2. Requests by individuals, groups or organizations for time to discuss their views on controversial public issues should be considered on the basis of their individual merits, and in the light of the contributions which the use requested would make to the public interest.

3. Discussion of controversial public issues should not be presented in a manner which would create the impression that the program is other than one dealing with a public issue.

C. Community Responsibility

1. Broadcasters and their staffs occupy a position of responsibility in the community and should conscientiously endeavor to be acquainted with its needs and characteristics to best serve the welfare of its citizens.

2. Requests for time for the placement of public service announcements or programs should be carefully reviewed with respect to the character and reputation of the group, campaign or organization involved, the public interest, content of the message, and the manner of its presentation.

D. Political Broadcasts

1. Political broadcasts, or the dramatization of political issues designed to influence voters, shall be properly identified as such.

2. Political broadcasts should not be presented in a manner which would mislead listeners to believe that they are of any other character. (Reference: Communications Act of 1934, as amended, Secs. 315 and 317, and FCC Rules and Regulations, Secs. 3.654, 3.657, 3.663, as discussed in NAB's "Political Broadcast Catechism & The Fairness Doctrine.")

3. Because of the unique character of political broadcasts and the necessity to retain broad freedoms of policy void of restrictive interference, it is incumbent upon all political candidates and all political parties to observe the canons of good taste and political ethics, keeping in mind the intimacy of broadcasting in the American home.

THE TELEVISION CODE: APPENDIX D

The Television Code, published by the Code Authority of the National Association of Broadcasters, Twenty-Second Edition, July 1981.

V. TREATMENT OF NEWS AND PUBLIC EVENTS

General

Television Code standards relating to the treatment of news and public events are, because of constitutional consideration, intended to be exhortatory. The standards set forth hereunder encourage high standards of professionalism in broadcast journalism. They are not to be interpreted as turning over to others the broadcaster's responsibility as to judgments necessary in news and public events programming.

News

1. A television station's news schedule should be adequate and well-balanced.

2. News reporting should be factual, fair and without bias.

3. A television broadcaster should exercise particular discrimination in the acceptance, placement and presentation of advertising in news programs so that such advertising should be clearly distinguishable from the news content.

4. At all times, pictorial and verbal material for both news and comment should conform to other sections of these standards, whenever such sections are reasonably applicable.

5. Good taste should prevail in the selection and handling of news. Morbid, sensational or alarming details not essential to the factual report, especially in connection with stories of crime or sex, should be avoided. News should be telecast in such a manner as to avoid panic and unnecessary alarm.

6. Commentary and analysis should be clearly identified as such.

7. Pictorial material should be chosen with care and not presented in a misleading manner.

8. All news interview programs should be governed by accepted standards of ethical journalism, under which the interviewer selects the questions to be asked. Where there is advance agreement materially restricting an important or newsworthy area of questioning, the interviewer will state on the program that such limitation has been agreed upon. Such disclosure should be made if the person being interviewed requires that questions be submitted in advance or participates in editing a recording of the interview prior to its use on the air.

9. A television broadcaster should exercise due care in the supervision of content, format, and presentation of newscasts originated by his/her station, and in the selection of newscasters, commentators and analysts.

Public Events

1. A television broadcaster has an affirmative responsibility at all times to be informed of public events, and to provide coverage consonant with the ends of an informed and enlightened citizenry.

2. The treatment of such events by a television broadcaster should provide adequate and informed coverage.

VI. CONTROVERSIAL PUBLIC ISSUES

1. Television provides a valuable forum for the expression of responsible views of public issues of a controversial nature. The television broadcaster should seek out and develop with accountable individuals, groups and organizations, programs relating to controversial public issues of import to his/her fellow citizens; and to give fair representation to opposing sides of issues which materially affect the life or welfare of a substantial segment of the public.

2. Requests by individuals, groups or organizations for time to discuss their views on controversial public issues, should be considered on the basis of their individual merits, and in the light of the contribution which the use requested would make to the public interest, and to a well-balanced program structure.

3. Programs devoted to the discussion of controversial public issues should be identified as such. They should not be presented in a manner which would mislead listeners or viewers to believe that the program is purely of an entertainment, news or other character.

4. Broadcasts in which stations express their own opinions about issues of general public interest should be clearly identified as editorials. They should be unmistakably identified as statements of station opinion and should be appropriately distinguished from news and other program material.

VII. POLITICAL TELECASTS

1. Political telecasts should be clearly identified as such. They should not be presented by a television broadcaster in a manner which would mislead listeners or viewers to believe that the program is of any other character.

STANDARDS OF CONDUCT AND TECHNOLOGY GOVERNING ELECTRONIC MEDIA AND STILL PHOTOGRAPHY COVERAGE OF JUDICIAL PROCEEDINGS IN THE STATE OF FLORIDA: APPENDIX E

1. Equipment and personnel.

(a) Not more than one portable television camera [film camera--16 mm sound on film (self blimped) or video tape electronic camera], operated by not more than one camera person, shall be permitted in any trial court proceeding. Not more than two television cameras, operated by not more than one camera person each, shall be permitted in any appellate court proceeding.

(b) Not more than one still photographer, utilizing not more than two still cameras with not more than two lenses for each camera and related equipment for print purposes shall be permitted in any proceeding in a trial or appellate court.

(c) Not more than one audio system for radio broadcast purposes shall be permitted in any proceeding in a trial or appellate court. Audio pickup for all media purposes shall be accomplished from existing audio systems present in the court facility. If no technically suitable audio system exists in the court facility, microphones and related wiring essential for media purposes shall be unobtrusive and shall be located in places designated in advance of any proceeding by the chief judge of the judicial circuit or district in which the court facility is located.

(d) Any "pooling" arrangements among the media required by these limitations on equipment and personnel shall be the sole responsibility of the media without calling upon the presiding judge to mediate any dispute as to the appropriate media representative or equipment authorized to cover a particular proceeding. In the absence of advance media agreement on disputed equipment or personnel issues, the presiding judge shall exclude all contesting media personnel from a proceeding.

2. Sound and light criteria.

(a) Only television photographic and audio equipment which does not produce distracting sound or light shall be employed to cover judicial proceedings. Specifically, such photographic and audio equipment shall produce no greater sound or light than the equipment designated in Schedule A annexed hereto, when the same is in good working order. No artificial lighting device of any kind shall be employed in connection with the television camera.

(b) Only still camera equipment which does not produce distracting sound or light shall be employed to cover judicial proceedings. Specifically, such still camera equipment shall produce no greater sound or light than a 35 mm Leica "M" Series Rangefinder camera, and no artificial lighting device of any kind shall be employed in connection with a still camera.

(c) It shall be the affirmative duty of media personnel to demonstrate to the presiding judge adequately in advance of any proceeding that the equipment sought to be utilized meets the sound and light criteria enunciated herein. A failure to obtain advance judicial approval for equipment shall preclude its use in any proceeding.

3. Location of equipment personnel.

(a) Television camera equipment shall be positioned in such location in the court facility as shall be designated by the chief judge of the judicial circuit or district in which such facility is situated. The area designated shall provide reasonable access to coverage. If and when areas remote from the court facility which permit reasonable access to coverage are provided all television camera and audio equipment shall be positioned only in such area. Video tape recording equipment which is not a component part of a television camera shall be located in an area remote from the court facility.

(b) A still camera photographer shall position himself or herself in such location in the court facility as shall be designated by the chief judge of the judicial circuit or district in which such facility is situated. The area designated shall provide reasonable access to coverage. Still camera photographers shall assume a fixed position within the designated area and, once a photographer has established himself or herself in a shooting position, he or she shall act so as not to call attention to himself or herself through further movement. Still camera photographers shall not be permitted to move about in order to obtain photographs of court proceedings.

(c) Broadcast media representatives shall not move about the court facility while proceedings are in session, and microphones or taping equipment once positioned as required by 1.(c) above shall not be moved during the pendency of the proceeding.

4. Movement during proceedings.

News media photographic or audio equipment shall not be placed in or removed from the court facility except prior to commencement or after adjournment of proceedings each day, or during a recess. Neither television film magazines nor still camera film or lenses shall be changed within a court facility except during a recess in the proceeding.

5. Courtroom light sources.

With the concurrence of the chief judge of a judicial circuit or district in which a court facility is situated, modifications and additions may be made in light sources existing in the facility, provided such modifications or additions are installed and maintained without public expense.

6. Conferences of counsel.

To protect the attorney-client privilege and the effective right to counsel, there shall be no audio pickup or broadcast of conferences which occur in a court facility between attorneys and their clients, between co-counsel of a client, or between counsel and the presiding judge held at the bench.

7. Impermissible use of media material.

None of the film, video tape, still photographs or audio reproductions developed during or by virtue of coverage of a judicial proceeding shall be admissible as evidence in the proceeding out of which it arose, any proceeding subsequent or collateral thereto, or upon any retrial or appeal of such proceedings.

8. Appellate review.

Review of an order excluding the electronic media from access to any proceeding, excluding coverage of a particular participant or upon any other matters arising under these standards shall be pursuant to Florida Rule of Appellate Procedure 9.100 (d).

STATEMENT OF PRINCIPLES OF THE BENCH-BAR-PRESS OF THE STATE OF KANSAS; APPENDIX F

This report was drawn up by a committee of the Kansas Associated Press Broadcasters but was never adopted by that body.

PREAMBLE

The Bench, Bar, and Press (comprising all media of mass communications) of Kansas:

(a) Recognize that freedom of News Media is one of the fundamental liberties guaranteed by the First Amendment of the Constitution of the United States and that this basic freedom must be zealously and responsibly exercised.

(b) Are obliged to preserve the principle of the presumption of innocence for those accused of a crime until there has been a finding of guilt in an appropriate court of justice.

(c) Believe members of an organized society have the right to acquire and import information about their mutual interests. The right to disseminate information should be exercised with discretion when public disclosures might jeopardize the ends of justice.

(d) Have the responsibility to support the free flow of information, consistent with the principles of the Constitution of this preamble.

To promote a better understanding between the Bench and Bar of Kansas and the Kansas News Media, particularly in their efforts to reconcile the constitutional guarantee of freedom of the press and the right to a fair, impartial trial, the following statement of principles, mutually drawn and submitted for voluntary compliance, is recommended to all members of these professions in Kansas.

PRINCIPLES

1. The News Media have the right and responsibility to print and broadcast the truth. A free and responsible news media enhances the administration of justice.

Members of the Bench and Bar should, within their respective Canons of Legal Ethics, cooperate with the News Media in the reporting of the administration of justice.

2. Parties to litigation have the right to have their causes tried fairly by an impartial tribunal. Defendants in criminal cases are guaranteed this right by the Constitutions of the United States and the various states.

3. No trial should be influenced by the pressure of publicity from News Media nor from public clamor, and lawyers and journalists share the responsibility to prevent the creation of such pressures.

4. All News Media recognize the responsibility of the judge to preserve order in the court and to seek the ends of justice by all those means available to him.

5. The News Media should strive for objectivity and accuracy. The public has a right to be informed. The accused has a right to be judged in an atmosphere free from undue prejudice.

6. Decisions about handling the news rest with editors and news directors, but in the exercise of news judgments the editors and news directors should remember that:

(a) An accused person is presumed innocent until proven guilty.
(b) Readers and listeners and viewers are potential jurors.
(c) No person's reputation should be injured needlessly.

7. The public is entitled to know how justice is being administered. However, no lawyer should exploit any medium of public information to enhance his side of a pending case. It follows that the public prosecutor should avoid taking unfair advantage of his position as an important source of news; this shall not be construed to limit his obligation to make available information to which the public is entitled.

8. Proper jounalistic and legal training should include instruction in the meaning of constitutional rights to a fair trial, freedom of the press, and the role of both journalist and lawyer in guarding these rights.

GUIDELINES FOR THE REPORTING OF CRIMINAL PROCEEDINGS

The proper administration of justice is the responsibility of the judiciary, bar, the prosecution, law enforcement personnel, news media and the public. None should relinquish its share in that responsibility or attempt to override or regulate the judgment of the other. None should condone injustices on the ground that they are infrequent.

The greatest news interest is usually engendered during the pretrial stage of a criminal case. It is then that the maximum attention is received and the greatest impact is made upon the public mind. It is then that the greatest danger to a fair trial occurs. The Bench, the Bar and the News Media must exercise good judgment to balance the possible release of prejudicial information with the real public interest. However, these considerations are not necessarily applicable once a jury has been empaneled in a case. It is inherent in the concept of freedom of the press that the News Media be free to report what occurs in public proceedings, such as criminal trials. In the course of the trial it is the responsibility of the Bench to take appropriate measures to insure that the deliberations of the jury are based upon what is presented to them in court.

These guidelines are proposed as a means of balancing the public's right to be informed with the accused's right to a fair trial before an impartial jury.

1. It is appropriate to make public the following information concerning the defendant:

(a) The defendant's name, age, residence, employment, marital status, and similar background information. There should be no restraint on biographical facts other than accuracy, good taste and judgment.

(b) The substance or test of the charge, such as complaint, indictment, information or, where applicable and appropriate, the identity of the complaining party.

(c) The identity of the investigating and arresting agency and the length of the investigation.

(d) The circumstances immediately surrounding an arrest, including the time and place of arrest, resistance, pursuit, possession and use of weapons, and a description of items seized at the time of arrest.

2. The release of certain types of information by law enforcement personnel, the Bench and Bar and the publication thereof by News Media generally tends to create dangers of prejudice without serving a significant law enforcement or public interest function. Therefore, all concerned should be aware of the dangers of prejudice in making pretrial public disclosures of the following:

(a) Opinions about a defendant's character, any previous record, his guilt or innocence.

(b) Admissions, confessions or the contents of a statement of alibis attributable to the defendant.

(c) References to the results of investigative procedures, such as fingerprints, polygraph examinations, ballistic tests, or laboratory tests.

(d) Statements concerning the credibility or anticipated testimony of prospective witnesses.

(e) Opinions concerning evidence or argument in the case, whether or not it is anticipated that such evidence or argument will be used at the trial.

Exceptions may be in order if information to the public is essential to the apprehension of a suspect, or where other public interests will be served.

3. Prior criminal charges and convictions are matters of public record and are available to the news media through police agencies or court clerks. Law Enforcement Agencies should make such information available to the News Media after a legitimate inquiry. The public disclosure of this information by the News Media may be highly prejudicial without any significant addition to the public's need to be informed. The publication of such information should be carefully reviewed.

4. Law enforcement and court personnel should not prevent the photographing of defendants when they are in public places outside the courtroom. They should not encourage pictures or televising nor should they pose the defendant.

5. Photographs of a suspect may be released by Law Enforcement Personnel provided a valid law enforcement function is served thereby. It is proper to disclose such information as may be necessary to enlist public assistance in apprehending fugitives from justice. Such disclosures may include photographs as well as records of prior arrests and convictions.

6. The News Media are free to report what occurs in the course of the judicial proceeding itself. The Bench should utilize available measures, such as cautionary instructions, sequestration of the jury and the holding of hearings on evidence after

empaneling of the jury, to insure that the jury's deliberations are based upon evidence presented to them in court.

7. The use of tape recorders, television cameras and other tools of the electronic news media should be considered just as important a piece of equipment as the pencil and pad of the newspaper or magazine reporter. Arrangements for the use of such equipment should be made prior to the trial proceedings commencing and the use of such equipment should be left to the discretion of the individual trial judges. Trial reporters should observe every available precaution to prevent the disruption of courtroom procedures.

8. Sensationalism should be avoided by all persons and agencies connected with the trial or reporting of a criminal case.

9. It is improper for members of the Bench-Bar-News Media or Law Enforcement Agencies to make available to the public any statement or information for the purpose of influencing the outcome of a criminal trial.

GUIDELINES ON THE REPORTING OF JUVENILE COURT PROCEEDINGS

1. News Media and Judges should work together with confidence in, and respect for, each other.

2. News Media should be welcome to all sessions of the Juvenile court. If the privilege is exercised and cases are reported, News Media should not disclose names or identifying data of the participants unless authorized by the court.

3. Responsibility for developing sound public interest in and understanding of the child, the community, and the court must be shared by the Judge and the News Media.

4. Representatives of the Electronic News Media should not attempt the use of tape recorders or television cameras to record the proceedings of the Juvenile Court.

5. All official records should be open to the News Media with the Judge's consent, unless inspection is prohibited by statute.

6. Confidential reports, such as social and clinical studies, school or personal records, should not be open to inspection by the Press, except at the express order of the court.

7. The Judge, at his discretion, may release the name or other identifying information of a juvenile offender in his court.

8. The court should strictly adhere to the Canons of Professional Ethics, which generally condemn the release of information concerning pending or anticipated judicial proceedings.

9. If an alleged act of delinquency is publicized, News Media should be informed of the disposition of the case to complete the original story.

10. In the handling of juvenile matters the basic principles of fairness and cooperation summarized in the Preamble and Principles of the Bench-Bar-Press Committee of Kansas shall apply. The possibility that any juvenile matter may ultimately be handled as a criminal case should be borne in mind.

11. Nothing in the foregoing guidelines shall be construed to prevent News Media from exercising their constitutional right to publish or broadcast any news about juvenile offenders from the time of their apprehension through the disposition of their

cases if such information can be obtained from sources other than the courts, should the latter not wish to release such information.

(a) In such instances due consideration should be given to recommendations of the Juvenile Court and its officers.

(b) In determining whether to disclose names or other identifying data pertaining to alleged juvenile offenders, due consideration should be given as to whether that information is of the type the public must have to be fully aware of its Juvenile Court and the delinquency situation.

GUIDELINES ON THE REPORTING OF CIVIL PROCEEDINGS

1. THE NEED FOR BROADER COVERAGE: Although far more numerous than the trials in criminal courts, civil trials receive only a fraction of the attention devoted to criminal proceedings. One reason may be the brevity of the civil case; another may be its apparent lack of human interest. Judges and Lawyers should recognize a third reason: That Newsmen do not understand some civil proceedings and pass them up for want of sufficient time to study or do leg work.

The courts and their officers should give special attention to the need of the reporter to have background information of evidence as it is presented. Only the News Media can give the public an objective and adequate explanation of civil actions and the reasons for judgments, orders and verdicts entered in such matters.

2. INTERPRETING LEGAL TERMS: Judges and Lawyers traditionally have employed legal phrases with special meaning to the profession. Unless these terms are interpreted faithfully by the Newsmen, the public cannot be expected to understand their significance. It is the duty of judicial officers and their staffs to assist representatives of the News Media to report accurately in lay language. Written judicial decisions should be so drafted that selected portions briefly summarizing the court's ruling may be quoted by the press.

3. LEGAL PLEADINGS: Allegations in pleadings should not be reported as more than simple allegations. Judicial officers and the Press should be mindful of injustices or prejudice that may result from pre-trial publication of such matters.

4. FILES: Official files in civil actions and probate matters, including pleading, court orders and published dispositions, are official records and available to the news media.

5. DEPOSITIONS AND INTERROGATORIES: Until opened and filed by court rule and order, a deposition is not an official document, not a part of the clerk's file in the case and not available to the News Media. After court publication it may be extracted, quoted or copied for public dissemination except any portions which may have been stricken.

Reporting prior to trial what was said in a deposition may prejudice prospective jurors. Premature reporting may be unfair if, on the reading of the deposition in open court, portions are stricken.

Answers to written interrogatories, filed with the clerk, are as much a part of the public record as are depositions which have been opened and filed.

News reports should reflect whether the statements in depositions or answers to interrogatories have been uttered in open court or only in a filed document.

6. CONFIDENTIAL PROCEEDINGS: Adoptions, mental illness and family court cases are by their nature and often by statute, entitled to special protection by the court.

Investigative reports are generally confidential. In those cases where the News Media desire access to such records or hearings, application may be made to the discretion of the court.

7. ESTATES AND GUARDIANSHIPS: The probate of estates of decedent and the administration of guardianships are usually non-adversary proceedings, conducted in open court without verbatim reporting by an official reporter. Newsmen should have access to all such hearings, to the official files concerning them and to such information as can be supplied by counsel and court attaches. Because of the nature of estate matters, personal and financial data concerning the decedent and his family must be revealed to the court. Whether it should be given to the public by the News Media should be governed with good taste, and the public's need to know, balanced against the potential effects on the survivors.

8. SUMMARY DISPOSITIONS: Disposition of civil actions by summary judgment or dismissal is a judicial determination which may appropriately be reported. The News Media should be encouraged to report the reasons for the Court's action. The court should make these reasons available.

9. FAIR TRIAL: Litigants in civil causes, including causes having special news value because of public interest in the subject matter, are as much entitled to a fair trial by an unbiased jury as is a criminal defendant. Jurors summoned to decide questions of civil liability or damages should be free from public clamor and special influences. News Media should be wary of contrived information, the effect of which would be to influence potential jurors as to liability or amount of damage awards. The Media acknowledge that the pretrial reporting of civil cases may involve the same risks to the administration of justice as the pretrial reporting of criminal cases. Pretrial coverage of civil cases should be balanced to minimize the risk.

Newsmen should use care in reporting portions of jury trials which take place in the temporary absence of the jury. To publicize the court's rulings as to evidentiary matters, may cause jury prejudice.

10. SUCCESSIVE RELATED CASES: When two or more related civil jury cases are being tried in series, the reporting of one disposition may prejudicially affect subsequent trials. The Media should exercise restraint to minimize influence on jurors in such matters.

11. PUBLIC UNDERSTANDING: Representatives of the News Media should be encouraged to attend trials and other steps of civil matters to the end that the public may understand the judicial process.

12. NAMES OF COUNSEL: Counsel should not use a court proceeding to advertise his skill. Lawyers present evidence and should seek no plaudits in the public press if courts or juries accept their arguments. It is unethical for a lawyer to seek personal publicity following a jury verdict or court determination.

13. INCOMPLETE REPORTING: Civil suits have two sides. It is unfair to report only a portion of the facts presented at a trial, as though they were the only facts. Trials proceed without regard to deadline. Reporting only one aspect of a case to meet a deadline may give the public a distorted view. Good coverage requires that the News Media follow up in a subsequent report with the other side of the story. Incomplete reporting of civil trials or reporting only those cases on which the newsman has had a helpful tip can give a distorted picture of courthouse news.

14. PERSONAL OPINIONS OF COUNSEL: The Canons of Professional Ethics forbid a lawyer from arguing to the court or jury his personal belief in his client's innocence or in the justice of his cause. He should also refrain from similar statements to the Media.

15. JUDGE AS A NEWS SOURCE: Because the trial judge has notes of the trial, he may be the best source of verification of evidence introduced in open court, other than the official court reporter. In the absence of other sources available to the newsman, he may ask the judge for verification of facts, but not for comment on the merits of the case prior to judgment or verdict. The judge should avoid any public statement which might prejudice rights on appeal.

16. MUTUAL CONFIDENCE: Judges should show appreciative courtesy to newsmen assigned to courthouse beats. They should recognize that newspapers and broadcasters have deadlines and that newsmen must complete their daily assignments within those prescribed times. There should be mutual confidence between the two. The judge may supply background information with the understanding that he will not be quoted and that the information will not be misused. The newsman is under no obligation to withhold publicity or judicial comments made to third persons.

17. TAPE RECORDERS AND CAMERAS: Except in those cases where coverage is prohibited by law or by previous guidelines set forth in this statement of principles and guidelines, judges should recognize the importance of tape recorders and cameras, both television and still, to the members of the Electronic News Media. In accordance with agreements reached between the News Media and the Judge, the use of such devices shall not be prohibited.

Newsmen should exercise every precaution to see that their use does not disrupt the proceedings of the Court or cause prejudicial information to reach the public ears and eyes.

The use of tape recorders and cameras shall be subject to the discretion of the individual trial judges.

GUIDELINES ON PUBLIC RECORDS

1. Free access to public records is of paramount importance if the public is to be fully informed, and the Bench, Bar and Press have an equal interest in and responsibility to see that this access is maintained.

2. Except where confidentiality is specifically provided for in statutes, all records which must be maintained by law are clearly open to the public.

3. Every effort should be made to educate not only those among the Bar, Bench and Press but other public officials as well to the Statutes, Supreme Court Decisions, Attorney General Opinions and other authorities bearing on the subject of public records.

4. Any effort by an individual or group to suppress or conceal a public record should be resisted and exposed by the Bench, Bar and Press.

5. The subcommittee should work toward persuading all persons involved to transcribe public records as quickly as possible and make them available to the public.

6. In cases involving matters of public interest, it is entirely proper for the Judge writing the opinion or decision to summarize his holding in a paragraph or two to aid the News Media in properly interpreting the decision to the public. This is especially important in cases where the opinion is technical or involved.

7. Members of the Bench and Bar should make every effort to be available to answer questions by communications media representatives regarding public records, and representatives of the media should be sufficiently trained to properly interpret legal actions.

8. The committee urges that public records of arresting officers, whether state, county or city, be kept in numbered sequence.

Third, the report recommends that after the adoption of a Bench, Bar and Press preamble and set of guidelines, the KAPBA members working on this report select a series of courts from several suggested by the general membership and approach those courts with requests for entrance into the courtroom with tape recorders and cameras.

Fourth, the report recommends that resolutions be sent to the various county commissions recommending that as improvements are made in their court facilities, special arrangements be included to accommodate the most efficient and practical use of electronic devices in the coverage of court proceedings.

Those improvements might include special glass booths for use by television sound cameras, special audio arrangements to facilitate recording, and more adequate lighting for photographers.

The Topeka Bar Association has already suggested court improvements to the Shawnee County Board of Commissioners. This would present an ideal opportunity for the media to suggest additional improvements such as those mentioned above.

CONCLUSIONS OF THE REPORT:

Much of the original difference of opinion between the Media and the Bar has been resolved through hard work and statesmanship on both sides. However, there are still some big issues to be resolved and if Kansas is to join the forefront of efforts to iron out these remaining problems, the time to start is now.

A set of guidelines is essential to a continued atmosphere of cooperation and trust between the Bench, the Bar and the Press. And such a set of guidelines is the first logical step toward problem solving.

We should be allowed access to the courts with electronic equipment, but we must recognize and understand the apprehension of judges and attorneys. We must make every possible effort to see that our presence does not affect the trial or we endanger the very premise of the First and the Sixth Amendments to the Constitution. We should urge modification of courtroom facilities to better utilize the tools of the electronic media.

We must come to an agreement with the Bar concerning the right of subpoena versus the right of the newsman to protect those confidences which are entrusted to him. This can only come about through responsible negotiation with members of the Bar and the various law enforcement agencies we deal with.

Finally, there is no time for waiting. There should be no reason why working broadcast newsmen should not be the ones to negotiate our problems with the Bench and the Bar instead of leaving the job to be done by management and the newspapers. We must move to the forefront of efforts to resolve our differences and be successful if responsible crime reporting is to emerge in the State of Kansas.

INDEX

A Wire 176-177
Abbreviations 13-14
ABC 182-183, 204
Accuracy 158
Active voice 55-56
Action news 215, 222
Actualities 206, 213
Adjectives 34-35
Adverbs 34-36
Ages, use of 16
Air Florida crash 213
Airplane registrations 190
Alleged, use of 49
All Things Considered 183
Ambulance records 189
APTV, see Associated Press 178
Assignment editor 185
Associated Press 176-179
 A Wire 176-177
 APTV 178
 B Wire 176-177
 laserphoto 180
 radio wire 178-179
 research 206-208
Attribution 42-47
 dangling 44
 delayed 45
 primary 46
 secondary 46
 source 42-47
Audio services 179

Beats, news 191
Beeper 247
Bleyer, Willard G. 159, 163
Boat ownership records 189
Bridges 110
Bulletins 179-180
Bump 220
Burger, Warren 238
Bust shot 217

Cable news 50, 115-151, 183-184, 204, 214-231
 Cable News Networks 50
 CNNI 183-184, 204
 CNN2 183-184, 204
 growth 214
 writing 115-151
Cameras in courtrooms 258-259
Canon 3A(7) 258-259
Carson, Johnny 217
CBS 144-147, 182-183, 204, 211-212
 radio news format 211-212
 Sunday Morning 204
 television news example 144-147
Character generator 121-123
Chromakey 125, 127-129
 examples of 127-129
Clarity in writing 158
Clauses 47-48
 dependent 48
 independent 47-48
Clergy titles 12
Cliches 29-30, 36
Coleman, John 184
Color in writing 50-52
Communications Act, 1934 238, 239-247, 256-258
 Fairness Doctrine 242-245
 indecent language 256-258
 personal attack 245-247
 Section 315 239-242
 telephone recording 247-248
Complexity in writing 31, 33

Computers 121
Consultants, news 204-205
Contractions 18-19
Corporate records 189
Court records 188
Cover video 132-138
 examples 133
Cronkite, Walter 204
Cuts, sound 93

Daily electronic feed (DEF) 183
Day book 185-186
Declarative sentences 31, 47
Defamation 250-255
Drive times, radio 205-206
Dun and Bradstreet 190

Eavesdropping 248
Echoing in writing 107
Editing news copy 104-106
Elite type 4
End signs 5
Electronic news gathering (ENG) 214, 166-167, 229
 co-ordinators 229
 ethics 166-167
 live 166-167
 real time 166-167
Estes, Billy Sol 258
Ethical judgements 166-168
Experts 187-188
Eyewitness news 215, 222

Fairness doctrine 238, 242-245
 controversial issues 243
 balanced coverage 243-244
 public importance 243-245
 reasonable opportunity 245
 sponsorship 245
Federal Communications Commission (FCC) 203, 257, 248-249
 indecent language 257
 news staging 248-249
Federal Election Campaign Act 241-242
Figuratively, use of 36-37
Film in news 132
Financial News Network 184
First Amendment 237-239
Flash 179
Flight information records 189
Font, see also Vidifont 217
Foreign words 30
Format, page 1-7
 radio script 2
 television script 3
Former, use of 36
Fractions 16
Frank Magid Associates 205
Free Press-Fair Trial 258-260
Freedom of Information (FOI) 262-263
Future file 185-186

Gag rules 259
Government agency records 190

Halo effect 203
Hauptman, Bruno 258
Headlines, newspaper 67
Health department records 190
Holmes, Oliver Wendell 238
Hyphenation 17-18

Indecent language 256-258
Independent Network News (INN) 184
Interviewing 93-103
 concluding 103-104
 cuts 93
 defining purpose 98
 hazards 103-104
 obtaining access 98-99
 research 100
 role 100-101
 six steps 98-103
 sound bites 93
 strategies 100-101
Invasion of privacy 255-256
Inverted pyramid 32
Investigative reporting 185-190

Job specialization 121-122
Jones, Clarence 187

KOA television 226
Kuralt, Charles 204

Land-mortgage records 188
Laserphoto 190
Late Night with David Letterman 204
Latter, use of 36
Leads 65-78
 broadcast 65-78
 comprehensive 75-78
 elements 67-68
 hard news 71-73
 newspaper 66
 purpose 65
 soft news 73-75
 throw away 70-71
Lead-ins 106-110
Legal terms 30
Libel 250-255
 broadcast 250-255
 defenses against 252-253
 elements of 251-252
 malice defined 254-255
 participation 253
 Per Quod 251
 Per Se 251

private laws of 254-255
public laws of 254-255
retractions 253-254
Literally, use of 36-37
Live openers 133
Localizing 78-79
Logo 217
Lower case 54

Magid, Frank 205
Malice, definition 254
Margins 4
Masterman, John 157, 204
Mayflower decision 242
McClosky, Robert 196
McLuhan, Marshall 115
Medical terms, use of 30
Middle of Road (MOR) 206, 210
Modifiers 48, 49
misplaced 48, 49
More, use of 5
Morning Edition 183
Mutual Broadcasting System 182
My Lai 159

Names 8-12
deleting 9
unknown 8
widely known 8
National public Radio 183
Morning Edition 183
All Things Considered 183
NBC 182-183
television news example 148-150
overnight news 204
Network services 182-238
New York Times 180, 238
libel decisions 254
News beats 191
News elements 163
conflict 159
human interest 159, 160
market size 164-166
prominence 164
proximity 164
time 166
News gathering, telephone 193-195
News judgement 157-172
News production 227-229
News script, radio 2
News script, television 3
News sets, television 223-227
News sources 175-198
News staging 248-250
deliberate distortion 249
extrinsic evidence 249
material significance 249
News stringer 197-198
News tipsters 198
Newsworthiness 255
Nightline 50, 183, 204, 217
Ninety-five (95) 190
Numbers, use of 14-17

Objectivity 158
Obscenity 256-258
Omnibus Crime Control Act, 1968 248
Order, chronological 84
Organization 83-88

Packages 132,138,140, 141-143
television news 132,138,140, 141-142
structure 143
Parroting 107
Personal attack 246-247
exclusions 246
political editorials 246-247
same day requirement 246
Personal pronouns 59-60
Pica type 4
PM Magazine 215
Police records 189
Political broadcasting 239-242
Positive writing 58-59
Privacy 255-256
newsworthiness concept 255
trespass 255-256
Privacy Protection Act 261-262
Private figure 254
Privilege 260-261
Producers, news 227-229
Production 115-121
field news 115-116,118
live field 115-116, 119-121
studio news 115-117
Pronouns 59-60
Pronunciation 19-21
Pronunciation guide 20
Proofreader's symbols 21
Propaganda 28, 158
Public officials 254
Public relations 195-196
Public service monitors 190-191
Punctuation 12-13

Quotations 40-42

Radio drive time 205-206
Radio Act, 1927 242
Radio formats, music 206-210
all news 209
adult contemporary 209
album oriented rock 208
beautiful music 209
contemporary hit 209
country & western 209
middle of the road 206, 210
Radio news
formula 213-214

news formats 210-213
scheduling 207-208
scripts 2
wire 178
Rapport 102-103
Real time coverage 166-167
Records, public 188-190
airplace registration 190
ambulance 189
boat ownership 189
corporate records 189
court records 189
flight records 189
financial information 189
government records 190
health records 190
land-mortgage records 188
police records 189
tax records 188
vehicle registration 189
voter registration 188
Reference books 187
Renick, Ralph 204
Reportedly, use of 49
Research 100, 204-208, 213-214
Respectively, use of 36
Reuters 180-182
Reuters monitor 180-182
RKO 183

Scientific terms, use 30
Section 315 238-242
censorship 241
debates 241
election periods 242
equal opportunities 240-241
legally qualified candidates 239
use 242
Sheppard, Sam 258-260
Sibilants 38-39
Simplicity in writing 31
Slander 250
Slang 31
Slug 4
Sound bites 93,105,132, 138-139
Sources 42-47, 175-198
news 175-198
Specialization 121-122
Stand up 138, 143
Statistics, use of 14-17
Still visuals 8-9, 125-127, 130
Stringers 197-198
Style, conversational writing 1
Subscriptions 191-192
Sunday Morning 206

Tag lines 110
Tandem anchors 230
Tax assessors records 188
Tease 220
Telephone 193-195, 247-248
call sheet 194
cross directory 193
recording 247-248
Television
block format 215-216
cover video 132-138
cover video example 133
CBS example 144-147
growth 214
integrated news formats 217-220
newscast formats 222-223
news formula 230-233
news sets 223-227
packages 132,138, 140-142
package structure 143
sound bites 132,138-139
script formats 125-127,133, 139-150
writing 115-151
Tense 52-55
future 52
present 52-54
That, use of 37
Those, use of 37
Timeliness in news 159
Tipster 198
Titles 8-12
Today, use of 53
Tongue twisters 37-40
Tonight Show 217
Trespass 255
Transitions 50
Type size 4

Unifax 180
United States Criminal Code 157
United Press International 178-179
Updating 79-81
UPI 178-179
unifax 180
audio 179
World in Brief 178-179
World News Roundup 179
UPITN 184
Upper case 5, 107
Urgent 180

VDT, see video display terminal 124
Vehicle registration 189
Verbs, active 56-57
Video display terminal 121
Video news formula 134-136
Video tape 131
diagram 131

Vidifont, see character generator 217
Visnews 184
Visuals, moving 130-151
Voicer 213
Voter registration 188-189

War of Worlds 248
Weather 231
Welles, Orson 248
WESH Television 225
Westinghouse broadcasting 204
Wire services 176-182
Wiretap 248
Word choice 28-30
WPLG Television 187
WTVJ Television 204
WUFT Television 224